Arctic governance

Manchester University Press

Arctic governance

Power in cross-border cooperation

Elana Wilson Rowe

Manchester University Press

Published by Manchester University Press
Altrincham Street, Manchester M1 7JA
www.manchesteruniversitypress.co.uk

British Library Cataloguing-in-Publication Data
A catalogue record for this book is available from the British Library

ISBN 978 1 5261 2173 8 paperback
ISBN 978 1 5261 3164 5 open access

First published 2018

The publisher has no responsibility for the persistence or accuracy of URLs for any external or third-party internet websites referred to in this book, and does not guarantee that any content on such websites is, or will remain, accurate or appropriate.

Typeset by Out of House Publishing
Printed in Great Britain
by CPI Group (UK) Ltd, Croydon, CRO 4YY

Contents

Figures

Tables

Acknowledgements

This book would have been impossible to carry out without the contributions of others.

I am grateful to all of the interviewees from many years from Moscow; Murmansk; Ottawa; Washington, DC; Iqaluit; Copenhagen; Oslo; Anchorage; and elsewhere. All of these interviewees are busy practitioners, whose responsibilities and schedules are not necessarily designed to accommodate discussing questions with a researcher. Yet they found the time and energy to meet with me, and their insights have been invaluable.

The enthusiasm of these practitioners is matched by a thriving world of Arctic social-science scholars, who continuously produce so much new, interesting research that I had to keep updating the references of this book until the very last minute. Discussions with this community of scholars, established and junior, at project workshops, at the International Congress of Arctic Social Sciences, Arctic Circle and Arctic Frontiers have been inspiring and formative. My 'long ago' friends and teachers from student days at the Scott Polar Research Institute continue to shape my thinking. My 'part-time' colleagues, Frode Mellemvik, Anatoli Bourmistrov and Elena Dybtsyna, as well as students at the High North Centre for Business at Nord University in Bodø, have increased my understanding of Arctic politics.

I also appreciate the efforts of the anonymous reviewers who took time to comment, and of Jessica Shadian, who looked closely at the manuscript for me at an important juncture. Tony Mason, Robert Byron and the team at Manchester University Press have been supportive of this project all along.

I am a lucky person who gets to work with talented, encouraging colleagues every day. I received helpful feedback from Ole Jacob Sending, Helge Blakkisrud, Wrenn Yennie Lindgren, Pernille Rieker, Indra Øverland, Francesca Jensenius, Bjørnar Sverdrup-Thygesen, Benjamin de

Carvalho, and Julie Wilhelmsen at a Norwegian Institute of International Affairs (NUPI) book workshop. Helene Asmussen provided helpful assistance with the references. Iver Neumann has been a great 'book buddy', providing encouragement and critique. The theory seminar and masterclasses organised by Ole Jacob Sending have also been a source of inspiration. Jan-Morten Torrissen and Ulf Sverdrup have invested themselves in making NUPI a good place to work, and their efforts have mattered greatly to me as a working parent of three small children.

The writing of this book has been financed by the Norwegian Research Council Polar Research programme through the research project 'Science and Business in Arctic Environmental Governance' (#257664).

Lars, Samuel, Vera and Isak have not made direct contributions to this book (beyond where otherwise referenced), but make immense contributions to my happiness. This book is dedicated to my parents, in memory of my Dad, John Wilson, and with gratitude to my mother, Carole Wilson, who were always there to answer the phone as curiosity took me further from home.

Abbreviations

ACAP	Arctic Contaminants Action Program
AEC	Arctic Economic Council
AEPS	Arctic Environmental Protection Strategy
AMAP	Arctic Monitoring and Assessment Programme (of the Arctic Council)
AMEC	Arctic Military Environmental Cooperation
CAFF	Working Group on the Conservation of Arctic Flora and Fauna (of the Arctic Council)
CBSS	Council of the Baltic Sea States
CITES	Convention on International Trade in Endangered Species of Wild Flora and Fauna
COP	Conference of Parties (of the UNFCCC)
DEW Line	Distance Early Warning Line
DNV	Det Norske Veritas
DOTS	directly observed treatment, short-course
EPPR	Emergency Prevention, Preparedness and Response Working Group (of the Arctic Council)
HoD	Head of Delegation (of a state, to a working group or to Arctic Council meeting)
IASC	International Arctic Science Committee
ICC	Inuit Circumpolar Council
IPY	International Polar Year
IR	international relations
MFA	Ministry of Foreign Affairs
NATO	North Atlantic Treaty Organization
NEFCO	Nordic Environment Finance Corporation
NGO	Non-governmental organisation
NPA-Arctic	National Plan of Action for the Protection of the Marine Environment from Anthropogenic Pollution in the Arctic

	Region of the Russian Federation (Global Environmental Fund-supported major project of the 1990s)
OGA	Oil and Gas Assessment
PAME	Working Group on the Protection of the Arctic Marine Environment (of the Arctic Council)
POP	persistent organic pollutant
PSI	Project Support Instrument
RAIPON	Russian Association of Indigenous Peoples of the North
SAO	Senior Arctic Official (of the Arctic Council)
SDWG	Sustainable Development Working Group (of the Arctic Council)
STS	science and technology studies
SWIPA	Snow, Water, Ice and Permafrost in the Arctic
UNCLOS	United Nations Convention on the Law of the Sea
UNFCCC	United Nations Framework Convention on Climate Change
WG	Working Group (of the Arctic Council)
WHO	World Health Organization
WWF	World Wide Fund for Nature

Introduction: a power perspective on Arctic governance

> I have reached these lands but newly
> From an ultimate dim Thule –
> From a wild weird clime, that lieth, sublime,
> Out of Space – out of Time.
> (Edgar Allan Poe, 'Dream-Land' (1844))

From the days of the Greek cartographers dreaming about Ultima Thule at the edges of the known world, the cold reaches of the northern hemisphere have inspired grandiose caricatures of risk and opportunity. The region is often imagined from a distance as sublime, exceptional and prone to extremes. Out of space and out of time, as Poe put it, the circumpolar North is frequently envisioned as fundamentally apart from the complexities, indeterminacies and intricacies of life and politics in other parts of the globe.

We see some of this exceptionalism in the application of dichotomies to the Arctic: the Arctic will either be preserved as humanity's last wilderness, or plundered by coastal states jealously guarding their natural resource treasure chests. All Arctic states are completely equal in Arctic governance, or the USA and Russia dominate militarily and diplomatically against a veneer of regional multilateralism. The region must be on the brink of a new cold war (a common media representation) or saturated with warm, comprehensive cooperation (a counter-representation by Arctic states, including Russia).

This book avoids testing the outer extremes of these 'either/or' dichotomies about the cross-border politics of the Arctic. Rather, the volume seeks to pose and explore a question that sheds light on the contested, but largely cooperative, nature of Arctic governance in the post-Cold War period: how have and how do relations of power matter in shaping cross-border cooperation and diplomacy in the Arctic? By illustrating relations of deference, plumbing episodes of controversy, and highlighting the quiet 'work' of various kinds involved in sustaining and expanding cooperation in the Arctic, I hope to show how dynamic and layered with power relations Arctic cooperation itself is. Acknowledging the exercise of power without positing the existence of open conflict allows us to consider how Arctic cooperation is constantly shored up through various kinds of context-specific performances and broached and resolved contestations, rather than a static output of stale agreement.

The chapters that follow are analytical windows on how relations of deference and dominance – and the disciplining logics, representations and norms produced within and maintained by these power relations – shape Arctic cooperation. The cases presented and associated concepts borrowed from geography, international relations (IR) and science and technology studies (STS) are chosen to sensitise readers to important aspects of power in the region that may matter in a more generalised sense (applied to other similar cases in the Arctic) or abstracted (as features of governance in the Arctic or global governance more broadly). However, the book's primary aim is to be selective, rather than encyclopedic, and concrete, rather than abstract, even if this leaves reassembling some of the broader lines on Arctic governance to the conclusion (and to further research).

The first chapter that follows provides background for readers unfamiliar with the Arctic context. Subsequent chapters are each meant to function as a window on power relations. Chapter 2 explores how defining/representing the Arctic region matters for securing preferred outcomes. The examples used to illustrate framing include a deeper exploration of how 'outside' geopolitical strife is handled in circumpolar cooperation, the place of non-Arctic states in the Arctic Council and the 2013 debate over new permanent observer applications, and the longstanding and ongoing balancing act between conservation and economic development in the region. Chapter 3 examines how circumpolar cooperation is marked by regional hierarchies and draws attention to the various kinds of roles available to those active in Arctic governance. Chapter 4 examines how Arctic governance has become a global social site in its own right, replete with disciplining norms for steering diplomatic behaviour. The chapter draws upon Russia's role in the Arctic Council as an extended case study. Chapter 5 looks at how Arctic cross-border governance can be understood as a site of competition over the exercise of authority, and uses the examples of science-political and indigenous diplomacy-state diplomacy interfaces at high-level Arctic Council meetings to illustrate how the performance of authority is varied, contested and certainly not only reserved for State actors.

This introductory chapter provides an argument for why an analytical focus on power in Arctic governance is a productive choice. It also provides a set of definitions on how power is understood here. Secondly, we turn to the seemingly simple question of 'where is the Arctic' and review both cartographical/natural-science-informed understandings and where the boundaries of governance are drawn in political practice. Next, existing research on cross-border cooperative politics of the Arctic is reviewed, with an aim of highlighting the strong scholarly baseline and teasing out where this book's power perspective and selected cases make a contribution. The chapter structure and the related propositions about power in Arctic governance that the chapters highlight are then presented. Finally, the chapter concludes with a brief note on methods, sources and the approach to theorising utilised in the book.

Why power? And how is the concept applied here?

A look at power relations sustaining and shaping Arctic cooperation and governance is timely. Broader scholarship in IR and critical geo-politics has illustrated well the key shifts that have taken place in global politics since the end of the Cold War. It is against this background of shifting power landscapes that Arctic cross-border cooperation has expanded.

The anxiously defensive black-and-white dichotomies about Arctic politics presented above tie into a wider uncertainty about how to inter-pret and cognitively map the post-Cold War world. As scholars working in a critical geopolitics vein have illustrated, the end of the Cold War dissolved a geopolitical imaginary of the globe as neatly divided between two superpowers. In this imaginary, the Arctic was a frozen front between the United States and the Soviet Union (Dittmer *et al.*, 2011; Powell and Dodds, 2014; Steinberg *et al.*, 2015). Lines of interest, cooperation and conflict that are exceedingly more complex and intertwined have replaced the Cold War geopolitical images of a spatial 'Iron Curtain' and a world divided, but stable, between the forces of Communism and democracy (Murphy *et al.*, 2004; O'Tuathail and Dalby, 1998). The rumpled geopol-itical backdrop of the post-Cold War years was important to reframing the Arctic as location for innovative forms of cooperation. The post-Cold War period saw the establishment of the circumpolar Arctic Council and the Council of Baltic Sea States, and formalised structures for cross-border contact in the Barents region of the Nordic Arctic (discussed in detail in Chapter 1).

Simultaneously, the impacts of globalisation and new networks of interest, influence and interaction have vastly broadened the range of actors and sites of politics that need to be taken into any account of global politics (Held and McGrew, 2002). Some argue that the nature of polit-ical power itself has been transformed by rapid post-Cold War global-isation, with economic interdependence, international institutions and new technologies rendering military force and deterrence less useful and other forms of influence more important or efficacious (e.g. Deudney, 2006; Keohane and Nye, 1989; Nye, 2002; Pape, 2005; Paul, 2005).

In some ways, power as relations of dominance and deference fell out of the analysis of IR in the first heady decade of theorising around a new post-Cold War liberal world order (for more on this critique, see Neumann and Sending, 2010). Global governance suddenly seemed mostly about processes of learning, spread of norms, deliberation, and persuasion amongst motley groups of non-governmental organisations (NGO), business and State representatives. Power, when addressed, was primarily the power of discourse to shape the thinkable and the doable rather than the existence of inequality between relevant actors. The unequal power relationships and exclusions within seemingly democratic or open global governance policy networks were largely overlooked until recently and are now the focus of a burgeoning research programme (Davies and Spicer, 2015; Seabrooke and Henriksen, 2017).

However, these lacunae probably tell us more about IR as a discipline than about how global politics has been perceived and understood by those active on global issues. Goddard and Nexon (2016) argue that sub-disciplinary battles within IR have set up an attending and odd dichotomy with military might and *Realpolitik* ('hard' power) on the one side and the liberal institutional order, attraction and marketplace of ideas ('soft power') on the other side. This obfuscates the fact that the institutions of liberal order are, of course, also marked by the dynamics of dominance and subordination, as well as contestation, and that relationships of power are often upheld by simultaneous deployment of soft competencies and hard resources.

The growing scholarly interest in bringing to light the performance of power in situations within the liberal world order and unmarked by military or open conflict is an analytical cue I pick up on to analyse the cooperative politics of the Arctic. Rather than trying to theorise what power *is* in today's global political landscape (or who *has* power), I draw upon IR scholarship suggesting that we need to look at the *performance of power* and *what power does* in practice (Guzzini, 1993; Adler and Pouliot, 2011; Cooley and Nexon, 2013). More recent work in political geography and critical geopolitics points us in the same direction with calls for attention to how geopolitical framings mould the world they represent. This entails directing greater attention to the everyday political practices and techniques of actors in global governance that constitute the performance of 'geopower', and draw sustenance from and sustain certain geopolitical representations (Thrift, 2000: 381; Mamadouh and Dijink, 2006; Muller, 2012; Jones and Clark, 2015). Practices of 'geopower' that can matter in facilitating the circulation and increased purchase of certain representations include techniques of mapping; cultural propagation in films and art; organisational routines; and, I would add, the practices of diplomacy (Dodds, 2010; Jones and Clark, 2015; Muller, 2012; Wilson Rowe, 2015).

The understanding of power relations within the liberal order that I utilise in the chapters that follow can be illustrated more specifically by three questions. What are we looking for? When are we looking? And where is the arena in which power relations are playing out?

First, *what* we are looking for is the successful deployment of relevant competence vis-à-vis other actors in a governance field, resulting in a heightened direct or indirect capacity to shape outcomes. As Adler-Nissen and Pouliot argue, potentially valuable structural assets, such as military might or geographic vastness or diplomatic finesse, do not automatically bring power, as it 'requires constant work to turn structural assets into power in practice'. This work involves positioning yourself as a 'competent player' by seeking to shape the rules of engagement, engaging in social negotiation to achieve recognition for a desired position or preference within the governance field and, finally, shaping outcomes by successfully deploying the competencies that have been privileged in that policy field and/or by capitalising on the relations established via social negotiation (Adler Nissen and Pouliot, 2014: 6).

All of these steps, which can occur simultaneously or consequently, direct our attention towards governance actors successfully or ineffectively 'performing power' rather than 'having power'. Power is therefore manifested in relations that secure/maintain positions of influence and deference, but those relations require work, and what counts as an effective performance of power will be historically contingent and context-dependent (Neumann and Sending, 2010).

When we look for power is a tricky question, as the power relations that are constituting a particular site of governance probably saturate the site in constant and subtle ways. However, power relations are easier to identify from an analytical perspective at key moments where the status quo is contested in some sense or another. This helps us denaturalise and highlight the effects of power, even if these effects are also present at moments less obviously oriented towards securing deference.

The question of *where* Arctic governance takes place seems at first glance straightforward. However, even from a purely natural-science or technical perspective, the question of where the Arctic is remains tricky. Some rely upon the lines of latitude with which our cartographic practices have encircled the globe. In this perspective, the Arctic is simply everything above the 'Arctic Circle': 60°N latitude. Natural-science-based definitions include using the varying extent of the tree line (the maximum point beyond which trees will not grow) or using average soil temperatures (the isotherm) (see Dodds and Nuttall, 2015 for a detailed discussion of these factors and delimitations).

For the purposes of this book, however, it is more relevant to trace the different ways that the Arctic has been defined in political practice. At times, these definitions have relied heavily on the natural-science-based definitions outlined above. At other times, the idea of 'what' or 'where' the Arctic is have been fascinatingly fluid and contested, depending on the political context and constellation of actors at hand. For example, in defining the eight countries of the Arctic Council, Iceland was included even though its coastline falls below the 60° latitude line above which all of the other Arctic Council member states are present. Or – to take another example – in vying for its permanent observer status to the Arctic Council, China worked to increase its relevance by forwarding the notion of itself as a 'near Arctic' state, introducing a new cognate to the geographical conception of Arctic space. Likewise, the American state of Maine picked up on China's near Arctic category in conjunction with its lobbying to host an Arctic Council Ministerial during the US chairmanship (2014–2016) and attendant efforts to position itself as a key gateway for Arctic shipping.

We see the same variations in Arctic definitions at the domestic level. The Russian internal definition of the Far North long included an important equivalency caveat. Russian policies were directed to both the 'Far North' and 'areas equivalent to it.' This expanded category of the North included the landlocked Tuvan republic found on the same latitude line as Amsterdam, simply because of its distance from federal centres of power, harsh climate and limited economic opportunity (Blakkisrud and Hønneland, 2006). The Norwegian usage of the High North can be as narrow as the land and sea territories above 60°N or nearly the entire state of Norway, given the country's 'northness' in a global perspective (Jensen, 2013).

As we will see in subsequent chapters, these definitions of what an 'Arctic issue' is (and where the Arctic is) are often an output of power relations and contestation. How natural-science-based or other definitions are activated by political actors has consequences for who the policy audience is, which kind of policy actors belong, and what kinds of knowledge and statements are deemed relevant and appropriate in a policy debate. Arctic politics can remain stubbornly, surprisingly regional or can be global in scope. Keil and Knecht (2017) suggest we should consider the Arctic as a global embedded space criss-crossed by different kinds of imagined communities, while Depledge and Dodds suggest we should think of Arctic politics as a 'bazaar' (2017) with both formal centres and unregulated peripheries or markets of ideas. Young has argued for understanding Arctic cooperation as a 'mosaic' making up a broader regime complex (Young, 2005).

To capture the element of fluidity of the boundaries of Arctic governance and the intersection of global, local and national politics with Arctic regional politics, I suggest we conceive of the object of study in this book – Arctic cross-border cooperation – as consisting of many intersecting and some overarching policy fields. I make this choice as the literature on policy fields in global governance allows us to bring a certain rigour to considering power relations within – and between – policy fields. Furthermore, policy fields can easily encompass the many actors of global politics today – from indigenous peoples' organisations through scientists and to NGOs, as well as State representatives – without losing sight of the enactment of power relations amongst these diverse field participants.

For example, the eight-country Arctic Council has a broad mandate and 'gathers' many issues that belong to other global or local policy fields, from global climate change to local economic development, into one conversational clearing house. I suggest that the Arctic Council can therefore be usefully analysed as one umbrella policy field in its own right, without necessarily requiring a strong focus on the institutional aspects of the multilateral forum (an already well-researched topic; see below). At the same time, the issues discussed in this umbrella field are clearly embedded in other global/local/national policy fields and associated networks. To take one illustration, the Arctic Marine Shipping Assessment produced by an Arctic Council Working Group (WG) identified many of the regulatory gaps that were important in developing the Polar Code to regulate ice-covered waters, negotiated by Arctic and non-Arctic states alike within the International Maritime Organization (Brigham, n.d.).

The notion of a policy 'field' draws upon sociologist Pierre Bourdieu's work, as interpreted by IR researchers. In this perspective, a field delineates a particular realm of interaction with internal rules about appropriate behaviour. Sending (2015) argues that fields in global governance should be understood as organised around concepts of governance on which actors can hold different conceptions. What unites them is a 'thin' interest in what is at stake and (more or less) agreed-upon ways of approaching the problem. To find a global policy field, we need to look for agreement about what is at stake and a shared sense that this problem should be governed – not necessarily agreement about what the governance outcome should be.

The notion of overlapping or nested Arctic policy fields serves to delimit the scope of study in this book, while retaining the sense that these cross-border policy fields are intimately connected to both local and national settings and other global governance issues. We can thus conceive of cross-border Arctic cooperation as consisting of an ecosystem of 'policy fields' that have important overlaps, shared contours or key disjuncture from other more local, national, regional or global policy fields relating to Arctic governance issues. This helps to overcome the problem of 'scalar fix', which can be understood as the analytical shortcomings that result from the standard scholarly practice of identifying a 'scale' of governance (local, national or global) at the start of a study. Fixing the scale first can easily overlook or exclude important intersections between these levels of socio-political life (Hakli and Kallio, 2014).

Overcoming the scalar fix is especially important in an Arctic context, as a key aspect of setting the Arctic agenda is determining the scale at which or location where the problem will be and should be addressed (and, by extension, who will play a key role in addressing it) (Shadian, 2017). So, rather than assuming that the problems addressed at regional or international levels are intrinsically 'international' or 'regional' ones, we seek to denaturalise and explore how and why these problems are addressed through cross-border efforts. This approach to scale speaks to Monica Tennberg's suggestion that we analyse the Arctic through a 'politics of relationality', following actors navigating Arctic politics within and across various temporal and spatial dimensions with a focus on the management of change (Tennberg, 2015).

A second important wager that speaks to this book's focus on power relations is that 'fields' are sites of equality and inequality – and have outer delimitations. Not all field participants have equal access to and facility in wielding the resources that matter to that particular policy field. The argument is that within this field there are, of course, all actors (networks, organisations, country representatives, business and so on) that characterise global governance. However, not all of these actors are equally well-positioned to 'play the game'. Agents in a field occupy unequal positions, and control over relevant economic, social and symbolic resources is usually unevenly distributed, causing various 'player[s] to play the game more or less successfully' (Pouliot, 2010: 34). The field, and its particular constellation of unevenly distributed resources relevant to maintaining power relations, also has an outer edge. Nexon and Neumann (2017) argue that the edge of a field is where we notice the features and effects of the field (over participant behaviour or outcomes) tapering off. Thus, to take an example from Chapter 5, when the Arctic Council is unable to agree on if and how to represent itself as a group at the United Nations Framework Convention on Climate Change (UNFCCC) Conference of Parties in Paris in 2015, one could argue that the edge of an umbrella Arctic policy field, greatly concerned with regional climate change, has yet to extend its policy field boundaries to the global climate policy field. By contrast, dealing with the global challenge of persistent organic pollutants, actors within the Arctic policy field have indeed exerted substantial and coordinated influence (Leonard and Fenge, 2003; Selin, 2017), which would indicate strongly overlapping circumpolar and global policy fields.

How does this approach fit in? Intellectual traditions and knowledge gaps

The compelling political nature of the Arctic – its indigenous sovereignties meeting state governance, management of a rapidly changing physical environment, and of intersecting national boundaries and transnational ecosystems, resources and legal regimes – has attracted a good deal of rigorous scholarly attention. Contributions to research on the cross-boundary relations of the Arctic come from many different social-science fields. This is important as it brings variety – and varied analytical wagers and pursuits – to the table. In other words, the scholarship discusses similar political phenomena in quite different ways as the authors are also engaged with their respective disciplinary communities.

Despite key disciplinary differences, it is perhaps most constructive to think of extant scholarship on cross-border cooperation as grouped around objects of study, even if various disciplinary angles are taken and methods used. These contributions to analysing the politics of the circumpolar north fall along three main lines.

Regional Arctic institutions/legal frameworks/regimes

One might argue that this research is focused on the following questions. What are the legal and institutional governance structures in the Arctic? How do they connect with global or other regional legal and institutional structures? And how well/sufficiently do they function to address specific governance challenges, singly and in concert?

Legal and political science scholars have analysed to what extent governance outputs interact with other existing legal regimes, draw upon different sources of legal precedent, promote particular norms or are sufficient to the policy problems at hand (e.g. Bankes and Koivurova, 2014; Beyers, 2014; Koivurova and Alfredsson, 2014; Humrich, 2017; Jensen, 2015). Pan-Arctic social and economic assessments also tend to include useful overview chapters on 'governance' that present formal Arctic political structures; their competencies; and challenges relating to the division of responsibility between non-regional governance and national, local and indigenous governance structures (Nymand Larsen and Fondahl, 2015; Poelzer and Wilson, 2015). The Arctic Council itself as a political institution has garnered a particularly high level of attention and generated strong scholarship (Dodds, 2013; English, 2013; Graczyk and Koivurova, 2014; Nicol and Heininen, 2013; Pedersen, 2012; Rottem, 2013). Local, cross-regional diplomacy and people-to-people contacts has also garnered attention (such as Olsen and Shadian, 2016; Tennberg, 2012).

On a similar note, a focus on the development and effectiveness of regimes has long been a key contribution from the Arctic political science community (Hoel, 2015; Hønneland and Stokke, 2010; Young, 1998). Regimes can be understood as sets of rights and rules around a policy object and patterns of interaction that make the regime not just a formal structure, but also a social institution within which expectations converge (Young, 1998; Krasner, 1982). Early studies of Arctic regimes examined the membership/participation structure of new regimes and also how the regimes define a policy issue or the mandate of the regime (broad or narrow) (Caron, 1993; Stokke, 1990; Young, 1998). The regime-theory literature does engage explicitly with questions of power, and the definition utilised is that power is demonstrated through overt exercise of will or willingness/ability to walk away from an established regime. However, a key aspect of regime-building theory is that, while regimes are pushed forward by entrepreneurs or exogenous 'shocks', new regimes usually only come about if they are attractive to all relevant parties (Stokke, 1990: 61). We therefore rarely see the overt demonstrations of power anticipated in regime theory.

A more recent turn in these institution-/law-focused studies of Arctic governance is assessing how the intersecting and complex web of governance structures is efficient or suited to purpose. Should Arctic governance be harmonised, with such overlaps and repetition removed or rationalised (Koivurova and Molenaar, 2009), or organised differently to take active advantage of the multiple levels of government involved in Arctic questions (Stokke, 2011)? One can also understand the complexity and fragmentation of Arctic politics as bringing about important possibilities for enmeshing Arctic questions in key broader fora across the globe (Stokke, 2015: 329).

Studies of regime complexity elsewhere in the world have noted that it creates useful ambiguities that are often actively guarded or promoted by states. Key politics, therefore, happen at the interstices of overlapping regimes and, with the sheer complexity of the obligations entailed in and produced by regimes, a higher reliance on personal relations and cognitive shortcuts is promoted (Alter and Meunier, 2009). As discussed above, the aim of this book is to understand better the power relations that undergird the informal politics of the interstices of Arctic policy complexity, and the resources, representations and positionings involved in delivering a performance of competence that matters in Arctic politics. In other words, the book draws upon the insights and findings of this literature on Arctic institutions and regimes, but does not seek to add to our understandings of the formalities, efficacy and shortcomings of governance structures and governance outputs.

Articulating and pursuing Arctic interests

A second set of contributions focuses on the interests identified as 'Arctic' by states (and other non-state actors as well). State interests are often understood from both a realist perspective, in which a state's interest in territory, sovereignty or security is taking as given analytical starting points, and a constructivist approach, which seeks to unpack what premises, actors and inter-state dynamics produced a set of interests. Many of the studies focusing on state-level Arctic politics and interactions among states in the Arctic have focused on security questions – both broadly construed (e.g. Heininen, 2015; Hoogensen Gjørv *et al.*, 2013; Huebert *et al.*, 2012; Sergunin and Konyshev, 2015; Wegge, 2010) and more specifically focused on the military preparedness and capacities of Arctic states (e.g. Blunden, 2012; Kraska, 2011; Zysk, 2011). Several studies have examined the positions of key Arctic states (Jensen, 2013 and Jensen, 2015 on Norway; Wilson Rowe, 2009, Laruelle, 2013 and Sergunin and Konyshev, 2015 on Russia; Griffiths *et al.*, 2011 on Canada). There is also growing attention to the roles played by indigenous peoples' organisations, non-state actors and non-Arctic states in shaping Arctic governance (Knecht, 2017; Shadian, 2014; Spence, 2016; Wehrmann, 2017). This book builds upon the scholarship illustrating the various positions and interests of key Arctic actors and seeks to understand how these interests fare when brought into the social space of Arctic cross-border governance. Why do some actors (and their interests) matter in shaping cross-border cooperation while other interests and actors do not? What relations of power undergird whose interests count most?

Discourse and representation

A third strand focuses on long-lines studies of changes in how the region is represented, including how particular understandings of its problems (and of the region itself) are 'talked into being' (Neumann, 1994; Jensen, 2013; Keskitalo, 2004; Keskitalo, 2007; Tennberg, 2000) or shored up by certain kinds of geopolitical framings and cartographic representations (Aalto *et al*, 2003; Dittmer *et al.*, 2011; Powell and Dodds, 2014; Steinberg *et al.*, 2015; Wilson Rowe, 2013a). On a related note, several scholars have carried out research on the new kinds of identities fostered by new regional framings, including on the individual level. This line of enquiry is exemplified by Hønneland's work on the 'Barents Generation' of cross-border actors in the European North (2013), Shadian's work on the emergence of an Inuit polity (2014) and Medby's work on Norwegian 'Arctic' identity (2014), among others. This focus on representation/identity-building also includes important contributions on the material aspects used to produce and shore up these representations. Several scholars have sought to highlight the material/technical resources available to the State in making the Arctic land, sea and seabed legible for statecraft (Dodds, 2010; Luedtke, 2013; Strandsbjerg, 2012; Stuhl, 2016).

In this strand of research, power is generally seen as embedded within and exercised by these discourses and representations because they define (to greater and lesser degrees) the realm of possible actions and speakable words in a given setting. As outlined above, there are growing efforts in both political geography/critical geopolitics and international relations to build upon this existing scholarship. In a critical-geopolitics vein, there have been calls for greater attention to the concrete power relations involved in constructing geopolitical representations – and closer study of how these representations are brought to bear on cross-border relations in practice. The Bourdieu-inspired research on global policy fields in IR discussed above is likewise meant to capture the disciplining effects of discourse, while dedicating greater analytical attention to the improvisational and instrumental ways in which policy field actors navigate and improvise against and along the limits of discourse.

While these studies are valuable in mapping and analysing key governance outcomes, none aims to take a systematic and theoretically informed look at how power relations are enacted, maintained and contested in the production of Arctic cross-border governance. This book seeks to address this small, but important, lacuna by bringing to light some key manifestations of power relations in circumpolar cooperation.

Four propositions on power relations and the structure of the book

Although the chapters that follow seek to unravel or question some of the established narratives of Arctic space and politics as a window onto power relations, Chapter 1 aims to initiate readers new to circumpolar politics. This background chapter looks at the longer lines of different governance actor groups in the region and introduces Arctic regional governance over time, with emphasis on the cross-border politics of the 1990s and onwards.

The subsequent chapters explore *four propositions* about the development and maintenance of power relations in key cases of Arctic cross-border cooperation. Chapter 2 takes a bird's-eye view of power in Arctic governance by exploring the proposition that *power relations are manifested in and shaped by the definitions and representations of Arctic policy objects and the region more broadly.* The chapter illustrates how 'framing' is about laying the ground for policy actions. In other words, a robust policy frame will address what the problem is and its causes, who can do something, and who should do something. The politics of framing is approached from three angles. The first examines how key political actors worked to shore up a cooperative frame of the Arctic region in a time of geopolitical crisis outside the Arctic itself, following Russia's annexation of Crimea in 2014. From there, we move on to a more granular policy scale seeking to see how particular types of representations of the Arctic matter for specific political outcomes. The two remaining case studies look at concrete consequences for what kind of actors seem to belong in Arctic politics, and focus on debates around the participation of non-Arctic states and business representatives in Arctic governance.

Chapter 3 explores relationships of power that come from occupying certain kinds of advantageous positions. The proposition explored here is that *as policy fields come together and endure, some actors will find themselves in occupation of a more advantageous position for securing desired outcomes because of effort and success in defining what matters in the policy field.* This discussion is informed by an emerging literature in international relations seeking to come to grips with the function of hierarchies in global politics. In an Arctic context, we could see forms of hierarchy in achieving a 'club' status, for example the 'Arctic 8' (members of the Arctic Council) vis-à-vis the rest of the world, or the politics of being an 'Arctic power' or a leading Arctic state. Questions include: How do 'global powers' matter in regional development? And what kinds of creative status seeking can be pursued – and recognised by others? The roles of Russia, the United States and Norway are explored as cases of hierarchies amongst states in Arctic Council diplomacy, and hopefully further research will pick up on this line of thinking to extend the conceptualisation of hierarchy to other key actors in the Arctic region, such as indigenous peoples' organisations and NGOs. Chapter 3 does, however, also look at questions of hierarchy in cross-border people-to-people relations, examining a circumpolar (Canada-to-Russia) development project and a health-focused cooperation within the Nordic Arctic. Here we will see how roles of students and teachers had been intrinsic to these projects of the 1990s and early 2000s – and protested by the target audiences in Russia.

Chapter 4 looks at the informal workings of power by examining what is accepted as a legitimate statement, policy concern or actor in the Arctic Council. We also explore what kind of interventions and persons fall outside the remit and how these exclusions are effected or maintained. This line of enquiry envisions global governance policy fields as social spaces with 'place-specific' norms and ways of enforcing these norms (Wilson Rowe, 2015). Acknowledging that performances of power – including developing and enforcing norms – have an inherently 'local' and setting-specific aspect is important to grounding broad statements about power in global governance. The proposition about power here is that Arctic cross-border cooperation *plays out in an environment that has social constraints and norms. These constraints allow for the performance of Arctic diplomacy to more and less successful degrees, and shape the behaviour even of the 'great powers' in the region.* Chapter 4 seeks to illustrate some of these key social constraints by examining how Russia – a major Arctic country by geography – has been disciplined by these constraints and also sought to transform them.

In Chapter 5, we explore how *power relations are malleable and constantly refined/redefined, especially between different 'kinds' of actors.* To get at this sense of the different forms of influence that can be exerted – without positing that non-state actors engage in global governance in fundamentally different ways than state actors – we will be utilising the concept of authority. Authority can be broadly construed as the capacity to secure deference from others by using whichever forms of capital or relations of power lend themselves to that particular policy field. The chapter suggests that a systematisation of what counts currently/at a given moment as authoritative performance (civic epistemology) can be a useful tool to borrow from science and technology studies when the classic IR tool – a genealogy of the field – is too difficult to carry out (which I hazard is the case for the complex ecosystem of the cross-border Arctic policy fields of today, although particular strands of these fields or actors could benefit from a genealogical analysis). To get a sense of the kind of authority that science diplomacy actors may achieve in Arctic governance, we zero in on high-level diplomatic debates over how to draw the line between knowledge and policymaking at the Arctic Council. Likewise, to understand some aspects of the authority sought and exercised by the Permanent Participants in the Arctic Council, I summarise some of the key diplomatic interventions made by indigenous peoples' organisations at Arctic Council high-level meetings.

The concluding chapter seeks to account for how the windows on power presented in each chapter can perhaps be reassembled into a broader view (and where this remains empirically or analytically challenging).

Note on methods and use of theory

In attempting to get at this relationally, situationally enacted exercise of power, IR theorists have engaged in their own 'practice' turn, arguing that it is not enough to look at state rhetoric, stated interests or potential resources to understand power. Rather, to grasp the workings of power one needs to look at an entire range of power performances (Sending, Neumann and Pouliot, 2015). This often involves field work in multilateral or bilateral settings and/or extensive qualitative interviews with field participants about discussions, outcomes and roles of the various participants in a policy field. Fieldwork or physical presence can be important for understanding the non-verbal performance of power. For example, at the climate success meeting in Cancun in 2010 after the debacle the previous year in Copenhagen, the 'unanimous' decision in the UNFCCC process was only achieved by simply overlooking the vocal objections of Bolivia as the country's representatives sought – and failed – to gain the attention of the chair as she invited celebration and applause (Lahn, 2016).

I had the privilege of conducting field research on cross-border people-to-people cooperation between 2003 and 2004 within a Canadian-sponsored development project promoting dialogue around natural resource management in the Russian North (see Wilson, 2006). The findings of this fieldwork are discussed in Chapter 3. I have also had informal discussions with Arctic policy actors at regional conferences, such as Arctic Circle and Arctic Frontiers, and in various gatherings of stakeholders at my workplace in Oslo and abroad, where discussions often go under Chatham House Rules. A broader challenge, however, with fieldwork in IR or on diplomacy is that key settings may often be closed to researchers with an active political-science agenda. Interviews and archival, media and policy document analysis, however, can help fill the gaps (Schia, 2013).

The volume revisits and interprets anew an interview set with 105 Arctic cross-border actors. These interviews took place between 2004 and 2017. Especially intense periods of formal qualitative interviewing took place in 2004 (resulting in Wilson, 2007a, b), 2007 (resulting in Wilson Rowe, 2009), 2011 (with Helge Blakkisrud, resulting in Wilson Rowe and Blakkisrud, 2014) and 2013 (with Per Erik Solli and Wrenn Yennie Lindgren, resulting in Solli *et al.*, 2013). These interviews were focused on Arctic actors from Russia, Norway, the USA and Canada, with a few interviewees with Finnish and Danish backgrounds as well. Gaining insight into practices – not just what is said but what is done and how – is a difficult pursuit. Given the conscious and unconscious commitments and tacit knowledge involved in diplomatic practice (or any practice for that matter), interviewees may often have difficulty reflecting on the implicit underpinnings of their daily, regular activities. Consequently, throughout I have taken a method cue from Vincent Pouliot (2010) and have asked Arctic policy field participants to reflect on other field participants' practices (their relative efficacy and intention) rather than just their own. In interpreting the interview sets, I have frequently kept an eye out for intersubjective agreement, indicated by more than one interviewee sharing an interpretation of a policy event or stakeholder.

Access to documents was an important source for triangulating data, and the policy documents of the Arctic coastal states are analysed in Chapter 3. Furthermore, the minutes from SAO meetings have been an important source of information (albeit probably highly filtered) about closed-door meetings. Nonetheless, the minutes most often report on disagreement and monitoring converging views, although the level of detail varies by chairmanship. On more controversial points, it is not always easy to determine which country or Arctic Council participant

Table 1 Comparison of bracketed text on point 7.2.10 from an SAO meeting preceding a ministerial meeting (PAME, 2015b) to the final version of the Arctic Marine Strategic Plan (PAME, 2015a)

Brackted text, two alternatives	Final text
[Advance the development of] [Implement] a pan-Arctic network of marine protected areas to strengthen marine ecosystem resilience and contribute to human wellbeing, including traditional lifestyles, within the broader context of Ecosystem Approach. es (e.g. LME Strategic Objectives, data sharing, risk assessments etc) [monitoring and climate change)]	Develop a pan-Arctic network of marine protected areas, based on the best available knowledge, to strengthen marine ecosystem resilience and contribute to human wellbeing, including traditional ways of life
[Develop [Advance the development of] [Implement] a pan-Arctic network of marine protected areas, based on the best available scientific knowledge, to strengthen marine ecosystem resilience and contribute to human wellbeing, including traditional lifestyles, within the broader context of Ecosystem Approach.]	

voiced concern or slowed a process. However, it has been possible to connect these indicated but not fully written-up disagreements to statements and perspectives from interviews.

An important analytical tool there, given the long timescale of documents now available online in the Arctic Council archives, is tracing the extent to which ideas that are introduced at early meetings in chairmanships succeed or fail to gain followers at subsequent meetings. The Arctic Council ministerial meetings that take place every two years are not usually marked by a lot of decision-specific diplomatic work. The Arctic Council is very much like many sites of global governance in this regard. The aim of the high-level civil servants representing their countries at more frequent intersessional meetings of multilateral bodies is to clarify options and texts so that little remains to be decided by top-level politicians. Much of this involves removing the brackets that are put around text or policy options or decisions around which disagreement remains. Removing 'bracketed texts' either involves reaching agreement by making needed adjustments or giving up on having the text included.

In rare occurrences, one or several country representatives may elect to push the issue to the ministerial or top-political level for decision and debate. The debate about admittance of additional observers to the Arctic Council, explored in Chapter 2, is one such rare example of a key issue remaining undecided and set for resolution at a ministerial meeting format.

Finally, a brief note on theory and how it is understood and used in this book. Theories and concepts generated by other case studies of global governance (or in other fields, such as psychology) are important to bridging the gaps of what is known, or can be known. I draw these theories primarily from the interpretivist social science tradition, in which interests, identities and cognitive frames are not immutable givens (even if they are only occasionally the object of active reflection by those enacting them). It is important to note that the abstracted ideas I utilise in this book are not put to use in the sense of 'grand theory' (Swedberg, 2014). I do not expect the abstracted ideas I utilise to predict that similar situations in Arctic governance would play out in similar ways. Rather, I employ them as sensitising theories that can point us in research directions and help us delimit data-gathering strategies. In other words, the book engages in theorising by bringing hitherto underused concepts generated by research on other global policy fields and empirical findings on Arctic governance into productive, if not predictive or generalisable, conversation.

1

Arctic international relations: new stories on rafted ice

In October 1988, an Inupiaq hunter saw that three grey whales were trapped in the sea ice off of Point Barrow (Nuvuk), Alaska. These younger 'teenage' whales were on a migratory route between Arctic waters and the warm seas of southern California and Mexico, but they had failed to leave their northern feeding ground in time and had become trapped. The North Slope community immediately set to work attempting to break the ice and create breathing holes for the trapped whales. An attempt to borrow a barge from the nearby oil and gas development at Prudhoe Bay failed. As attention to the whales' plight and the villagers' efforts grew, national resources were brought in to cope, with whale biologists from the National Oceanic and Atmospheric Agency lending assistance.

Eventually, the issue went international. The United States State Department contacted the Soviet Union to secure the cooperation of two icebreakers stationed in the Russian Far East – the *Admiral Makarov* and the *Vladimir Arseniev*. Over the course of several days, Soviet icebreakers rammed the tough ridge of sea ice attempting to make a path through the Arctic sea ice.

Federal authorities had closed the airspace above the ships, thinking that the Soviets would appreciate all efforts made to ensure secrecy during their volunteer effort in American waters. However, the spirit of glasnost was in the air and the American media were invited aboard the Makarov to take a look. One of the ship's officers, Vladimir Morov, told American reporters that the Russian audience was following closely too: 'Our whole country is watching, just like everyone else. We love animals, just as anyone' (Mauer, 2010).

By the time a channel of ice-free water was opened, the whales had been given names in both English (Bone, Bonnett and Crossbeak) and Inupiaq (Putu, Siku and Kanik). One whale died during the wait, but it was hoped that the two surviving, but weakened, whales had escaped via the channel opened by the Soviet icebreakers and resumed migration.

Figure 1 North Slope (USA) villagers passing a Soviet icebreaker, flying a Soviet flag in 1988.

'Operation Breakthrough' received high levels of media attention and was also the object of critique from those who found the use of resources disproportionate to the likelihood of successful survival for the whales or the importance of the effort (Archer, 1988).

The whale rescue incident brings into focus many of the actors, ideas and physical elements that continue to shape Arctic politics today. Migratory species, interlinked Arctic ecosystems gathered around the narrowing circumference of the globe, and vast distances challenged the ability of one country – even a global superpower – to bring its 'own' military/coast guard resources to bear. The Soviet icebreakers were the best alternative. Local indigenous villagers – inspired by the animals' plight and relations to the whale extending back to mythological timescales (Bodenhorn,1990) – took action. The problem triggered the application of resources and expertise from the national level. The quick mobilisation of resources possibly drew steam from the campaigns of environmental NGOs that had sought to limit commercial whaling and had used the whale as a flagship 'charismatic megafauna' in their campaigns to raise global environmental awareness (Epstein, 2008).

This book is designed to give us insight into how power relations have been important to structuring and sustaining cross-border Arctic cooperation and cooperative governance of the region. Taking a close look at power necessitates jostling and unpacking established narratives about regional history and key actors. This chapter, however, aims to provide readers less familiar with Arctic settings with important background and, therefore, draws upon established narratives and classifications that later chapters may re-examine. We begin with an introduction to various Arctic actor groups in a brief historical context. The difficulty of keeping these actor groups separate from one another underlines the complexity and interconnectedness of Arctic governance today, and it is on this topic of Arctic multilateralism and cross-border innovation that the chapter concludes. In preparing the ground for the contemporary chapters that follow, a lot of the richness of detail that historians of the Arctic have brought to light is, by necessity, glossed over. Hopefully, however, the referenced works used in this brief long-lines look at the Arctic past will point the curious reader in the right direction for comprehensive historical works.

Politics on rafted sea ice: a bird's eye view of Arctic political actors

This section introduces actor groups in a historical perspective, rather than trying to use a chronological approach that pulls these actor groups into particular eras. Of course, the emphasis on actor groups may delineate too sharply among them, just as a purely chronological approach could gloss over the different ways in which key historical events or eras were experienced by differently positioned actors at the time. However, the focus on actors serves the book's purpose well given the emphasis on power relations (which are manifested among individual actors and sets/kinds of actors). Secondly, the emphasis on actor groups in a historical perspective – and in the more contemporary chapters that follow – encourages us to see how Arctic politics today is shaped by layers of historical experience that are authored and narrated from multiple perspectives.

Indigenous peoples and their organisations

The high northern latitudes of the globe have long been occupied by humans, and one could argue that the region's political history started with them. The peopling of the Americas is believed to have occurred via a land bridge between today's Chukotka in the Russian Far East and today's Alaska at the height of the last ice age, although the theories of how America was populated are frequently revised and revisited (Schweitzer, Sköld and Ulturgasheva, 2015). Much of the world's ocean water was then bound up in ice, which exposed new tracts of land connecting the continents. In the North American Arctic and Greenland, the archaeological record and Inuit oral histories document occupation by the mysterious Tuniit people, who are understood to have been distinct from and displaced by a twelfth-/thirteenth-century migration of Inuit from Eurasia and Alaska (McGhee, 2006). The migration and success of the Inuit people over a wide range of territory that came to be encompassed by the emerging Russian, Canadian, American and Danish states were later a key element underlining the regional nature of the Arctic and challenging the primacy of state borders in the international politics of the Arctic (English, 2013; Shadian, 2014).

In the Nordic and Russian Arctic, many of the indigenous peoples also shared – and many continue to share – traditions surrounding a reliance on reindeer herding, in addition to the opportunities for fishing, hunting and gathering afforded them in their particular territories. The state borders that grew up around Saami territories in today's Nordic Arctic also served to catalyse cross-border Saami connections, starting in the 1950s. These organisations, like the Inuit Circumpolar Council, made a similar contribution to a conceptualisation of the Arctic as a region that transected state borders (Vik and Semb, 2013).

It is important to keep in mind that the indigenous Arctic has long been a place of mobility and interconnection, even as North–South ties remained non-existent, weak or contested (see Dodds and Nuttall, 2015; and McGhee, 2006 for a circumpolar discussion). Historical interconnections in the Bering Strait are an interesting example of this (Fitzhugh and Crowell, 1988). While the Cold War period made the expanse of Arctic seas separating Alaska and Chuktoka seem like an insurmountable geopolitical distance, the Bering Sea had, for indigenous communities, been no obstacle. Kinship ties, visits, trading routes and marriage journeys criss-crossed the region.

For example, the Inupiat living on Big and Little Diomede Islands had cousins, friends and trading partners on each island and up and down the Alaskan and Russian coasts. Residents of Big Diomede Island regularly traded and intermarried and visited residents of Little Diomede. Even as these territories became gradually more incorporated into the new 'motherlands' growing up on both sides of the Bering Sea, the travel and interconnection continued across the 2.4-mile separation. The school-teacher on Little Diomede recorded 178 people visiting in a six-month period during 1944 (Alaskaweb, 2015). However, as the uneasy alliance of the Soviet Union and the United States grew chillier after the end of the Second World War, and eventually cooled into the strategic stand-off of the Cold War, these longstanding connections and visits ceased, and travel between the islands was no longer permitted.

Reactivating these kinship and language ties across a geopolitically significant border was an important catalyst in the active Arctic region-building of the immediate post-Cold War era. In John English's wonderful account of the history of the Arctic Council, he describes the first North American Inuit delegation to travel across the 'Ice Curtain' of the Bering

Figure 2 Big and Little Diomede Islands and the Alaskan and Chukotka coasts.

Sea to Chukotka in the waning days of the Soviet Union in 1988. The delegation was inspired and led by the Inuk leader and later Canadian Circumpolar Ambassador Mary Simon, and was part of a broader exploration of the ground for interconnected, innovative forms of circumpolar governance. Moments of the joyful, tearful reunion, which also brought together some family relations who had been separated for four decades, took place in the border-crossing Inupiaq language of the Bering coasts. This was to the consternation of the English-speaking KGB 'listeners' assigned to monitor the delegation (English, 2013).

Likewise, the ICC had always kept an empty chair for the Russian Inuit of Chukotka (Chukchi) since the organisation was first established in 1982. The aim of the newly founded organisation had been to bring together all the Inuktitut-speaking peoples of the Arctic – the Inuit people – to develop a shared voice. The driving forces behind this increased political organisation were growing interest in the Arctic's natural resources (oil, gas, mining) and an increasing impact from global environmental movements, such as the anti-whaling movement, on Arctic communities (Shadian, 2014). The Chukchi finally joined a meeting of the ICC in Iqaluit in 1988.

Similar international organisations were established by the Saami people (Saami Council, founded in 1956), the Athabaskan peoples of the North American sub-Arctic (Arctic Athabaskan Council in 2000), the Aleut International Association (1998), Gwich'in Council International (1999) and the indigenous peoples of Russia (RAIPON, 1992). These organisations vary in their staffing and ability to represent their interests in all forums (see Knecht, 2017, for an overview of Arctic Council participation), but are generally active in the UN Forum for Indigenous Peoples and meet in the Arctic Council as 'Permanent Participants'. We return to the topic of the diplomacy of indigenous organisations in the international Arctic in Chapter 5.

While indigenous contact with 'outsiders' between the sixteenth and nineteenth centuries had generally been based around mutually beneficial exchange of goods (Dodds and Nuttall, 2015), the intensity of contact between indigenous peoples and 'outsiders' increased with the advent of modern states extending and asserting their sovereignty over their putative Arctic 'backyards' in the nineteenth and twentieth centuries, as we shall see below. These colonial efforts included the growing use of native lands for non-renewable resource extraction (Mitchell, 1996; Berger, 1985), religious conversion processes (Balzer, 1999), extension of law and justice (Grant, 2002), residential schools, medical care (including isolation of those with infectious diseases, such as tuberculosis) (Shkilnyk, 1985), and forced relocation and settlement policies (Marcus, 1995; Damas, 2002; Vitebsky, 2005). The effects of this internal colonialism and the rapid social and economic disruption that accompanied it continue to be felt (for scholarly works on these dynamics, see Alfred, 1995; Mitchell, 1996; Shkilnyk, 1985; Irlbacher-Fox, 2009; Vitebsky, 2005).

A passage from Hugh Brody's book *The Other Side of Eden* gives one vivid illustration of the colonial legacy. Brody was collecting interviews for a film in northern British Colombia, amongst the Nisga'a people. He decided to interview an artist assisting with the film, George Gosnell, about his experience in the residential school system in the 1950s. Gosnell recounted his travel to St George's residential school; the first night in a huge dormitory too frightened to sleep; the incomprehensibility of the sole language used, English; and the four times he was strapped across the hands with a belt for speaking his Nisga'a language. He said:

> I don't why the residential school ... I don't know why they had such far distant places for education. To get torn apart from, from your parents and your brothers and your sisters to educate us ... they made us forget our own language ... And then in the summer, after the school was finally finished with our one year, spending our time in the residential school was over, we came back on the train. Again the trip took three days. I got off the train. I looked in my mother's face. And I used English. She asked me why I used the English. I told her that's what we went away for.
>
> (Brody, 2000: 170–172)

George Gosnell relearned Nisga'a languages at the insistence of and with help from his parents. During this interview, the film's sound recordist had searched desperately to eliminate what seemed like a source of background noise in the room. Listening to the recording later, they realised that the noise they had picked up – a faint beating – had been the sound of George Gosnell's heart suddenly pounding as he recalled, thirty-five years later, his return home and his mother's shock that he could only speak English to her. It is important to keep in mind that it is against this legacy of colonialism, and partly in pursuit of its redress, that internationally active Arctic indigenous organisations engage in cross-border politics.

Commercial actors

The Arctic gradually moved out of the realm of myth and into a realm of opportunity for European kingdoms, as Spain, Portugal, England and others built out their status as maritime powers. The quest for a sea route to China, as well as rumours of the riches of the New World, encouraged sailing into the relative unknown (Craciun, 2009). Many of the early explorers were supported by consortiums of business actors, often interconnected with royal or political patronage, and military actors as well. Frobisher was patronised by Elizabeth I with the equivalent of £80 million in today's currency, while William Barentsz, whose sixteenth-century exploration reshaped the map of the Arctic from Spitsbergen (today known as Svalbard) to Novaya Zemlya, was supported by wealthy Dutch merchants (English, 2013). Barentsz' travels and reports, followed by William Baffin's journey of 1615, did much to undermine the hope that the Arctic would present new trade routes to China or any other easy opportunities for transit and riches. The next phase of Arctic exploration, therefore, had the emphasis on national glory, heroism and science, rather than the prospect of great riches, and we return below to this era in connection with the State.

The Arctic colonial periphery has long supplied more southerly markets with valued goods from the fur trade of the past to the diamonds, oil and gas, and fish of today. For example, the comparatively temperate Arctic Norway – with its long coastline and robust seafaring traditions and sea-based trade routes – has centuries-old connections southwards. Portuguese vessels plied Arctic fisheries off the Lofoten Islands to fish cod. Additionally, the pursuit of whales and other migratory marine mammals brought European whalers and hunters to the Arctic archipelago of Spitsbergen (Pederson, 2006). Likewise, trading in furs and the quest to map the eastern edges of the Russian empire pushed Russian actors towards the outer edges of the Eurasian Arctic in the 1730s and 1740s (Bonhomme, 2012) Exploration was often succeeded either by the establishment of State-supported trading monopolies, such as the Hudson Bay Company, or by missionary-controlled contact with outsiders, as we saw develop in Greenland.

Figure 3 Hudson's Bay Company Building in Apex, Iqaluit, Nunavut.

Companies became an especially prominent feature of the Soviet and now Russian (again) Arctic. Industry and exploitation of the Arctic's natural resources were seen as important pursuits in Stalin's 'revolution from above' to promote Soviet economic independence and prosperity (Rowe, 2013; Bruno, 2016). Mining and metallurgy became key parts of this from the 1950s onwards, followed by an oil-and-gas era in Siberia from the 1970s. The Russian Arctic is highly urbanised – an anomaly in the otherwise small-community Arctic landscape. These towns are 'one-industry' cities (*monogorody*) with industries that typically took responsibility for education, community health, pensioner travel, and support and accommodation. While these State–business relations have been rapidly changing in the post-Soviet Arctic, the companies remain the touchstone for how corporate citizenship and environmental and social responsibility of new companies are assessed (Kelman *et al.*, 2016; Wilson Rowe, 2017b).

Business interests and related forms of new or different activity in the Arctic have also served to highlight weak spots or disagreement in international law. Canada, the United States and the Northwest Passage provide an interesting example in this regard. The USA adheres to the doctrine of the freedom of the seas and characterises the Northwest Passage as an international strait, whereas Canada seeks to define these as internal waters (Elliot-Meisel, 2009). One of the contested voyages was the 1969 'Manhattan Voyage', in which the Humble Oil Company (later Exxon) wanted to take a modified oil tanker through the Northwest Passage. The company requested customary permission from the Canadian Government, which was granted. By contrast, the USA announced that it would send an icebreaker into the Northwest Passage to accompany the commercial tanker, but did not ask permission in light of the US assertion that the passage is an international strait

Navigating relations with business and consideration of different economic possibilities has also been a key aspect in asserting or winning greater degrees of self-determination. The considerations Denmark and Greenland weigh as they tackle the question of full economic independence for the Arctic island state illustrate this well. Like many Arctic national/local economies, Greenland is characterised by a narrow economic base and a reliance on natural resources (Bertelsen *et al.*, 2015). Full independence for Greenland from Denmark will be highly dependent upon diversifying the economic base and gaining additional sources of income beyond fisheries and hunting, tourism, raw materials and land-based industries. The questions of what kind of economic development opportunities (large vs small scale; extractive vs renewable) should be pursued – and what kind of actors should represent Greenlandic interests – are hotly debated in Greenlandic society (Nuttall, 2015; Wilson, 2015).

Today, corporate actors are arguing for an increasing place at the table in questions of Arctic economic governance. Financial actors/banks who lend money to key Arctic projects play an instrumental role in setting and enforcing various standards of relevance to the Arctic natural and project environment (Alto and Jaakkola, 2015). More specific to the Arctic itself, the establishment of the Arctic Economic Council (AEC) in 2015 and the new Arctic Investment Protocol, forwarded by a working group at the World Economic Forum, are two key new initiatives (see Chapter 2 for more on this).

States and their representatives

It seems almost strange to need to introduce 'states', as they are the taken-for-granted building block of most IR scholarship. However, when it comes to the Arctic, especially the cold reaches of the Eurasian and North American North, the State could almost be considered a newcomer. The expansion of the State – in earnest and with the aim of pursuing sovereignty through the incorporation of indigenous lands and peoples into the polity – happened as late as the 1920s, 1930s and 1940s in the American and Eurasian Arctic. The growth of the State into the Arctic was accompanied and facilitated by the presence of military, police and military-related activities (Grant, 2010). This expansion also involved generating State-friendly knowledge of the region (for example, through cartography and census-taking) and establishing physical presence and ways of monitoring or maintaining vision over the Arctic region, largely through scientific and military endeavours (Wråkberg, 2013).

The nineteenth and twentieth centuries also saw a new phase of exploration in conversation with the State more directly, rather than the broad consortiums representing various economic interests that drove previous phases of exploration. Sir John Franklin, and later Fridtjof Nansen, Roald Amundsen and Robert Peary are prominent names in this regard. For example, Franklin's journeys with the *Erebus* and *Terror* in 1845 were motivated in part by the British empire's naval strength. The thirst for exploration also connected to an increasingly literate British public, eager to consume reports of distant land and imperial heroism. This reading public was a market for publishing revenues, and a key audience for narratives of imperial greatness and national identity (English, 2013: 47–48).

The disappearance of Franklin's crew and ships sparked rescue expeditions throughout the late 1840s and 1850. The location of the sunken ships was deemed a mystery until Parks Canada divers identified the wreckage in 2014. However, local Inuit had long told stories of the boat their great-grandparents had collected items from for years before it was eventually crushed and sank – and of the journalists, cavalry officers and other explorers to whom they had tried to show the resting place of the *Erebus*. In fact, the Inuktitut placename given to where the ship was eventually found translates to English as 'the boat sank here', and appeared on a map of Inuit testimony collected by an American explorer as early as 1867 (Ducharme, 2017). The obstinate overlooking of Inuit knowledge about the *Erebus'* whereabouts as reliable information for over 147 years, and the downgrading of Inuit knowledge and contributions in the initial reporting of how the *Erebus* was 'found', are vivid examples of the knowledge politics of the Arctic. We return to this question of knowledge and authority in Chapter 5.

During the Cold War, the Arctic had heightened significance as a military theatre in the stand-off between the era's two superpowers – the United States and the Soviet Union. Young (1985: 61) points to geography as an important feature here, noting that it was 'hard to ignore the facts that the United States and the Soviet Union [were] immediate neighbours in the Arctic (western Alaska and eastern Siberia are only 57 miles apart at the Bering Strait), that the shortest route between the two superpowers [was] across the North Pole'. The Arctic became dotted by a range of early warning sites and radar listening stations. These characteristic, space-age-looking facilities were called – in North America – the Distance Early Warning (DEW) Line. The DEW Line, which was built in the 1950s and rejuvenated in the 1980s, increased threat awareness in the Arctic (Young, 1985). Similar kinds of radar listening stations are still active along the Norwegian–Russian border. At the same time, the performance of national 'softer' security functions was also an opportunity for cooperation and drew upon some of the same kinds of resources that could be applied in a hard security logic. For example, in 1988, Norway and the Soviet Union signed a bilateral agreement on search and rescue in the Barents Sea, which specified procedures and methods of cooperation in the event of maritime accidents (Archer, 1988).

These early State–military cooperative agreements also point us to an important feature of Arctic governance. Dodds and Nuttall (2015: 41) coin the term 'legalization' of Arctic space to capture the growing layers of soft and hard law, produced specifically for the Arctic or for global application with important Arctic repercussions. At the end of the Cold War, the only multilateral agreements in place specific to the Arctic were the Svalbard Treaty and the 1973 Polar Bear Convention, which was originally an initiative of the Soviet Union (Roginko and LaMourie, 1992; Young, 1992, 1998). The development and ratification, by most Arctic states, of the United Nations Convention on the Law of the Sea (UNCLOS) in 1982 was also another key milestone for the legal harmonisation of interests amongst the Arctic coastal states (Harders, 1987). At a recent Arctic conference, the Norwegian Foreign Minister Børge Brende described UNCLOS as the 'Constitution of the Arctic' (Nilsen, 2017). Gerhardt *et al.* (2010) suggest that the key legacy of UNCLOS is the definition of various zones of ocean space (exclusive economic zones close to the coast, outer continental shelf, high seas and so on), and a specification of a suite of rights and responsibilities of users.

The framework was provided by UNCLOS for Norway and the Soviet Union/Russia to identify and negotiate overlapping claims about extended continental shelves in the Barents Sea (see Beyers, 2014, for an overview of the various overlapping claims and their process towards resolution). Long-term bilateral negotiations resulted in the 2010 Barents Sea Delimitation Agreement. Likewise, the USA (albeit as a non-signatory to UNCLOS) and the Soviet Union/Russia had an overlapping claim in the Bering Sea resolved in 1990 under these same principles. Although the agreement was never ratified by the Soviet Union because of dissent in the Russian Parliament (the Duma), both countries operate with respect to this agreement (Berbrick, 2015). Arctic states' public respect for the practices and frameworks identified in UNCLOS has been an important resource for counteracting the occasionally popular notion of the Arctic as 'ungoverned' and undergoing a 'scramble for resources', as will be discussed in greater detail in Chapter 2.

The migratory nature of many Arctic species also brings a layer of international law to the Arctic. Norway and Russia had long cooperated on fisheries-management of joint stocks in the Barents Sea (Hønneland,

2013), utilising international frameworks (International Council for the Exploration of the Sea standards, the UN Fish Stocks Agreement) to inform the establishment of fishing quotas (Churchill, 2015). For example, the harvesting of whales is managed through the International Whaling Commission, which was established by the International Convention for the Regulation of Whaling in 1946 (Churchill, 2015). These same whales – and many other Arctic plants and animals – are also covered by the Convention on the Conservation of Migratory Species and the Convention on International Trade in Endangered Species of Wild Flora and Fauna (better known as CITES).

Scientists

Scientific knowledge and endeavour have been intimately intertwined with Arctic states' pursuit of sovereignty over their own territories. In their examination of scientific debates in early modern England, Shapin and Schaffer famously asserted, 'solutions to the problem of knowledge are solutions to the problem of social order' (1985: 332). In many ways, this description of early modern England holds true today and also points us in the right direction for understanding the relationship between science and politics in the international and national Arctic as well. As Sverker Sörlin has argued, the relative scarcity of people and the absence of major agriculture and settlements made scientific activity an even more important marker of State presence in the Arctic than elsewhere in the world. He cites, for example, Norway's slogan for visibility on Svalbard as 'flag-waving, hunting/fishing and research' ('flagg, fangst og forskning') (2013: 7).

However, the international nature of the scientific disciplines and the interconnected nature of Arctic ecosystems have been push factors for international cooperation (Bravo and Sörlin, 2002). Western scientists were long hindered from understanding the specificities of Arctic Ocean circulation patterns because of incomplete access to physical data from the Soviet/Russian Arctic (Harders, 1987; Brosnan *et al.*, 2011). These patterns included the Transpolar Drift, which brings ice from east Siberia across the North Pole and into the Atlantic Ocean via the eastern shores of Greenland; and the Pacific Gyral, which is a clockwise rotation above the North American Arctic (Harders, 1987). These ocean-spanning circulation patterns make any pollution originating in national coastal waters (or in polluted rivers flowing north) an international problem. The work of scientists, albeit restrained by the strategic stand-off of the Cold War, was essential to documenting how some environmental problems were indeed crossing borders within the Arctic, including the challenges of migratory species and regionally driven atmospheric issues, such as 'Arctic haze' from the burning of fossil fuels in a cold environment (Friedheim, 1988).

Cooperative efforts have long been made to supersede these access and data challenges, as well as to seek to combine resources in the high-cost, high-technology fields of oceanography, geology, mapping and so on (see Lajus, 2013, for an example of international field stations around the White Sea). The International Polar Year (IPY) was first carried out in 1882–1883 and involved the cooperation of scientists from twelve countries in establishing twelve international research bases in the Arctic. This tradition continued at regular intervals, even taking place as the 'International Geophysical Year' at the height of the Cold War in 1957–1958, and most recently with a diversity of natural- and social-science activities in the period 2007–2009 (Elzinga, 2013). In 1972, the USA and the USSR signed an agreement on Cooperation in the Field of Environmental Protection (Harders, 1987), which included clauses on exchange of information on marine pollution prevention and cooperative study of Arctic ecological systems. However, despite an emphasis on sci-entific work as an area of potential cooperation in the Cold War Arctic, and strong national communities of knowledge relating to Arctic science, the direct military and industrial applications of some fields (oceanog-raphy, upper-atmosphere physics and Arctic engineering) limited in-depth sharing of data and scientific expertise (Stokke, 1990: 28; Young, 1985: 177–178).

Scientific efforts have been important for states in building sover-eignty, as they allow them authoritatively to claim to 'know' their own Arctic. Science, as we will see in Chapters 3 and 5, is also one of the most important diplomatic 'coins' that can be used in the coopera-tive forums of Arctic governance today. This is not to say that scien-tific findings are political or that scientists are biased. Rather, the point is that states have long been reliant upon building both political and knowledge orders and, therefore, the activities of statecraft and pro-ducing, managing and applying knowledge should be understood as closely intertwined.

NGOs and their representatives

Historically, many of the non-state and non-commercial actors present in the region had a religious mandate. Moravian, Russian Orthodox and Catholic representatives sought converts and took responsibility for residential schools, but also engaged in linguistics (including pro-ducing orthographies for translating the Bible) and collected phys-ical observations of the Arctic as hobby scientists typical of the time (Bravo, 2005).

In more recent history, NGOs of various stripes have played an important role, often through their ability to provide input and assist in processes in ways seen as relevant by other actors in the policy field. Mainstream environmental NGOs, such as the World Wide Fund for Nature (WWF), and scientific organisations, such as the International Arctic Science Committee (IASC), have been longstanding participants in the politics of the Arctic Council, and many other NGOs have observer status as well. Seconding scientists to Arctic Council WGs and otherwise providing inputs into ongoing science diplomacy efforts are a key activity in this regard.

The role and presence of NGOs in the Arctic policy field remains somewhat understudied. Duyck (2012) notes that NGOs may play an important role in linking different levels of governance or by rallying public support in national contexts. Wehrmann (2017) suggests that on certain technical issues, such as oil-spill prevention, NGOs may be important at early stages but are increasingly seen as irrelevant if not able to provide specific, technical expertise on the issues at hand. She also notes that NGOs may have better access to and influence within the Arctic Council WGs, as opposed to task forces established by the Arctic Council states to facilitate binding agreement on an Arctic issue (Wehrmann, 2017).

Environmental organisations have also been decisive in promoting a vision of the Arctic that emphasises the region's global environmental significance to a greater degree than some Arctic governments and indigenous governance organisations would themselves emphasise. Greenpeace – an NGO that has not gained observer status at the Arctic Council – has drawn attention to their standpoints through dramatic branding of its core positions. It has done this notably in connection with the Arctic oil and gas sector, seeking to block oil exploration activity with activists in kayaks or by boarding the Russian Prirazlomnoye platform (Palosaari and Tynkkynen, 2015). The impact of its efforts to sway global audiences has, at times, put the organisation at odds with local Arctic actors. For example, Greenpeace, in cooperation with high-profile celebrities such as Brigitte Bardot, was instrumental in raising the seal hunt as an issue of concern, later resulting in the European Union's ban on seal-product imports (Airoldi, 2014). The 1980s campaign highlighted graphic images of seal cubs clubbed to death, their blood spattered across the white Arctic snow (Wenzel, 1991).

For Inuit communities, the seal hunt and trading of seal furs were longstanding, key elements in a sustainable, mixed economy of the North. Seal fur was an important source of cash and also a source of cultural continuity, as it made livelihoods based on traditional activities financially rewarding. The European market's 1982 trade ban on seal furs from harp seal and hooded seal pups resulted in collapse of this Arctic economy (Wenzel, 1991), even though an exception had been made for the indigenous hunt. Greenpeace later apologised for this unforeseen impact on an Arctic sustainable economy, and its cooperation with indigenous organisations is growing, but still frequently rocky, as a consequence (Kerr, 2014).

Letting the lines cross: actors in Arctic governance today

The astute reader may have noticed that the actor categories described above were challenging to keep disentangled from one another. In any one section about a particular actor, nearly all of the other actor groups required mention in order to deliver a sensible account of key trends and events. In the post-Cold War period of cooperation, the actor picture becomes even more interconnected in fascinating ways, and the power relations involved in these interconnections is a topic that the subsequent chapters explore. We see indigenous organisations and states seeking to 'sing from the same songsheet' to maximise their success, businesses hammering out regulations to be ratified by states, NGOs working with the finance sector to promote responsible development of the Arctic and so on.

In 1988, Mikhail Gorbachev gave his famous 'Murmansk speech', in which he outlined how tension in the Arctic region could be decreased and cooperation increased (for an analysis, see Åtland, 2008). A series of events drew attention to the environmental vulnerability of the Arctic. Radioactive fallout from the Chernobyl disaster and sulphur dioxide from Soviet nickel smelters, as well as the oil spill from the *Exxon Valdez* and the loss of the Soviet nuclear submarine *Komsomolets* in April 1989 in the Barents Sea, highlighted the fragility of Arctic ecosystems (Graczyk and Koivurova, 2014).

The immediate post-Cold War years witnessed the establishment of the many new forums and network. The Northern Forum was launched in Alaska, bringing together regional (sub-state) governments, indigenous organisations and engaged academics (Young, 2002). The Barents Euro-Arctic Region and Council brought together a similar set of actors at the Nordic/Russian Arctic level. The establishment of IASC highlighted the potential and desire for more cooperative work in the Arctic, while the debate over which countries belonged in the forefront of the initiative highlights an early tension between the participation of 'Arctic' and 'non-Arctic' states to which we return in Chapter 2 (Stokke, 1990; Śmieszek, 2016).

The Arctic Environmental Protection Strategy (AEPS) was launched from Finland in 1991. The strategy focused on new opportunities to address the problems of Arctic pollution. Many of the pollution issues to be addressed tied into testing, transport, storage and decommissioning of nuclear weapons and nuclear-powered vessels, and thus were only possible to address in the radically changed post-Cold War geopolitical climate (Roginko and LaMourie, 1992; Keskitalo, 2004). The AEPS focused on six key pollution issues: (1) acidification in the Arctic; (2) persistent organic pollutants (POPs); (3) oil pollution in the Arctic (from vessels, offshore development); (4) radioactivity in the Arctic; (5) heavy metal pollution through long-range atmospheric transport; and (6) the monitoring and conservation of flora and fauna (Scrivener, 1999; Caron, 1993).

Later the AEPS became absorbed into/served as a partial structural basis for the Arctic Council in 1997 (Scrivener, 1999). The five Arctic Council WGs came directly from the AEPS: AMAP, PAME, the Working Group on the Conservation of Arctic Flora and Fauna (CAFF), the Emergency Prevention, Preparedness and Response Working Group (EPPR), and a sustainable development working group. This last group had been contested by those concerned that including a sustainable development group would water down the environment/conservation focus of circumpolar cooperation. However, the sustainability focus was championed by the ICC and they carried the day (Scrivener, 1999).

Today, the Arctic Council remains a forum, increasingly referred to as an intergovernmental forum (see Olsen and Shadian, 2016, for a discussion), rather than a formal international organisation. It has enjoyed significant success in promoting innovative scientific assessments of the region and in influencing international environmental policy processes. Just as important, it has become a meeting place where states' interests and policy framings of the Arctic have become largely harmonised (see Chapter 2) and where the indigenous peoples of the region have made visible their rightful place in shaping Arctic governance (see Chapter 5).

However, as this book will illustrate, not all actors are equal in cooperation, even in more open or networked forms of cross-border cooperation. Rather, certain positions, resources and interests can matter more in shaping outcomes, and these reflect (and amplify) power relations. Turning our attention to a theoretically informed concept of power politics adds important insights to our existing understandings of Arctic politics, allowing us to see how cooperation is dynamically maintained and contestation managed. Building out this argument about power and contestation within cooperation in Arctic regional governance is the main task of the coming chapters.

2

The power politics of representation

Saami poet Nils-Aslak Valkeapää called for a vision of the Arctic as a horizontal highway of movement and conversation, with its treeless expanses providing opportunity to roam and the long polar nights providing opportunity to talk and listen (1998). This evocative image of a highway of interconnection is a counterpoint to the typical ways in which the Arctic is divided by standard maps and globes, with North–South political lines transecting the Saami homeland in the European North. Maps, films, poetry and policy documents can all tell a story about the region. This chapter seeks to highlight how these representations of the region – or the way in which circumpolar policy issues are framed by narrative and images – are a manifestation of and serve to shape power relations in the region. Consider the selection of the three maps in Figures 4–6 as an illustration of the various ways of representing the region.

Figure 4 illustrates the bird migration routes connecting one nesting ground in Arctic Alaska with populations around the world. Like the ice-locked whales discussed in Chapter 1, these kinds of ecosystemic connections serve to unsettle political boundaries and tie into the logic presented by several of the non-Arctic states in their applications for observer status at the Arctic Council, as we will see below. In this illustrative map, political boundaries are completely absent. Figure 5, by contrast, with its satellite view centred on the Arctic, highlights political boundaries and presents a view that brings to the forefront Arctic states (see Steinberg *et al.*, 2015: 29 for a close analysis of a previous version of this map). Figure 6 shows a view of the Arctic where the relevant lines are neither political borders nor bird migration routes, but a comparatively local view of usage pathways of Inuit hunters moving on the land. The lines were created through GPS mapping software that Inuit hunters attached to their snowmobiles. A fourth map, not reproduced here but available in Jakobsen (2010: 4), was made by Hao Xiaoguang and was utilised by the Chinese Arctic and Antarctic Administration from the

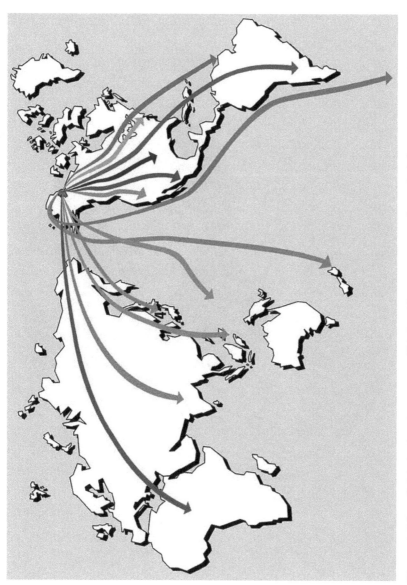

Figure 4 Map of global migration routes of birds with nesting grounds in Alaska's Arctic National Wildlife Refuge.

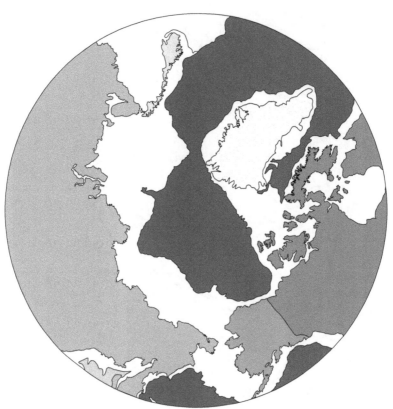

Figure 5 Map of North Circumpolar Region (polar projection).

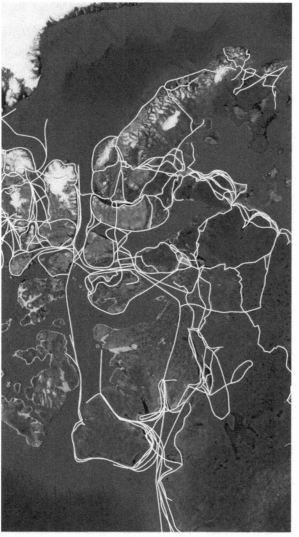

Figure 6 Map of a use-based demarcation of the Arctic from the Pan Inuit Trails project.

early 2000s, but fell into disuse as China escalated its efforts to secure Arctic Council permanent observer status (see discussion below). The map has a flattened perspective allowing for a viewing of both poles at once. The boldest lines are not political boundaries, but rather potential transpolar shipping routes in bright red and blue that could bring Chinese goods to European and North American markets in the rapidly warming Arctic.

These broader representations of the Arctic are well analysed in the literature, with key sources of empirics coming from photography, film, mapping, and broad policy narratives and media representations (Powell and Dodds, 2014; Steinberg *et al*, 2015). While the broad strokes of how the region can be framed and is represented have been well examined, we still need to know more about how these frames are brought to bear on the political practice of engaging across borders in the Arctic – and how they tie in with (or undermine) existing relations of power. Whether the Arctic is framed as a resource frontier or an indigenous homeland has consequences for the kinds of politics that can be pursued (and who can pursue them and to whose benefit).

So, how do actors go about deploying regional frames in practice? The chapter illustrates how 'framing' is about laying the ground for policy actions. In other words, a robust policy frame will address what the problem is and its causes, who can do something and who should do something. The first case examines how key political actors worked to sustain a representation of the region as cooperative in a time of geopolitical crisis outside the Arctic itself, following Russia's annexation of Crimea. From there, we move on to a more granular policy scale seeking to see how particular types of representations of the Arctic matter for specific political outcomes. The two remaining examples look at framings relevant for clarifying policy debates around what kind of actors belong in Arctic politics, namely the participation of non-Arctic states and business representatives in Arctic governance.

Framing for policy action: more than just pretty pictures

How something – a place, a policy problem, an historic event – is 'framed' says much about what kind of political action is deemed possible and justified. As Jasanoff and Wynne (1998) put it in their discussion of the framing of environmental problems, a frame is a robust interpretation that gives the policy public a sense of what the problem is, what the cause of the problem is and, most importantly, what can and should be done to address it. In this way, 'framings' or representations of the Arctic as a political space set the parameters for possible political action. A robust representation of any policy object most often delimits the kinds of actors, rhetoric and practices that are recognised as 'relevant', 'practical' and 'useful'.

Analytical attention to framing is a feature of the broader literature on the social construction of space. This literature resulted from a sense for the shortcomings of purely temporal explanations in accounting for how the fabric of everyday life gets made – including local, national and international politics (Foucault, 1980; LeFebvre, 1991; Soja, 2003; Unwin, 2000). For example, work in the vein of critical geopolitics illustrates how particular outcomes in inter-state relations stem from constructed (not given) spatialisations of world politics (O'Tuathail and Dalby, 1998). These may be broad categories, such as developing vs developed world or the 'first' (western capitalist, developed), 'second' (socialist) and third (poor, developing) from the Cold War.

Acknowledging that our ideas of space are socially constructed is not the same thing as asserting that space is socially constructed (Unwin, 2000: 26). The Arctic environment is not just a blank slate upon which the powerful get to write their discourses, as we will discuss further in the conclusion of this volume. Physical realities, like changes in Arctic sea ice due to climate change, matter. Rather, underlining the social construction of our ideas around space serves to highlight that how places and attending policy problems are packaged for political action is just one representation out of many theoretically possible representations. This line of thinking brings us to relations of power: What does the resulting idea of space do and whose interests does it serve? One way of identifying empirically how frames undergird relations of power and promote interests is to zoom in on what political actors actually do with particular framings in their meetings with other political actors. My emphasis here on how regional or policy frames get deployed is part of a growing literature from geographers focusing on the concrete practices of those who personify and enact geopolitics in global governance settings (Jones and Clark, 2015; McConnell *et al.*, 2012; Hakli and Kallio, 2014).

Frame 1: a cooperative Arctic in rough winds

The Arctic as a zone of peace

At the 2013 Kiruna ministerial session, Foreign Minister Sergey Lavrov recalled a special 'symbolic trip' of the senior officials of the Arctic Council to the North Pole in April of that year. The trip was organised by the Russian Security Council and accompanied by a well-known polar explorer and Russian Arctic policy actor, Artur Chilingarov. Chilingarov had been part of the Swedish–Russian expedition that had planted a Russian flag on the Arctic seabed in 2008, causing much consternation. Minister Lavrov noted: 'It is hard to overestimate the value for history of the photos [of the SAOs from all eight Arctic countries] against the background of the flags of our eight countries and the flag of the Arctic Council made by them.' He also commented on the signing of the second legally binding circumpolar agreement – on marine oil pollution preparedness and response, underlining how this was 'another evidence of high responsibility of Arctic countries for the state of affairs in the region' (MFA, Russia, 2013).

This statement was not just pretty, diplomatic words – it also tallied well with how the Arctic was discussed at the time by Russian civil servants working on Arctic issues more broadly. As a Russian high-ranking civil servant had also noted in a 2011 interview, image was important for Russia and for the Arctic space more generally, as it was seen as essential to work against Cold War narratives: 'We have to be proactive in telling others about Russia and what we do. We leave it too much to others, and this does not always work out. We are a normal people in a normal country with strengths and weaknesses.' Another Russian interviewee put it this way in 2011: 'Russia plays by the rules. The process of carving up the Arctic does not pull Arctic states apart, in fact it brings us closer.'

Statements like these from the Arctic states have been regularly forwarded to counteract another framing of the region – the Arctic as on the edge of geopolitical chaos. In attempting neatly to package an Arctic that is undergoing complex and unpredictable ecological 'state change' (Young, 2009), the familiar narrative of competitive geopolitics lent itself well to popular imagination. 'Race for the Arctic', 'Arctic scramble' and the 'new Cold War' have been common newspaper headlines when it comes to the coverage of Arctic affairs (Wilson Rowe, 2013a; Powell and Dodds, 2014 and Steinberg *et al.*, 2015). By contrast, the Arctic states have, in recent years, become a coordinated chorus extolling the peacefulness of the region and the sufficiency of existing international law for dealing with eventual issues (Bailes and Heininen, 2012; Wilson Rowe, 2013a). The 2008 Ilullissat Declaration issued by the 'Arctic 5' coastal states was an important milestone in calming, if not eliminating, concerns about potential Arctic conflict (see Steinberg, *et al.*, 2015, for an extended discussion of this political moment). One study found a remarkable drop in coverage of or reference to the possibility of conflict in the Arctic in Russian State-owned media following the Ilullissat Declaration (Wilson Rowe and Blakkisrud, 2014).

However, a mere two years after referencing the symbolically significant and hopeful snapshot taken at the North Pole, Lavrov did not even attend the ministerial session held in Iqaluit during the Canadian chairmanship. Russia was instead represented by its Minister of Environment. Russia's annexation of Crimea and continued interventions in eastern Ukraine in spring 2014 had triggered a sanctions regime by European and North American countries, and a war of words and non-military reactions in many bilateral and multilateral settings (Legvold, 2016). Arctic military cooperation, for example the Chief Heads of Defence cooperation, had been immediately suspended (Østhagen, 2016). Indeed, the region had been buffered from external disagreements in the past – for example, after Russia's armed conflict with Georgia in 2009 (Wilson Rowe and Blakkisrud, 2014) – but the broader impact of these earlier conflicts paled in comparison to 2014.

Buffering a peaceful frame in cold geopolitical winds

So, how did high-level diplomats shore up and utilise their longstanding framing of the Arctic as a zone of cooperation and peace at a historic low in East–West relations? To get at this question, we are going to take a small trip in time and space to the 2015 Arctic Council ministerial meeting held in Iqaluit, Canada.

Although little diplomatic work on specific decisions takes place at the ministerial meetings (see Introduction for a discussion), they are an excellent place to observe the symbolic work of framing the Arctic for political purposes in a broad way. Relieved of debating policy minutiae, Arctic Council ministers often use their time at the meeting to present once again their general understanding of the purpose of the Arctic region and recommit their countries to work towards that vision.

Consequently, the archival documents from the meeting give us some interesting insights. At the ministerial meeting in Iqaluit, the ministers of foreign affairs actually read their prepared remarks in full. This 'sticking to the text' is a sign of a more uncertain and restricted atmosphere (as a high-level Arctic official commented to me off the record in June 2014), rather than the sometimes free-flowing discussions that had characterised previous ministerial meetings.

From Table 2, we can see only six participants addressed the problem of international conflict directly, beyond general statements about regional peace and cooperation. For example, Finland's foreign minister addressed the geopolitical environment this way:

> the question whether and to what extent the strained international situation will affect Arctic cooperation can be answered in a positive tone and quoting our declaration saying that we are committed to maintaining peace, stability and constructive cooperation in the Arctic. It is in no-one's interest to let problems elsewhere to impact [*sic*] negative on Arctic cooperation and the Arctic Environment.
>
> (MFA, Finland, 2015: 3)

Sweden's statement highlights the more oblique way that most of the other Nordic countries addressed the question of broader issues in international relations between the countries gathered in Iqaluit: 'there is no

Table 2 High-level statements at the Iqaluit ministerial meeting

Polity	Addressed conflict?	If yes, how?
Finland	Yes	Noted strained international relations, and underlined importance of peace and cooperation in the Arctic.
Denmark/Greenland/ Faroe Islands	No	
Norway	No	
Iceland	No	
Sweden	Yes	Noted the peacefulness of the region and the increased importance of the forum during times of tension.
Russia	Yes	Acknowledged strained relations as 'external circumstances', emphasised peacefulness of the region and applauded progress in Arctic (despite external challenges).
Canada	No	
USA	No	
Saami Council	Yes	Emphasised interconnected nature of region, and the importance of securing and stabilising the region in times of geopolitical instability.
Arctic Athabaskan Council	Yes	Concerned about Lavrov's absence, concerned about unacknowledged tension in the region.
Aleut International Association	Yes	Concerned about geopolitical issues affecting the Council's work.
ICC	No	

Sources: MFA, Finland, 2015; Arctic Council, 2015b; Saami Council, 2015; MFA, Norway, 2015; US Department of State, 2015; Persson, 2015; ICC, 2015b; Arctic Council, 2015c; Arctic Council, 2015a; MFA, Denmark, 2015; Aleut International Association, 2015; Arctic Athabaskan Council, 2015; MFA, Canada, 2015; Ministry of Environment, Russian Federation, 2015.

problem that cannot be solved through cooperative relations. The Arctic Council's role as a forum for political dialogue is especially important in times of conflict and tension' (Persson, 2015: 3).

Interestingly, nearly all the Permanent Participant representatives expressed concern over the possibility of global problems becoming circumpolar regional ones. Reflective of most statements made by the Permanent Participants, the President of the Saami Council addressed geopolitical tension head-on:

> The representatives around this table represent the generation that has seen the Cold War come to an end. The Saami Council has seen the relationship with our brothers and sisters in all countries flourish again after decades of separation. Since 1992, the Saami Council has worked in all four countries the Sami people reside in ... Most of the Permanent Participant organisations represent an indigenous people that reside in more than one country. In times of geopolitical instability and changing economies, the indigenous peoples' communities will be the first to be negatively affected. Our pledge to you all is that we need to safeguard the unique work of the Arctic Council. We need to continue to cooperate as one Arctic family learning from each other and respecting each other. That is our responsibility and is important for sustainable development and well-being of all.
>
> (Saami Council, 2015: 1)

The Aleut International Association likewise expressed concern that 'geopolitical issues not related to the Arctic might threaten the discourse on Arctic issues and consensus based approach to decision making that is such a strength of the Council' (Aleut International Association, 2015: 1). On a similar note, Michael Stickman from the Arctic Athabaskan Council noted that they had to speak openly about the tensions between Russia and the West and about the absence of Lavrov: 'We are not naïve, but this Council and its individual members should shield our co-operation from broader political and geopolitical rivalries' (Arctic Athabaskan Council, 2015: 3).

Minister of Environment Sergey Donskoy represented Russia at the ministerial meeting, and also addressed the difficult political atmosphere between Russia and Europe/North America, expressing:

> appreciation of the fact that Arctic cooperation has been steadily developing despite the external circumstances ... Russia sees the Arctic as a territory of dialogue and cooperation and is interested in strengthening international cooperation in this region, both on a bilateral and multilateral basis ... Russia sees huge potential in the Arctic to promote and expand a constructive agenda for our common region, built on the basis of national interests of all the Arctic states ... There is no room for confrontation or aggravation of tension in the Arctic region – especially from outside sources – and there is strong public

demand for joint responses to common challenges and for joint use of shared opportunities in the Arctic. Russia opposes any attempt to politicize the development of Arctic cooperation.

(Ministry of Environment, Russian Federation, 2015: 1)

The USA, by contrast, focused exclusively on its aims for the upcoming chairmanship. This may suggest that the USA sought to naturalise the framing of the Arctic as cooperative by mentioning neither cooperation nor conflict (US Department of State, 2015). The absence of attention devoted to broader geopolitical tension also matches the United States' official reports and strategies relating to the Arctic. Though the USA ranked sovereignty and security as its top priority in its 2013 strategy, it characterised the Arctic region as 'free of conflict' and elaborated on the need 'to seek to work with other states and Arctic entities to advance common objectives in the Arctic region in a manner that protects Arctic states' (Obama, 2013: 6, 10).

Here, we see various kinds of diplomatic work in framing the region as cooperative, from oblique reference to the cooperative nature of Arctic politics, to direct calls for states to work to protect regional politics from outside conflict. This is not, however, the same as suggesting that the Arctic Council was unaffected by worsened East–West relations post-2014. In fact, the meetings leading to the ministerial session seem to have been more challenging than at other periods, if we judge by output alone. This renders the symbolic shoring up of the cooperative frame at the ministerial meeting in Iqaluit even more significant.

First, the minutes of the final SAO meeting held before the Iqaluit ministerial held some unusual appeals and exhortations from the Canadian chair. The chair made a general statement about the purpose and function of the Arctic Council to those assembled. He stated 'the Arctic Council is perceived as the preeminent intergovernmental forum in the Arctic, a model for international governance and a body that is moving towards policymaking and implementation'. He also noted that there was 'an increased interest in the Arctic Council', and 'urged delegates to rely on their spirit of cooperation and collegiality during the weeks leading up to the Iqaluit Ministerial' (Arctic Council Secretariat, 2015a: 4). Likewise, at a meeting six months earlier, an output on Arctic marine oil pollution prevention was touted as being of key importance for 'public diplomacy' (Arctic Council Secretariat, 2014: 8). These stated emphases on the diplomatic and symbolic traditions of the Arctic Council suggest that delegates were aware there was an audience watching to see how Arctic Council work proceeded in a new atmosphere of inter-state strife.

Secondly, the Canadian ministerial meeting did not produce a binding agreement as the previous two ministerial meetings had done (2011, Search and Rescue Agreement; 2013, Oil Spill Pollution and Response). Several initiatives under the 2013–2015 chairmanship seemed to be aiming for high-level agreement in various task forces, but failed to reach it within a two-year chairmanship. Task forces are often established on areas of high political priority and have previously enjoyed rather quick progress to completed goals under each chairmanship. This probably relates to the fact that task forces are ad hoc and established at the political level (by the SAOs), probably in issue areas where there is already agreement about the potential scope of outcomes and political goodwill. This contrasts with the rather more 'bottom-up' approach that generates a lot of the other Arctic Council outputs, which frequently come from the WGs.

For example, as late as 2015 at the final pre-ministerial SAO meeting in Whitehorse, the hope remained that the Task Force for Action on Black Carbon and Methane would invite observers to join and work towards a politically binding agreement that could reduce the presence of so-called short-lived climate forces in the Arctic. However, during the discussions, it became clear that this policy area did not yet have the needed support for a legally binding agreement by the Iqaluit ministerial meeting, and that the group needed to work further in incorporating various 'national priorities' into their work (Arctic Council Secretariat, 2015a: 10–11). The same seems the case for the Arctic Council Task Force on Oil Pollution Prevention, which had been working in earnest with one meeting in Nuuk in September 2014 and another in Ottawa in June 2014 (Arctic Council Task Force on Arctic Marine Oil Pollution Prevention, 2014b, c). This task force, however, also decided that working towards a non-binding document was preferable, but with a binding agreement coming later.

The seemingly slower progress within these task forces could be explained in part by the generally more challenging atmosphere between Russia and the other Arctic states outside the Arctic. Even if all the states were committed to keeping conflict out of the Arctic Council, as the review of ministerial statements above would support, Arctic Council representatives still needed to navigate their home environments to gain backing and clearance for their activities, particularly ones that might be novel or at the edge of existing mandates. An alternative or perhaps supplementary explanation is that the Arctic Council may be maturing and tackling an increasing number of questions that do not have clear policy solutions, and thus require more extensive handling and increased opportunity for discussion.

Nonetheless, as we have seen above, the conflict of Russia with European and North American states in the aftermath of Russia's military interference in Ukraine in 2014 resulted in a moment when all the Arctic states reiterated and underlined their commitment to representing and enacting the Arctic as a zone of cooperation and peaceful coordination. This was a coordinated display of diplomatic work from Arctic states and the Permanent Participants around the longstanding, state-supported framing of the Arctic as a zone of peace and cooperation. These displays were necessary because of the broader conflict lines between East and West and because this conflict had probably affected the Arctic Council's work in subtle ways, as suggested above in the work, slower across the board than usual, amongst the Arctic Council's task forces. Counteracting policy discourses around the Arctic as ungoverned or on the verge of conflict shores up a relationship that we examine in detail in the next chapter – a hierarchy of power established between Arctic and non-Arctic states. We also see traces of this Arctic/non-Arctic hierarchy in the more granular policy framings to which we turn now.

Frame 2: navigating global and regional framings of the Arctic

In their Arctic strategy documents, the five Arctic coastal states (Canada, Greenland/Denmark, Norway, Russia and the United States) all point to increased traffic and regional activity as a promising economic possibility and a security and governance challenge (Wilson Rowe, 2013a). These developments have not gone unnoticed by non-Arctic states, which have demonstrated an increasing interest in the region (Blunden, 2012; Manicom and Lackenbauer, 2013; Jakobsen and Lee, 2013, Wegge, 2012; Willis and Depledge, 2015). A key moment in which Asian states' interest was debated intensively was in connection to these countries' ultimately successful applications to gain permanent observer status on the Arctic Council.

As discussed in the methods section of the introductory chapter, the aim of the ministerial meetings is to have all the issues basically ironed out beforehand by high-level civil servants and their teams, and to work in home capitals and multilateral settings. It is, therefore, interesting that consideration of a new batch of observer applications, including China, Japan, South Korea, Singapore and the European Union, became a late-night, high-political affair prior to the end of the Swedish chairmanship ministerial meeting in Kiruna (2013). Some states, namely Norway and Denmark, publicly went out with their support for the impending applications early on, even flagging their support for some of their Arctic strategies (e.g. MFA, Norway, 2011: 78). Others, such as the USA, Canada and Russia were taciturn. Interviews conducted with decision-makers in 2013 indicated that the USA, Canada and Russia had not yet made their decisions plain – even at the behest of the Swedish SAO to put all cards on the table in advance of the ministerial session (Solli *et al.*, 2013).

The late-night, ministerial discussions around the topic were not because the question of observers was novel or had suddenly come on to the agenda. These observer applications had been delayed from the

2011 Nuuk ministerial meeting, where a decision had been made instead to revise application procedures for aspiring Arctic Council observers. The amendment (the 'Nuuk criteria') required aspiring observers to submit comprehensive applications detailing how they fulfilled the seven observer criteria, including demonstration of Arctic interests; financial and material contributions to the work of the Council; recognition of the Arctic states' sovereignty and jurisdiction over the region; and support for the UN Convention on the Law of the Sea, the prevailing legal framework for the Arctic. Furthermore, the Task Force on Institutional Cooperation had produced, during the Swedish chairmanship, an 'Observer Manual', which had been pushed for especially strongly by Russia and Canada (Solli *et al.*, 2013). The manual sets specific criteria across the board for both previous and incoming permanent observers with a focus on form and procedure within the Arctic Council – who sits where and who is allowed to speak in what order – as well as making specifications about expectations of and limits to the financial contributions of observers to Arctic Council work (Arctic Council Secretariat, 2013).

Table 3 Stated key interests of Asian states

Country	Stated key interests
China	Arctic's global environmental significance; climate change impacts (on food and agricultural productivity in China); new Arctic shipping routes and long-term economic picture; expansion of Arctic Council mandate from science/research to sustainable development work. (Bennett, 2015; Lanteigne, 2014; MFA, China, 2010; Jakobsen and Lee, 2013; Zhao, 2013; Zhang and Yang, 2016)
Japan	Maritime state with extended polar traditions; scientific presence on Svalbard; concern about global climate change. (Tonami and Watters, 2012; MFA, Japan, 2012; Ohnishi, 2016)
Korea	Environmental aspects and global impacts of climate change; polar research strengths/traditions; demonstrated ability to play role in global governance; long-term economic interests such as shipbuilding, shipping and energy. (Dongmin et al., 2017; Solli et al., 2013)
Singapore	Interests stemming from status as global maritime hub, including specific economic interests (expertise and experience in maritime traffic management, shipbuilding); concerns about climate change impacts as an island state. (Tonami and Watters, 2013; MFA. Singapore, 2012; Chen, 2016)

Asian countries' interests and global framing

So, why was the decision left until the ministerial meeting itself? Turning first to the East Asian countries that sought observer status, we see that the interests stated in their efforts to secure formal observer status were quite similar (see Table 3). All of the states demonstrated a concern for climate change (of which the rapidly warming Arctic is a key barometer) and most mentioned maritime traditions and economic interests. By the time of the Kiruna ministerial session, all of the East Asian observer applicants had underlined their respect for the pre-eminent position of Arctic states and accepted the premises of international law in governing the region, in particular UNCLOS (Solli *et al.*, 2013).

At the same time, these countries had, at times, engaged in some creative work in 'framing' the Arctic in a way that lent logic to their desire to secure their position within the Arctic Council. China; South Korea; Singapore; and, to a noticeably lesser extent, Japan underlined the global nature and significance of the Arctic region. As one interviewee from Singapore put it in 2013: 'It is our opinion that Arctic states should bear in mind that action in the region can affect the whole world and should include other states in polar matters' (in Solli *et al.*, 2013: 260). China had gone further than the other East Asian states in its framing of the Arctic as a 'common heritage of mankind', although this particular representation of the Arctic was noticeably dampened following the issuance of the Nuuk criteria, including suspension of the flattened polar map view discussed at the start of this chapter (Jakobsen and Lee, 2013). However, the emphasis on the global nature of the Arctic still remained, as demonstrated by the Chinese Ambassador to Norway's speech in 2013: 'In spite of their regional nature, the Arctic issues also include trans-regional ones, such as climate change, maritime shipping and so on, which need to be addressed with joint efforts of the international community' (Zhao, 2013).

Receiving a global framing: Arctic states' reactions

The Nordic countries were generally supportive of EU and East Asian states' observer applications. Norway has been forthcoming and welcoming of Asian states' Arctic interests. Norway proclaimed its support of the Asian states' inclusion on the Arctic Council early and continued to play a role in the states' ultimate acceptance and inclusion in Kiruna (MFA, Norway, 2011: 78; Bekkevold and Offerdal, 2014; Lunde, 2016). Denmark, Finland, Iceland and Sweden were also openly welcoming of non-Arctic states' applications to the Arctic Council after the Nuuk ministerial meeting in 2011. Denmark reiterated its support for observers in 2013 and noted that it looked forward to welcoming the EU (whose application was once again delayed in 2013). The Danes' argument was that observers can 'give valuable contributions to the work of the Arctic Council. By this decision, we show to the outside world that ensuring a sustainable future to the benefit of people living in the Arctic is a regional and a global responsibility' (MFA, Denmark, 2013). Iceland also expressed its support for meeting the interest of 'relevant stakeholders to contribute to the work of the Council [as it] will strengthen our ability to ensure the sustainable development of the North' (MFA, Iceland, 2013).

A largely positive stance from the USA with regard to an inclusive Arctic Council was also generally known, although not yet spelled out in any submissions or documents before Kiruna. A US interviewee in 2011 pointed to the question of expanding the number of observers as one of the biggest challenges for the Arctic Council, and outlined clearly the US position before Kiruna: 'For the US as a matter of principle it should be open and transparent. Some non-Arctic states and NGOs are upset that the process is taking so long.' It was also reported that the USA, represented by Secretary John Kerry, was catalytic in bringing about a united approval of the permanent observer applications (Solli *et al.*, 2013). In line with other Arctic states, the US reception of the Asian states came hand in hand with reminders of responsibilities. Tapping into the Asian states' own discourse about their Arctic interests being strongly linked to climate change, Secretary Kerry warned that proactive measures and efforts taken by the USA and other nations to combat climate change would be wiped out by 'China or another nation' using coal firepower, and he underlined the importance of countries, such as China and the United States, pursuing responsible growth (US Department of State 2013).

Both Canada and Russia had been more reserved, as had some of the Permanent Participants. Canada's concerns about the 2013 group of observer applications were primarily directed towards the EU's application for observer status, particularly considering the EU's ban on the import of seal products, despite an exception made for seal skin sold by indigenous hunters (see Introduction). There was also a concern cited, primarily by Canada and the ICC, about a possible reduction in permanent participants' ability to maintain a strong position in a broadened Arctic Council with a new batch of populous, wealthy observer states. At the Kiruna ministerial meeting, the ICC underlined that the 160,000 Inuit are vastly outweighed by the new sum of the Arctic 8 plus the observer states (3.5 billion people) and urged the US chairmanship to pay greater attention to 'specifically northern' – rather than global – concerns, such as food insecurity and inadequate housing (ICC, 2013).

A contrasting Permanent Participant position was forwarded by Chief Michael Stickman on behalf of the Arctic Athabaskan Council, who noted that most sources of pollution that affect the Arctic originate from outside the region, necessitating engagement of non-Arctic states

(Arctic Athabaskan Council, 2013). Likewise, the Aleut International Association's statement emphasised that they were not afraid of change or new voices and opinions in Arctic affairs, but also that the organisation wanted to preserve the pre-eminent positioning of Permanent Participants and Arctic states within the Arctic Council (Aleut International Association, 2013).

It is also important to keep in mind that China, as a major economic power, probably created some concern, even if its Arctic interests were clearly specified and in accordance with the dictates of the Observer Manual (Willis and Depledge, 2015). Russia was primarily opposed to China's application, as they felt it was purely 'economic reasoning' about China's size that spoke in favour of its application (Chernenko, 2013). Nonetheless, Russia did accede to the observer applications (MFA, Russia, 2013), although perhaps more to avoid 'breaking the consensus' (Kommersant, 2013) than from real enthusiasm or sense of possibility from an expanded contact network within the Arctic Council.

Russia's concerns also seemed to be anchored in broader debates about how Arctic cooperation can best serve Russia's long-term priorities. Rather than conflict or cooperation as the main Arctic dichotomy, studies of Russian media coverage have found that the primary tension is between the national and the international scales. In this discourse, 'internationalising' Arctic challenges is seen as a worst-case outcome, with national or regional circumpolar solutions being the preferred one (Wilson Rowe and Blakkisrud, 2014). As one Russian journalist from the State-owned *Rossiskaya gazeta* reported from Kiruna: 'Members of the council do not hide, that it is with difficulty that they find a balance between protection of the regional identity of the Council and development of mutually beneficial cooperation with non-Arctic states' (Vorob' ev, 2013).

At the 2015 ministerial meeting in Iqaluit, however, the Minister of Environment, Donskoy, took a departure from the previously cautions approach towards observers. He actively welcomed observers in the implementation of projects and underlined and argued that 'cooperation should not develop according to the "insider principle"'(Ministry of Environment, Russian Federation, 2015). This may be an interesting indication of both an acceptance of the status quo (the observers are there already, in the limited roles assigned to them by the Observer Manual) and of Russia's growing orientation towards China and the East as its transatlantic and European relations were challenged following the country's interference in Ukraine in 2014 (Blakkisrud and Wilson Rowe, 2017).

Balancing global and regional framings

Many of the reactions outlined above seem to have been more about how the different Arctic states envision the Arctic's place in the world than specific disadvantages or advantages tied to more observers or these particular potential observers. How tied into global process and politics do the key Arctic states like to envision the region? To what extent does a more 'global' vision of the Arctic serve to weaken or strengthen the positions of the Arctic states themselves?

The delimitation of global/regional issues in Arctic cooperation comes up repeatedly in a number of guises at the Arctic Council. For example, in a 2009 SAO meeting in Copenhagen, the question of whether observers should be included in the Search and Rescue Task Force was raised. A key element of search and rescue in the high seas is that it also relies on the input and participation of any vessel in the region – commercial, scientific and so on, and sailing under any flag. The minutes reflect disagreement, with some SAOs arguing the point that many countries in Europe and other continents have an Arctic presence and that 'perhaps [the Arctic Council] should not exclude parties that have legitimate interests from observing the Task Force'. Other SAOs are recorded as expressing doubts about observers at intergovernmental negotiations between member states (Arctic Council, 2009b: 6).

The same question arises on issues of a rather everyday nature as well. For example, in a discussion of how the Arctic Council should be communicating its outputs and decisions, the debate about target audience came up. The choices lay between primarily northern and Arctic audiences and/or non-Arctic states as well, and this question remained unresolved (Arctic Council, 2010a). In another discussion at the 2015 SAO meeting in Anchorage, we see that Permanent Participants and, to some extent, some of the SAOs found themselves surprised – or 'unaware of the extent and nature of these formal and informal relations' of Arctic Council WGs in global settings (Arctic Council Secretariat, 2016c). That WGs had independent, extra-regional diplomatic ties was seen as a problem. Concern was especially directed towards WGs with wide networks, such as AMAP (with its connections to UN bodies such as the UN Environment Programme and UNFCCC) and CAFF (which had a wide range of agreements with actors, organisations, research centres and NGOs) (Arctic Council Secretariat, 2015b). The conclusion was that WG secretariats were to report in these relationships too and also consult more with the SAOs on establishing new extra-regional ties.

The reactions of Norway, Russia and the United States to Asian states' Arctic interests have been marked by a number of specificities that could be contributed to national interests or foreign policy traditions. Such concerns could include, for example, that Russia overall prefers smaller multilateral clubs as opposed to broad tents in international relations, and fears China's rise, the strong outrage in Canada's domestic North over the EU's ban on seal products, Norway's interest in joining regional bodies in the Pacific as an observer and the USA's 'pivot to Asia'.

However, this varied reception of Asian states' applications also speaks to some divergences and questions about how the Arctic region should be understood – as global or regional or a mixture of both. In terms of the observer debate, we see how these competing broader framings of the region mattered for shaping the concrete policy debate on what kind of actors belong in Arctic governance – and how they should participate.

Frame 3: business in Arctic governance

Policy 'storms in teacups' may be a relevant cue for the analyst in identifying when broader issues or spatial frames – and the power relationships undergirding them – are at stake. The debate over the new batch of observers' applications seems to have been one such moment. Even with key interests at stake, it was surprising that the decision went to the ministerial level. Similarly, the formal considerations of economic development and business issues by the Arctic Council might seem another such surprisingly tempestuous issue. The Arctic has long been a place of regionally and sometimes nationally important industries (mostly extractive) and other forms of economic development (Huskey, Mäenpää and Pelyasov, 2014). However, as Kristoffersen and Langhelle (2017) note, the representation of the region as a frozen nature preserve or a booming resource extraction zone of opportunity (and a range of representations in between these visions of the Arctic) has long been contested. This provides a hint as to one reason why a focus on bringing business actors into circumpolar cooperation would be debated. If and how does such an effort unsettle broader regional framings?

Negotiating the Arctic Economic Council

As discussed in Chapter 1, the Arctic Council has long had scientific cooperation and coordination as its key mandate and has produced important conclusions about and engaged in global diplomacy on issues of climate change, conservation and biodiversity. The Council grew out of an even more specifically science-oriented cooperation, the AEPS. The introduction of 'sustainable' development issues was a key, and contested, expansion of mandate when the Arctic Council replaced the AEPS. The inclusion of sustainable development occurred despite US concern about lack of definition of the concept. The issue was of great importance to the newly minted 'Permanent Participants', who argued for a stronger focus on Arctic populations to weigh up against the heavily natural-science-oriented/conservationist traditions of the AEPS (English, 2013).

As Canada took the helm of the Arctic Council from Sweden in 2013, it was clear that business and economic development were flagship emphases for the chairmanship period. All Arctic Council states and Permanent Participants had stated support for the initiative and welcomed it as part of the Canadian chairmanship (Quinn, 2016). As the idea evolved within the 'Task Force to Facilitate a Circumpolar Business Forum', however, opposition began to crop up. A key element of change in this period is the relationship of the 'business forum' to the Arctic Council. Early documents had envisioned a special place for state representatives in the new forum. However, the end product was an organisation of and for business to be held at an arm's length from the Arctic Council (Loukacheva, 2015). Distance between the work of the Arctic Council and a business forum had been an important requirement forwarded by the ICC (Arctic Council Secretariat, 2014).

Non-governmental organisations involved in Arctic affairs had become concerned when it was clear that the evolving business forum was more about enrolling 'big' nationally significant businesses rather than an effort to support small and medium enterprises (Greenpeace, 2015; WWF, 2014). The WWF had encouraged the 'greater involvement of business in meaningful dialogue about sustainable Arctic development', but was concerned about transparency and accountability of a solely business organisation operating independently from the Arctic Council (WWF, 2014). Some key Canadian voices, such as former Foreign Minister Lloyd Axworthy and former Circumpolar Ambassador Mary Simon, had never supported the initiative. They were concerned about the role given to private actors pursuing private concerns at a potential crossroads with the concerns of and directions given by participants in the Arctic Council (Axworthy and Simon, 2015)

Opposition, however, did not prevail, and the initiative resulted in a new organisation, the AEC, with a secretariat opening in Tromsø, Norway in 2015. The AEC describes itself as an independent organisation, aiming to facilitate Arctic business-to-business relations and positioning itself as the preferred advisor to the Arctic Council on business issues. Membership is open to all businesses active in the Arctic, with special positions reserved for key representative businesses nominated by the 'Arctic 8' states. These 'representative' companies range from the native corporations of Alaska, through shipping and shipowners' associations (Denmark, Finland, Norway and Russia), complex holding companies based in the North, federations of industries and chambers of congress (Iceland, Denmark, Norway, Russia), to Rosneft, which is one of the Russian national oil companies. Three representatives from each of the Arctic Council Permanent Participants' organisations are also present (AEC, 2017). The AEC is further organised into several WGs (e.g. infrastructure, maritime transport, telecommunications, traditional knowledge/stewardship in the years 2016–2017).

Statements by the AEC leadership and WGs emphasise a commitment to stringent regulatory regimes, as long as these regimes are predictable. In a commentary in the *Arctic Yearbook*, Tara Sweeney, then chair of the AEC, and Tero Vauraste, then vice-chair, stated that the AEC aims to make the Arctic a 'favourable place to do business', by working to remove trade barriers, forge circumpolar market connections, and ensure predictable and common-sense regulatory environments (Sweeney and Vauraste, 2016). The support for the regulatory regimes established by the Arctic Council and at the national levels in Arctic states received another vote of confidence from the maritime WG of the AEC: 'today's Arctic business environment is governed by stringent regulatory regimes … and so it should be – the Arctic is a pristine environment, where people have thrived for generations. The AEC will work to promote best regulatory practices and to the extent possible seek to align rules and regulations to ease the flow of business' (AEC, 2017). The WG on traditional knowledge, stewardship and small/medium business development likewise noted that the Arctic is ground zero for climate change, and emphasised the importance of providing a necessary framework for partnership with Arctic communities (AEC, 2017).

Overall, the goals are unsurprising and very much in keeping with broader Arctic efforts and discourses. However, the voices and an official role for this actor group are novel. On the whole, you do not see many business representatives present at Arctic Council meetings. One does note business actors at the WG or task force level. For example, oil and gas producers' associations have been active in ongoing work on prevention of marine oil pollution (Arctic Council Task Force on Arctic Marine Oil Pollution Prevention, 2014b, 2014c). This is striking in light of the fact that business is absolutely a target audience of much of the Council's work – most of which is about persuasion and best practices rather than enforceable regulatory initiatives.

A broader debate over framing: conservation versus sustainable development

To understand the degree of uncertainty and debate around the AEC, we also have to turn our attention to framing and representation. I would argue that the debate about business actors is closely tied to a broader uncertainty about how to balance conservation principles and economic development in the North. What is the Arctic for – and who is meant to benefit from it? Is the relatively undeveloped – and increasingly threatened by global warming – Arctic landscape something to be protected for a global audience and experienced through photos and documentaries? Or is the Arctic, like many other parts of the world, the physical base upon which people living there should attempt to support their communities, accessing and marketing the local resources at hand?

This is an ongoing tension that is evident in how individual states and communities debate their development strategies (Steinberg *et al.*, 2015). At the national/bilateral level, President Barack Obama's agreement with Prime Minister Justin Trudeau of Canada to protect the Arctic environment by banning offshore oil and gas development in the Arctic is a useful example (Trudeau, 2016a). This effort in Obama's last days of office was a follow-on from an earlier 2016 bilateral agreement to protect 17 per cent of Arctic land and 10 per cent of Arctic marine areas by 2020 (Trudeau, 2016b). The bilateral agreement was received with jubilation by many national and global audiences, and with consternation and a sense of betrayal by many Arctic communities. The immediate direct economic costs were small, given that Arctic oil and gas production in the North American Arctic is yet to prove itself a feasible avenue for economic development.

However, Arctic communities reacted strongly, and these reactions are summarised thoroughly by Chater (2017). The Governor of Alaska, Bill Walker, stated that the agreement prioritised 'outside voices' above the 'voices, lives and livelihoods of Arctic residents'. Alaska's senators and congressional representatives put it even more pointedly: 'The only thing more shocking than this reckless, short-sighted, last-minute gift to the extreme environmental agenda is that President Obama had the nerve to claim he is doing Alaska a favor.' Canadian leaders objected to Ottawa acting on behalf of Canada's Arctic territories, pointing out that it went against the spirit of devolution. Peter Taptuna, premier of Nunavut, put it this way:

> We do want to be getting to a state where we can make our own determination of our priorities, and the way to do that is gain meaningful revenue from resource development. And at the same time, when one potential source of revenue is taken off the table, it puts us back at practically Square 1 where Ottawa will make the decisions for us.

The ongoing balancing act between the sustainable development and conservation 'pillars' of the Arctic Council is also evident in SAO and Permanent Participant commentary on WG activity. At the conclusion of Denmark's chairmanship in 2011, the Greenlandic representative made a statement that exemplifies some of these tensions: 'The Arctic is not just about polar bears and ice. What is most often missing from the discussion is the human aspect of the Arctic and the conditions in which we live' (my translation from Danish, Kleist, 2011: 3). In discussing CAFF's work, which is now focused on biodiversity challenges, several delegations at the first Anchorage SAO meeting pointed to the need for CAFF to use both conservation and sustainable use as guideline principles. The CAFF chair pushed back that they do indeed look at sustainable use. The chair then diplomatically intervened, stating that use and conservation are not inconsistent, and suggested that the conversation that had ensued around the Council's work on biodiversity 'may indicate a need to consider shifting emphasis and thus the Council's focus a little bit' (Arctic Council Secretariat, 2015c: 15).

Likewise, in discussing the oil and gas work of the Council at the same opening meeting of the American chairmanship, Norway pointed out that petroleum was a mature industry in Norway and an important 'driver of regional development in northern Norway'. The country asked whether the Arctic Council focuses enough attention on the economic development value of oil and gas, as opposed to merely 'source of environmental risk'. Russia supported the remarks by Norway, as did Denmark and Canada. Other states, which were not listed specifically, retorted that 'the substantial environmental consequences of oil and gas activity must be addressed' (Arctic Council Secretariat, 2016c: 21–22; see also US Chairmanship of the Arctic Council, 2016b).

Here, we can see how the framing of the Arctic as a space for economic development or a space for conservation is not a one-off effort supported by a one-time marshalling of resources and articulation of preferences. Rather, the preferred framing is constantly shored up and debated by actors seeking to present a picture of the region that makes their interventions and preferred outcomes sensible.

Representations and the 'constant work' of maintaining power

As Edward Soja puts it: 'it may be space rather than time that hides consequences from us, the "making of geography" more than the "making of history" that provides the most revealing tactical and theoretical world' (2003: 1). In this chapter, we have shown how broader framings of Arctic space do indeed matter in 'day-to-day' circumpolar diplomacy and are actively contested and enthusiastically marshalled by actors seeking to promote particular perspectives on the region. The active support given by most Arctic Council high-level representatives to buffering the region from external political strife was an important reflection of their foreign policy aspirations and interests in the Arctic. It also served as a display for non-Arctic actors who have frequently expressed concern about the potential for conflict over resources and boundaries and wondered if the Arctic environment should somehow be protected with a regime or a special set of globally endorsed rules. Reasserting the peaceful Arctic frame in Iqaluit in 2015 was an important message to others about the commitment of the Arctic states to governing the region peacefully – and primarily amongst themselves (an important hierarchy of players, which the next chapter addresses).

We may identify that frames – and the power relations implicated in these framings – are at stake when we witness policy 'storms in teacups'. The drawn-out consideration of a new batch of observer applications over two chairmanship periods, and the late-night, last minute discussions of those applications on the eve of the 2013 ministerial meeting in northern Sweden, may be one such policy storm that is difficult to understand without taking frames into account. The East Asian states that presented their applications did so in conjunction with the rules and preferences that had been articulated by the Arctic states and Permanent Participants formally and informally. Observers, permanent or not, have a limited role to play in the Arctic Council overall. What was also at stake, however, was a framing of the Arctic as regional or global. For some key participants, such as the ICC and Russia, the regional framing was the preferred one, as it ensures a smaller 'club' format where more purely 'Arctic voices' can be heard.

The contention around the development of the AEC can be seen in this light too. Commercial actors are one of the target audiences of many of the Arctic Council's policy efforts from conservation to economic development, and not newcomers to Arctic affairs, as discussed in Chapter 1. Yet the development of the AEC in its various early iterations attracted high-level debate from a number of key Arctic actors. This is probably in part because the enhanced presence of business actors ties into a longstanding tug-of-war or balancing act between policy frames of the Arctic that speak to conservation/environmental concerns and sustainable development. While we often see framing as an academic analytic, used to help us understand in a more abstract sense how representation, power relations and policy outcomes tie together, it is perhaps worthwhile to consider how framings, like rhetoric, are actively deployed and debated by policy field participants. This chapter took a cue from critical geopolitics and its growing emphasis on tracing what actors do with particular geopolitical framings. From the cases selected and empirical insights generated, we can see that experienced players in Arctic governance seem be highly aware of the importance of 'geopower' (Thrift, 2000) – anchoring their preferences in richly weighty narratives about space – to realise preferred power relations and political outcomes.

3

Power positions: theorising Arctic hierarchies

International relations scholars of the twentieth century operated primarily with a conception of states' interrelations as little more than billiard balls bouncing and crashing in trade, war and other forms of encounter. They posited anarchy as the only option in the absence of formal authority at the international level (Milner, 1991). In more recent history, IR scholars have sought to envision the international order as something more than anarchic and explain structured, repeated modes of interaction. Theorising dominance of key states – in empires, as great powers or as 'hegemons' – has been an important analytical avenue for understanding how stability is secured in the international system. These dominant states frequently do not rely solely on force or the threat thereof. Rather, singly or as groups of states, they take responsibility for the provision of 'public goods' in the international system, from security alliances, stable trade regimes, normative frameworks or leadership, currency stability or financial structures.

During the Cold War, many of these kinds of public goods were provided by the United States and the Soviet Union in their respective spheres of influence. In the post-Cold War period, the question of whether the USA can act as a fully global hegemon in delivering global public goods is actively debated. At the same time, US dominance in the international system has not been replaced by another power, however unevenly enacted or contested this American hegemonic position has become. This incomplete/partial hegemony thus ties back into broader debates discussed in the introduction to this volume about the changing nature of the post-Cold War international system (multipolar, concentric, anarchic) and the jumbled and untidy geopolitical imaginings of a new, arguably more chaotic, world order.

As discussed in Chapter 1, Arctic governance is marked by a number of initiatives that have been initially promoted by 'non-great-power' states in the international system (or indeed by indigenous peoples'

58

organisations, NGOs and other sectors of civil society). These include 'the Finnish Initiative', which became the AEPS (Keskitalo, 2004). Canada and the ICC drove forward the AEPS successor – the Arctic Council (English, 2013). At the same time, as we shall see below, it is the regional 'great powers' – the Soviet Union and the United States – that have been instrumental in clearing the political space for such initiatives. For example, Gorbachev's Murmansk speech was critical to reframing the Arctic as a location where former Cold War foes and all the countries in between them could meet to address shared environmental challenges (Åtland, 2008).

In this chapter, I suggest that hierarchy is a useful analytic for understanding Arctic governance. While the broader global-governance and security picture surrounding Arctic governance is indeed marked by some of the structuring aspects of (incomplete) hegemonic politics, I suggest that hegemony does not take us far enough in understanding the regional politics of the Arctic. Instead, hierarchy is a useful conceptual choice, as it does indeed allow us to acknowledge the presence of leading actors, while explicitly directing attention to many other important, flexible and dynamic roles available within a policy field. While hegemony is frequently tied to world-order thinking, hierarchies can differ across global policy fields and can change without disrupting broader stability in world politics. The literature on hierarchy directs us to the following questions. Who is seen to lead in circumpolar politics? What are the functions and benefits of different roles at different places on the hierarchy? How are hierarchies tied to more deeply held identities? These questions allow us to explore a second proposition about power: namely that *as policy fields come together and endure, some actors will find themselves in occupation of a more advantageous position. This position is a result of prior effort and success in defining what matters in the policy field, and brings again advantage in shaping further developments.*

The chapter proceeds as follows. After reviewing and taking cues from the literature on hierarchies in IR scholarship, 'circumpolar-wide' expressions of hierarchy are analysed, including the leading 'club status' of Arctic Council member states vis-à-vis the rest of the world. I also argue that Russia and the USA can be best understood as 'resting great powers' in cooperative Arctic governance. These resting powers structure only in broad strokes the room for manoeuvre in the region at key junctures, but their preferences (articulated or guessed at) are difficult to ignore because of their regional and global prominence. Secondly, we look at more transactional approaches to hierarchy, meaning how certain positions may provide certain privileges (and responsibilities). The existence and importance of hierarchy, I argue, are also demonstrated when policy field participants seek to change their position, using Norway and its seeking of Arctic leadership status as an example. Finally, turning away from states and towards the people-to-people relations in the Arctic, I suggest that it can be analytically significant to be attuned to potential manifestations of hierarchy in the more day-to-day dynamics of Arctic cooperation as well. Looking back to the 1990s and early 2000s at two projects directed towards transition and change in the Russian Arctic, we can see how hierarchical identities of students and teachers were intrinsic to these projects – and protested by the target audiences in northern Russia.

Why hierarchy?

The recent scholarship on hierarchies and status-seeking has three insights that I wish to bring into conversation with the dynamics of Arctic governance. First, the literature documents how relations of hierarchy have long been important in structuring world politics, from the age of the Greeks through imperial politics and through to the present (Cooley, 2005; Lake, 2009; Nexon and Wright, 2007; Hobson and Sharman, 2005; MacDonald, 2018). The presence of hierarchy, however, has long been analytically overlooked because of the IR discipline's commitment to anarchy as the fundamental feature of the global system (for an early corrective, see Luard, 1976). It was, therefore, difficult to clear the analytical space for understanding how certain relations between states were structured on enduring, if unequal, interactive relations. The now documented ubiquitousness of hierarchy in global politics makes it a reasonable assumption that it is worthwhile to explore how hierarchy may account for and structure some of the more systemic aspects of Arctic international relations.

So, hierarchies are ubiquitous in international relations, but, importantly, can vary over space and by policy field. In other words, hierarchies can, but do not necessarily, reflect broader positioning in global politics or in other policy fields. Hierarchies may rely upon resources and relations of power unique to particular policy fields and different from those realised in other bilateral or multilateral settings. For example, in climate negotiations under the auspices of the United Nations, small island states occupy a special position – and are invited to be at the table when major economies meet to discuss mitigating climate change. This has to do with the particular moral status conferred on them as the most immediately affected by rising sea levels in a changing global climate (Lahn and Wilson Rowe, 2014). To take another example from climate negotiations, forested countries, such as Brazil, have gained a new climate leadership standing since their vast tracts of rainforest were assigned a concrete carbon mitigation value as 'carbon sponges'. Likewise, Norway has gained status beyond its size or economic value in contributing to bringing about this framing of the world's rainforests (and then becoming one of the largest donors to this climate mitigation effort). By contrast, the Philippines' negotiators have established themselves as institutional memory repositories on the land-use related negotiations themselves, thereby acquiring a status as key negotiators by gaining a capital intrinsic to the land-use policy field itself (Wilson Rowe, 2015).

This brings us to the second point of usefulness of hierarchy thinking for understanding Arctic governance: interplay between different positions and the politics of status-seeking. Hierarchy allows us to think about enduring relations and expectations (privileges, responsibilities, norms of behaviour) between actors in global governance without losing sight of power relations and the attendant production of advantage and disadvantage. The literature on hierarchies systematically examines how specific forms of power are at play in maintaining these superior and subordinate positions in international relations (Zarakol, 2017). Importantly, this literature also theorises and directs analytical attention to the function of roles below the 'top' – exploring the question of how other positions within a hierarchy (such as intermediaries between different kinds of actors, brokers between great powers) matter for upholding power relations within a policy field (MacDonald, 2018).

Seeking 'status' in international relations is a good indication that actors recognise themselves as engaged in policy fields structured by hierarchy. In other words, one indication of hierarchy mattering in a governance field is seeing involved actors actively seeking to change their position vis-à-vis other policy field participants (Larson and Shevchenko, 2010; Wolf, 2011; Wohlforth and Kang, 2009). Within hierarchies, participants may actively seek to change or maintain their status and draw upon a variety of resources, if those resources are recognised by other field participants as valuable. As we will see below in the cases of Norway's status-seeking in Arctic international relations, different resources can be creatively applied in seeking a circumpolar leadership position.

On a related note, and of critical importance to understanding Arctic governance, hierarchies can be held open conceptually in terms of the kinds of actors involved in shaping outcomes. The analytical openness to the kinds of actors that may matter is important for applying hierarchy to Arctic governance. As discussed in Chapter 1, the actors of importance to shaping Arctic cross-border relations have been multitudinous. There is also nothing intrinsically predictive or limiting to the concept of hierarchy when it comes to what types of resources (political, social, economic, cultural/moral capital and so on) matter for maintaining a certain position. An important extension of the analysis below would be to theorise in the positions of other actors prominent in Arctic cooperation, such as indigenous peoples' organisations, NGOs and the semi-independent working groups, for example.

Thirdly, the literature on hierarchies makes a useful distinction between two kinds of hierarchies that reflect and serve to uphold relations of power in different ways – transactional and structuring. These two main categories are not at odds with each other, but rather distinguish between how superficially or how 'deeply' a hierarchy is entrenched (Mattern and Zarakol, 2016). In the transactional category, we see how hierarchies are not about direct coercion or dominance, but about relations that are seen as mutually beneficial or where the perceived costs of hierarchy are outweighed by perceived benefits (Lake, 2017). Actors will support and participate in hierarchies where positive consequences of subordination (or leadership) can be produced. In the Arctic context, the fact that Norway seeks, for example, status as an Arctic leader – and must invest significant resources in order to maintain this role – dovetails with a desire to shape international regimes around principles and practices enshrined in Norwegian political discourse and practical regulation (see below).

Alternatively, hierarchies may be expressions of more embedded forms of power in which actor identities are so structured by longstanding forms of hierarchy that hierarchy becomes difficult to identify and, by extension, difficult to contest: for example, arguments that illustrate how discourses make superior and inferior spaces of politics and mark actors as superior and inferior (OECD countries vs the 'developing world'; 'transitional countries') (Mattern and Zarakol, 2016). Below, we will explore such dichotomous hierarchies in looking at Arctic/non-Arctic states in the discussion of circumpolar governance dynamics and western/post-Soviet states in people-to-people cross-border politics. One could also argue that the Arctic/non-Arctic dichotomous framing, explored in Chapter 2 and in the next section here, is illustrative of an increasingly strong form of structuring hierarchy, anchored deeply in the politics and experiences of identity and geographical representation.

Circumpolar hierarchy in a satellite view: club status and resting great powers

The 'Arctic 5' and 'Arctic 8' can be seen as a 'club status' (Wohlforth and Kang, 2009) position at the top of a hierarchy, conferring upon all Arctic states a shared, privileged position in relation to non-Arctic states. Today the idea of the Arctic 8 is so naturalised in our understanding of regional politics that it is almost banal to point out that this is an important expression of hierarchy. One must remember that, in the early days of negotiating the AEPS, ideas of who belonged in Arctic politics were more open and fluid. For example, Canada had been concerned that the AEPS structure should be open to all interested and affected parties, given the global nature of the Arctic (English, 2013: 19). Likewise, the United

States had long sought to include major environmental organisations involved in southern polar issues at the table in Arctic coordination as well (English, 2013: 266).

The significance of this club status is often expressed in the friction between global and regional framings of Arctic governance. For example, as discussed in Chapter 2, it was difficult to ascertain from the actual observer applications and the circumscribed role of observers in the Arctic Council why the issue would become the topic of unusual late-night, high-level negotiations. Among other concerns, including a non-regional state of global importance, such as China, was probably perceived by some states as having potential to weaken the Arctic 8 club status. It is telling that a key aspect of the revised rules on application for observer status and aspects of the Observer Manual produced in 2013 were acknowledgement by the applicant of the pre-eminence of the Arctic coastal states under UNCLOS and the unchallenged position of the Arctic Council (for an extended discussion, see Graczyk *et al.*, 2017).

Here we see that of key importance is being on the 'inside' of the Arctic 8 club and ensuring that this privileged position in a hierarchy of states is recognised. But what about within that club? Does position matter? Are there leaders and followers in Arctic cooperative governance?

Leading in the Arctic

A look at self-definition of Arctic countries in their national policies gives insight into the kind of role they expect to play in Arctic politics. Several countries do indeed underline 'power' status or leadership in their strategies. Canada's strategy discusses how the Arctic – which makes up 40 per cent of Canada – is 'fundamental to Canada's national identity'. The strategy also underlines that how the region evolves has implications for Canada's status as an 'Arctic power' and the country's intention to play a 'robust leadership role' (Government of Canada, 2010: 4–5; see also Burke, 2017). Russia's short-format Arctic strategy paper from 2008 identified Russia as a 'leading Arctic power' (*derzhava*) and emphasised Russia's interest in an active international role in Arctic cooperation (Security Council, 2008: 5). Norway, as will be discussed below, has long sought to be a 'leader' by generating knowledge and practices relevant to handling Arctic challenges (MFA, Norway, 2011: 19). However, the claims to leadership in an international setting in the most recently released policy document of that country are more focused on specific goals, rather than a particular position, and status as an 'agenda-setter' (Government of Norway, 2017: 14).

For other countries, the statements are not about seeking a particular leadership position, but rather firming up their status and visibility as

Arctic countries. Iceland underlines its identity not only as an Arctic state (because of a location 'by the Arctic Circle') but also as a coastal state, given the close ecosystemic connections between the North Atlantic and the Arctic Ocean: 'Icelanders, more than other nations, rely on the fragile resources of the Arctic region, for example the industries of fishing, tourism and energy production. Therefore, it is of vital importance that Iceland secures its position as a coastal State among other coastal States' (Althingi, 2011: 6). Finland's strategy describes the country as 'an active Arctic actor' with a key objective to 'bolster its position as an Arctic country' (Prime Minister's Office, Finland, 2013: 9, 43). The Kingdom of Denmark's Arctic strategy does not take an explicit stance on the status of Denmark, Greenland and the Faroe Islands in the Arctic, although modestly and accurately it takes note of the Kingdom's central location in the Arctic (MFA, Denmark, 2011: 7). On a similar note, Sweden's strategy takes as a starting point that Sweden is an Arctic country, but does not make any claims to particular forms of status beyond that (Government Office of Sweden, 2011). The United States defines itself as an Arctic nation yet refrains from making any status claims at all (Bush, 2009; Obama, 2013).

Here we see that several Arctic states claim a central role in Arctic governance, including the notion of leadership and 'Arctic power' (reminiscent of 'great power' and the leadership responsibilities and privileges that this notion entails). Can there be multiple leaders? What might it mean to take leadership in Arctic cross-border governance? Do Arctic states that do not claim a leadership status in their key policy texts lead in the Arctic anyway?

When it comes to taking on practical leadership roles in the Arctic Council, the Arctic Council's Amarok project overview guide is one useful resource to consider (Arctic Council Secretariat, 2016a). This document provides an overview of Arctic Council projects and also main contact person(s) and their home country, and is now being updated regularly, after the practice began in 2016. As those listed as contact persons tend to be from the country providing substantial financing or leadership in supporting the project, the contact lists can be understood as a reasonable source of proxy data for engagement in leadership/coordination activities at the Arctic Council. Working Group secretariats, as well as the few projects where indigenous organisations and other international organisations, such as NEFCO, are given as key contacts, are listed under 'Other' in Figure 7. Each contact listed was given one 'point' whether listed as first, second or third contact and, in this way, this analysis gives a leadership point to countries, regardless of size, ambition or number of involved countries in a given project. In reality, some contact points are probably much more heavily involved, both with in-kind contributions and financial contributions, than other contact points.

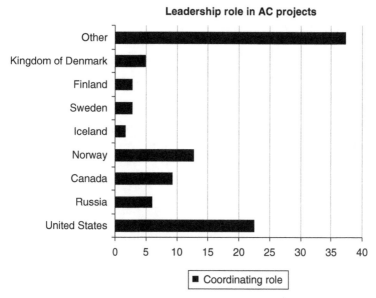

Figure 7 Graph of Arctic Council project leadership by country.

This limitation of the data and their interpretation should, of course, be kept in mind.

What are held outside this list of ongoing projects are financial or in-kind contributions made to supporting the Council's Task Forces, which are often established in areas where the Arctic Council seeks to create binding agreement. As we see in Chapter 4, Russia has invested significantly in creating binding agreements, including co-chairing all three of the binding agreements concluded under the auspices of the Arctic Council (see Table 4).

Another key source of financial contribution that is not reflected in Figure 7 is direct financial support to the substantial coordination work carried out by various WG secretariats (PAME, CAFF, AMAP) and the main Arctic Council secretariat in Tromsø. The Arctic Council main secretariat was, as of 2016, receiving 42 per cent of its funding directly from Norway, with remaining funds coming from other Arctic states. Norway and Denmark largely fund the Indigenous Peoples Secretariat, with smaller contributions from Finland and Canada. The funding of the AMAP secretariat also comes from Norway, while Iceland pays 40–50 per cent of CAFF and PAME secretariat costs (Arctic Council Secretariat, 2016b).

What we can see in Figure 7 is that the Arctic coastal states do indeed seem to be leading on more projects under the auspices of the Arctic Council. The outsized bar of the United States in Figure 7 should,

Table 4 Countries chairing binding treaties produced in connection to the Arctic Council

Agreement on	Year concluded	Chaired by
Cooperation on Aeronautical and Maritime Search and Rescue in the Arctic	2011	Russia, USA and Norway
Cooperation on Marine Oil Pollution Preparedness and Response in the Arctic	2013	Russia, USA and Norway
Enhancing International Arctic Scientific Cooperation	2017	Russia, USA

however, be partially understood in light of its chairmanship activities in 2015–17. It is customary for the chair to have a more active portfolio of projects than may be normal at other times.

One can also see the same amplified role for the coastal states in the chairmanship of binding agreements under the auspices of/related to the Arctic Council (Table 4). As these binding legal agreements necessitate their own forms of negotiation and process, it is incorrect to see them as products of the Arctic Council itself. However, much of the idea of development, and discussion of policy lacunae and options, took place within the Arctic Council, even formally through Arctic Council Task Forces. The agreements are also officially unveiled in connection to Arctic Council ministerial meetings and mean to be seen as an outcome of that forum, even if that is not entirely the case in a legal sense.

The sponsorship of projects and the chairmanship of flagship Arctic governance agreements do indeed point to, within the Arctic 8, a leadership position assumed by the Arctic coastal states in recent years, in terms of diplomatic and, probably, financial resources. This may indicate a certain hierarchy within the Arctic/non-Arctic states dichotomy, with the Arctic coastal states achieving a kind of additionally privileged position given their responsibilities for Arctic Ocean issues. Indeed, the coastal states have come together before to send a message about Arctic Ocean governance. The 2008 Ilullissat Declaration had a clear policy function and intervened successfully to dampen concerns about geopolitical rivalry in the Arctic (Wegge, 2010; Wilson Rowe, 2013a; Steinberg *et al.*, 2015). Importantly for our discussion here, it was an Arctic governance vision formulated by the five Arctic coastal states, rather than the Arctic Council as a whole.

This new delineation within the Arctic states themselves was contested. Problematically, the newly highlighted outsider group included Finland, Sweden and Iceland. These countries are members of the Arctic Council, but not coastal states as defined under international law. Both Russia and Canada were keen to promote the 'Arctic 5' as a new sub-grouping in Arctic politics. Russia was a supporter of the meeting that resulted in the Ilullissat Declaration and Canada called in to a follow-up meeting. Importantly, however, the USA has not promoted the use of the Arctic 5 brand. The then State Secretary Hillary Clinton even publicly rejected the Arctic 5 'club status' to the chagrin of a Canadian foreign minister extolling the concept to his home audience (English, 2013: 2). Thus the expanded role of the coastal states is something we can observe in the practical politics of Arctic cooperative governance, but not a status position celebrated in its own right.

The reluctance of the USA to use the Arctic 5 status widely politically points us to the role played by 'great powers' in the region. Do the USA and Russia occupy special positions in the hierarchy beyond their Arctic state club status? The analysis of some critical historical junctures in Arctic governance below suggests that the USA and Russia occasionally do intervene in the politics of the Arctic as 'great powers', with the caveat that the performances of global status need to be understood as temporally limited ones.

Resting great powers

'Non-great' powers have been instrumental in developing a suite of post-Cold War Arctic multilateral settings. The predecessor to the Arctic Council, the AEPS, was initially known as the 'Finnish Initiative', and Canada is further acknowledged as being critical to bringing the AEPS to life (Keskitalo, 2004). Initially, the United States had been sceptical of the initiative, noting that other areas of Soviet–American relations had higher priority (English, 2013: 107–108). The country had to be lobbied extensively, by Finland especially, to begin engaging in the emerging AEPS. Interestingly, despite the perceived importance at the time of involving the United States, the USA was not able to win its preferences on all fronts. For example, the involvement of NGOs in the AEPS, for whom the USA wanted a larger place at the table and with whom it had cooperated extensively on Antarctic-related issues, did not come about: this despite the USA having made frequent interventions to include large environmental groups at the Arctic table in the days leading up to the June 1991 Rovaniemi meeting, to the reported 'irritation' of other delegates (English, 2013: 134).

Turning to another great power, we see that, despite the extensive diplomatic footwork done by Canada and Finland, the trigger for the AEPS had been Gorbachev's Murmansk speech in 1987 (Åtland, 2008). The speech provided the opening for new initiatives in the Arctic and highlighted the Arctic as an area where cooperation with the Soviet Union could occur. This discursive shift in the landscape of how the Arctic mattered because of the status of the Soviet Union as a global superpower in charge of a great swath of circumpolar territories – and also the country's status as source of many of the Arctic transboundary pollutants that cooperation would seek to address (Darst, 2001).

As the 1990s progressed, Canada was once again a key driving force in seeking to amplify the reach and permanence of the AEPS into a circumpolar multilateral forum. As before, as Canada was lobbying to transform the AEPS into the Arctic Council, its key concern was how to get the USA on board. This is especially interesting, given that the Canadian initiative was initially poorly received by many other Arctic states. Finland had been concerned about undermining the AEPS, and Norwegians, Danes and Americans were all concerned about how to handle indigenous representation in the forum, and about duplication of diplomatic efforts (English, 2013).

The perceived importance of winning over the USA provided a platform for American representatives to set many of the ground rules. These included that the AEPS WGs be incorporated into the Arctic Council (thus eliminating duplication of efforts), that the body be consensus- rather than voting-based, and that there be no permanent secretariat or work on overarching Arctic treaties (English, 2013: 205). One scholar describes the USA's position as a 'take it or leave it one' on the points of a looser declaration rather than by a charter or convention document, and functioning without a secretariat (Scrivener, 1999). In the same negotiations process, the US also insisted on the inclusion of additional indigenous peoples' organisations from Alaska Athabaskan and Aleut groups, over the objections of the indigenous peoples' organisations already within AEPS who were concerned about the watering out of their positions with added numbers (Scrivener, 1999: 54).

In essence, the USA was able to call many of the shots while other countries, such as Canada, did the diplomatic footwork. In his comprehensive history of the establishment of the Arctic Council, John English also notes that the USA promoted a rather narrow, science-based focus on Arctic issues, preferring a tighter format. American diplomats used the first US chairmanship to 'refocus' the Arctic Council on these kinds of questions, rather than the broader mandate envisioned by early Canadian activists (English, 2013: 266).

Two decades or so into this new era of post-Cold War diplomacy, it seems that the division between globally 'small' or medium-status states, such as the Nordic countries and Canada, still mattered. In a set of interviews carried out between 2007 and 2011 with diplomats from many Arctic states, Arctic governance participants (broadly construed) were asked who led, who followed and who mattered (Wilson Rowe, 2013b). Interviewees from the non-great power states (Norway, Canada and

Denmark/Greenland) were unanimous in underlining the importance of the USA and Russia as the regional 'great powers'. Largely, the interviewees shared the aim of working to bring these two states more actively into the Arctic cooperative fold rather than seeking to counterbalance their influence. One North American interviewee noted in 2007 that this was one of the motivations for giving these two countries chairmanships so early in the life of the Arctic Council organisation to 'bring these countries further into the activities of the Arctic Council'. Another Norwegian interviewee urged that Arctic Council participants work hard to angle projects and elicit Russian interest, finding 'ways of making sure Russia stays involved' (Wilson Rowe, 2013b: 76). In fact, one of the accomplishments that one Norwegian foreign minister prided himself on was that 'the High North has been put on the map of many more capitols through our active High North diplomacy and international cooperation' (Gahr Støre, 2011a). The most trumpeted of these successes had been the participation of Secretary of State Hillary Clinton in the 2010 Arctic Council ministerial meeting in Nuuk, Greenland, marking the first time the USA sent such a high-ranking official to the Arctic Council.

The Arctic includes two countries – the USA and Russia – that can be assigned great power status from their historical or current global roles. 'Small-state' policy entrepreneurs focused intently on securing the participation of the USA and Russia. And the two countries played critical roles in the growth of circumpolar Arctic cooperation. The Soviet Union and Mikhail Gorbachev desecuritised Arctic space, and the USA agreed to support the AEPS and Arctic Council (in the end, and albeit on specific terms). This suggests that our understandings of Arctic power politics should remain attuned to 'resting great powers' in the region. They may regularly act like all other Arctic states (or at least similarly to the coastal states) in terms of their level and type of involvement; however, these powers can indeed wake up and play decisive roles in Arctic governance – beyond the roles that can be played by other members of the Arctic insider club – at critical junctures.

In the main, however, the club status of Arctic states keeps the great powers in rest mode. But what about the non-great powers – are the remaining roles and functions homogeneous? As we shall see below, Norway's foreign policy behaviour in the Arctic suggests that there are other useful, unique and politically valuable roles that can be pursued in this regional context.

Moving up? Norway and status-seeking in a circumpolar hierarchy

Social status is acknowledged as one of the most important drivers of human behaviour and research in psychology. Individuals may seek and prefer high status, even when they may not derive utility or material gain from a higher status (Wolf, 2011). However, high positions in hierarchies, political and otherwise, most often bring some benefits and advantageous power relationships to others. As noted above, the fact that actors seek particular positions in international relations is a strong indicator of the presence of hierarchy and associated power relations. After all, if all positions were equally advantageous to pursuing desired outcomes, the terms 'great powers' and 'small states' would not have entered commonplace political language and academic analysis.

The literature on status-seeking, however, has expanded the set of tools and vocabulary that can be applied to understanding different, hierarchical positioning in global governance. In particular, the research has focused around highlighting different techniques that global governance actors can apply in seeking better positions within a hierarchy. Social mobility implies a mimicking of top-status states' behaviour in order to achieve a higher place in an international hierarchy. Social competition may be trying to surpass a dominant group, or alter the criteria upon which high status is assigned. Social creativity means reframing a 'negative attribute as positive' or underlining different kinds of achievements in new fields (Larson and Shevchenko, 2010: 66–67).

To understand the role of non-great powers in regional politics, we now turn our attention to Norway and the various positions it has sought in Arctic politics. I will argue here that, even though Norway already occupies a privileged club status position as an Arctic coastal state, the country has additionally sought to increase its status through being a 'knowledge power' and through close association with Russia (until this association became too politically challenging after 2014).

The North has long been an area where Norway is an international-relations entrepreneur. Norway's first big post-Soviet foreign policy initiative in the Arctic was the Barents cooperation, which was established in 1993 between the Nordic countries and Russia. The aim was to promote regional peace and encourage economic growth through greater regional integration (Hønneland and Rowe, 2010; Hønneland, 2017). Although deemed a success in promoting people-to-people contact across the former Iron Curtain, Hønneland (2005) argues that by the turn of the millennium the Barents initiative had lost some of its original sparkle. By 2004, the idea of the 'High North' as a politically coherent concept emerged, accompanied by a cavalcade of policy documents relating to the Arctic published between 2003 and 2011 and, to a large extent, replacing the Barents focus of the 1990s (Jensen and Hønneland, 2011:1; Jensen and Skedsmo, 2010). Key goals of the slew of new policy documents published included: continuing to develop 'neighbourliness' with Russia, sustainable fisheries management, development of the Barents as a European energy province while balancing these pursuits with concern for the environment, promoting the application of international law to the Arctic, and ensuring the quality of life of indigenous and non-indigenous northerners (MFA, Norway, 2006, 2009).

While all these points speak to relatively longstanding Norwegian foreign policy interests, the strategy documents and surrounding political discourse also indicate a few points where Norway launches new ambitions – a desire to be at the 'forefront', from established sectors (e.g. fisheries) to new fields such as marine bioprospecting. To achieve this position, the policymakers who wrote the strategy put their faith in knowledge, arguing that 'knowledge is the heart of the High North policy' and that Norway needed to be at the 'forefront of knowledge in all of these [key] areas' (MFA, Norway, 2006: 6). In a speech to a home audience in southern Norway in 2011, the then Minister of Foreign Affairs, Jonas Gahr Støre, reiterated the point that the country should be a 'leader on Arctic knowledge ... because through competence and presence we will strengthen our ability to influence the development of the entire Arctic' (Gahr Støre, 2011a).

These lines of thinking were addressed further in the 2011 White Paper on the High North. The document underlines a number of ways in which Norway and its research networks can gain an important position. For example, the establishment of the Arctic Council's secretariat in Tromsø was seen to 'increase the possibility for Norwegian research networks to be even more important agenda-setters in international climate diplomacy', as well as strengthening 'Norway's position in Arctic cooperation and policymaking' and as a 'central agenda-setter in the High North' (MFA, Norway, 2011: 16, 24, 23). Likewise, it stated that 'Norway has an ambition to be leading in knowledge about, for and in the North. The High North Strategy defines knowledge as the heart of the High North policy' (MFA, Norway, 2011: 19). On a similar note, Norway aims to be 'leading on central wealth-creation activities in the North' and to be 'the most forward-looking manager of environment and resources in the North', as well as a 'driving force for strengthening the Arctic Council' (MFA, Norway, 2011: 20, 24).

The dedicated focus on the North and funding to the social and, especially, physical sciences have not only increased the expert capacity in the research sector, but also resulted in a strong capacity on northern issues amongst Norwegian civil servants and politicians. This becomes particularly clear if we take the example of Norway's efforts to influence EU policy on the Arctic (Wegge, 2012). After the EU Parliament passed a resolution in October 2008 calling, among other things, for an international treaty to protect the Arctic environment, Norway and Denmark immediately mobilised to prevent the EU Commission from supporting the Parliament's resolution. Multiple bilateral talks between EU leaders and senior Norwegian MFA officials took place, as well as a final meeting between Norwegian Prime Minister Jens Stoltenberg and Commission President José Manuel Barroso. After this meeting, Barroso declared that the Arctic was a sea and should be treated as such, implying that UNCLOS was on its way to being recognised as a sufficient legal framework – in line with the adamant position of the Arctic 'A5' states. Norway had been so active in this process that a senior EU official on Arctic affairs reportedly exclaimed that he felt 'surrounded by Norwegians' (Wegge, 2012: 12). Given the Commission's lack of experience on Arctic issues, Norway achieved a high level of influence because of its proactive role, and the expertise, information and competence it could contribute to (or bring to bear on) the process.

Overall, we see that Norwegian High North politics have placed great emphasis on leading through knowledge and science by knowing Norway's slice of the Arctic best. In the case of EU Arctic policy presented above, we also see how Norway achieved a high level of influence through its knowledge resources. Perhaps Norway's longstanding commitment to multilateralism, and its reputation as having a certain 'moral authority' in international politics more broadly (see Neumann and De Carvalho, 2015) allowed the country to play this role as a provider of 'information' to a Commission in need, rather than to be perceived as solely defending its national interests. This is what we might describe as a kind of status position assumed: that of a privileged yet responsible 'knowledge power'. This status allowed Norway credibly to defend a set of positions and perspectives without having those positions dismissed as driven by national interest.

Seeking a status within a hierarchy, however, only works if that position is acknowledged. After one decade of Arctic Council diplomacy, a group of interviewees pointed to the leadership role played by Norway in Arctic affairs (2007–2011, extracted from Wilson Rowe, 2013b). Norway was perceived as being a strong funder of Arctic activities, particularly in comparison to Russia and the USA. An American interviewee noted in 2007 that Norway 'often comes through with solo funding and pushes projects ... including facilitating the reorganization of the Arctic Council to include a secretariat in Tromsø' (76). North American interviewees suggested that Norway has achieved a special status in the Arctic as both a key player and as a 'convenor' and bridge-builder in Arctic relations. One North American interviewee put it this way:

> There is no question that Norway advances Norwegian interests first in the Arctic. They have been successful in marketing Tromsø as a locus for Arctic cooperation and they are definitely a big Arctic player. Russia and Canada are the geographically bigger northern states, and Norway navigates the waters between these two well. But then if you look at Norway's northern population, economy/wealth and the size of the sea areas that Norway manages, Norway is big too. (76)

Another North American observer noted that Norway has worked hard to:

> brand itself in the North and has done so successfully. If you look at the northern science locus at Ny Ålesund the role of Norway as a 'convenor' in Arctic relations is evident. Many nations have science stations there, under the auspices of Norway. This is like the Arctic Council secretariat in Tromsø. Norway has used this role as a convenor to good effect in pursuing strategic interests. (76)

The roles of 'convenor' or 'knowledge power' are somewhere outside the traditional status dichotomies of great power/small state. By creating an entirely different status for itself and devoting political and material resources to maintaining a unique role not easily filled by others, Norway occupied an important niche in the politics of the circumpolar North.

An important aspect of this niche is arguably the country's historically constructive relations with Russia (see Rowe, 2015; Hønneland, 2017). An oft-mentioned prerequisite and ambition for achieving Norway's Arctic policies was, at the time the White Paper was published, cooperation with Russia. In 2011, hopes for the potential cooperation were high: 'Norway emphasises the continuation of the development of a close and predictable cooperation with Russia in the North. The vision is that we are gradually able to develop the neighbourliness to encompass qualities we know from the open and trusting neighbourly relations Norway has with its Nordic neighbours' (MFA, Norway, 2011: 17).

Norway and Russia share a 196 km border in the High North, and the idea of being 'neighbours in the North' has been an important part of post-Cold War relations in this region (Holtsmark, 2015). Russia is mentioned as a cooperative partner in every single chapter (covering every imaginable sector) of Norway's northern policy document (MFA, Norway, 2011). Shortly after this policy document was released in 2011, Norwegian civil servants interviewed were overall very optimistic about their efforts and their relationship with their big neighbour, with whom they had just recently, and to great fanfare, settled overlapping continental shelf claims. One Norwegian civil servant noted: 'we have a very positive dynamic between the two countries ... because we work on concrete issues of mutual interest ... this gives us a platform to take up other issues'. Another stated that it 'is Norway and Russia in the Arctic. We are natural partners for cooperation' (Wilson Rowe, 2013b: 77).

At the same time, Norwegian interviewees underlined that it was changes internal to Russia that were critical to precipitating an agreement after forty years of intermittent negotiations around the delimitation line. One stated 'the Russians began to see the benefit of a settled border and wanted to be modern in the Arctic, taking the lead when they can ... The Arctic is a dream situation for them – they are recognised as a great power' (77). Another Norwegian interviewee put it this way: 'the Russians became more oriented towards clarity and law. For Norway, this was a window of opportunity because the Russian regime has legitimacy and the ability to ensure that the agreement went through' (77). Here we see that the power to move the negotiations forward or stall them was seen by Norwegian interviewees as resting primarily in the hands of Russia.

This suggests that Norwegian policymakers and diplomats have had few illusions about claiming or achieving a greater status directly in relation to Russia, despite all the references to neighbourliness. In referring to the Barents Sea agreement, Norwegian Foreign Minister Gahr Støre put it this way: 'good neighbours can resolve complex issues by means of peaceful negotiations. [It is an example of] big player–small player cooperation through agreed principles and international law. This is important for Norway' (Gahr Støre, 2011b). Here we see reference to the neighbourhood idea, but also to small and big states. Another more quotidian example of policymakers' awareness of this asymmetry comes from an interviewee with responsibilities in the Norwegian–Russian bilateral relationship. This official referred to a conversation with Moscow where they were working to plan their bilateral cooperative activities for the coming year. Their Russian counterpart put the ball squarely in the Norwegians' court, stating 'We are the great power [*velikaya derzhava*]. You make the suggestions' (Wilson Rowe, 2013b: 77).

While Norway retained its 'small state' role in relation to Russia, the historically strong bilateral relationship gave credibility to Norway's special role in Arctic politics in the eyes of *other* Arctic countries. As a Norwegian interviewee with responsibilities relating to environmental cooperation put it: 'The Canadians are envious of our relationship with Russia. How frank we can be with our Russian counterparts and what we achieve. They call upon us as bridge builders.' A North American interviewee echoed this point: 'Norwegians present themselves as a channel to the Russians and help other countries interpret Russian positions and messages. They are useful in playing this role and recognised by others as useful' (interview quotes from Wilson Rowe, 2013b: 77).

Russia's annexation of Crimea and the resultant sanctions regime triggered a low-point in Russian–western relations not seen since the colder days of the Cold War, albeit manifested in uniquely more modern ways (Legvold, 2016). Norway is a North Atlantic Treaty Organization (NATO) country – and significantly reliant for its own security on cooperation with other NATO countries – and also what could be described as an 'arm's-length' EU member (upholding all EU regulations, without formally belonging to the Union). Participating in the sanctions regime and demonstrating solidarity with NATO and EU partners has been a top priority for the country since 2014. This competing set of interests therefore complicated the position Norway could maintain as a key interlocutor for other Arctic states vis-à-vis Russia.

In an updated statement on Norwegian northern policy at this new low-point in East–West relations, the Conservative Prime Minister Erna Solberg put it this way:

> [T]he High North is Norway's most important foreign policy interest area. We are driving forces in international Arctic diplomacy and cooperate closely with other countries and organisations about how we can best develop the region. Our aim is to secure continued stability, predictability, and a peaceful development. The changing political and security picture in Europe of late underlines the importance of this approach to manage some of the richest, but also most vulnerable, natural areas on Earth.
>
> (MFA, Norway, 2014: 2)

The document later emphasises the choice Norway made in aligning itself strongly in its security and political alliances with NATO and the EU:

> Norway stands together with the rest of Europe and other allies in the defence of international law and norms in response to Russia's actions in Ukraine. Respect for the law of the sea and international cooperation contribute to stability and predictability in the North. Norway and Russia have many common interests as Arctic coastal states, not least defensible management of the environment, natural resources and shared fisheries in the Barents Sea. Our ambition is therefore to continue cooperation with Russia where we have shared interests.
>
> (MFA, Norway, 2014: 16)

This tallies with the broad lines of other statements made by the Conservative Coalition Government about how Norway will handle the once-again highly complicated relationship with Russia.

However, Norwegian authorities seem to have perhaps overestimated their country's status and the importance of the shared interests in the Arctic and the Barents Sea when it comes to holding a dual policy in relation to their 'great power' neighbour. Spring 2017 witnessed a much more assertive line from Russian diplomatic representation to Norway. An open letter published by the Russian Ambassador in a major Norwegian daily newspaper (Russian Embassy to Norway, 2017) challenged Russia's willingness to continue to allow Norway to pursue cooperation in areas of interest, while refusing to engage in high-level political dialogue. The absence of a visit from the Foreign Minister was one of the specific issues mentioned, and, on the same day the Embassy's letter was published in a major Norwegian daily newspaper, it was announced that Foreign Minister Børge Brende would be travelling to Russia to participate in an Arctic conference in spring 2017 (Norsk Telegrambyrå, 2017).

Looking at Norwegian foreign policy in the Arctic region, it is evident that there is indeed latitude for social creativity and definition of unique roles within an Arctic hierarchy. The role of an 'information provider' (e.g. to the EU), a 'convenor' and a 'bridge to Russia' that Norway achieved in Arctic multilateral settings gave the country an acknowledged status outside the more commonplace great power/small states hierarchy of international relations.

That Norway was able to pursue and utilise a creatively designed role in the Arctic as a convenor between states has much to say about the political climate of the region itself. As one European interviewee argued, 'it isn't what you are [great power or small state], but what you do and what you are interested in doing in the Arctic' (Wilson Rowe, 2013b: 78). Given the Arctic region's relatively peaceful nature and the emphasis on circumpolar cooperation, space has been made for creative approaches to status. Size and military or economic greatness can therefore be less decisive factors for taking a lead, although they can matter at critical junctures, as described above. As Vincent Pouliot argues (2010), status positioning is not solely about how much power or influence one country has, but what counts as power in a particular political setting in the first place. The challenges faced by Norway in navigating its relationship with Russia after 2014 do indeed show how certain resources of status – and options for status positions – become scarcer when the broader political picture changes.

It is therefore not surprising that the most changed element from previous High North strategic statements and a new strategy issued in April 2017 (MFA, Norway, 2017) is the relationship with Russia. In the 2011 strategy, hopes for the potential breadth and depth of cooperation with Russia were high: 'Norway emphasises the continuation of the development of a close and predictable cooperation with Russia in the North. The vision is that we are gradually able to develop the neighbourliness to encompass qualities we know from the open and trusting neighbourly relations Norway has with its Nordic neighbours' (MFA, Norway, 2011). The 2017 strategy, by contrast, reiterated Norway's commitment to having a good 'neighbourly' relationship with Russia and underlined how essential a broad suite of cooperative efforts have been for predictability and stability in the High North. However, the aspirations for trusting relations and the hope to extend the closely intertwined interests and political cultural traditions that bind the Nordics together to neighbouring Russia are now absent.

Hierarchies in time: positing Arctic 'pasts' and Arctic 'futures'

How might hierarchy – and its changing political backdrop – look at the level of non-state relations? The growth of people-to-people relations in the circumpolar North has blossomed since the end of the Cold War. The Soviet Union broke into fifteen successor states and the largest part of it became the Russian Federation – a new country and the largest Arctic state (see Chapter 4 for more on this). An interesting feature of the time that marked, in particular, the early days of post-Cold War Arctic cooperation was the expectation that Russia would be a 'transitional' country, with the end point of that transition being a democracy recognisable and pleasantly familiar to its European neighbours (Carothers, 2002). In hindsight, one could argue that western policy actors and, to some extent, scholars largely undervalued Russia's long traditions for defining itself *against* the idea of Europe (Neumann, 2017). Structural and geographical constraints – as well as the importance and slow evolution of political culture – were also largely overlooked.

I would, against this background, suggest that an important 'deep' hierarchy of the Arctic exists in privileging the historical approaches and current perspectives of the European/North American Arctic above the experience and perspectives of the post-Soviet Arctic space. The European/North American space was seen by Europeans and North Americans as the source of teachers and lessons, whereas the post-Soviet space and its representatives were cast as the students and learners. Historically, this has found interesting expression in people-to-people cross-border efforts that can be seen at both the European North scale and at a circumpolar scale, as I will illustrate with two examples. These examples are not meant to be full assessments of the success or relevance of these particular initiatives, which have been varied, extensive and of long duration, or the broader efforts in which they are embedded (for example, the Barents cooperation (see Tennberg, 2012) or intercity paradiplomacy in the Arctic (see Joenniemi and Sergunin, 2015). Rather, the aim is to illustrate features of deep hierarchy with a few vivid examples.

Turning first to the European Arctic, the growth of new regional cooperation initiatives – such as the Barents cooperation and cooperative initiatives around the Council of the Baltic Sea States (CBSS) – were key in the immediate post-Soviet years. The Iron Curtain had been pulled aside, and the Nordic countries were keen to build out relations on all fronts with their newly accessible Russian neighbours. This was both immediately pragmatic – much of the cooperation was oriented around cross-border challenges such as policing and border control; managing shared resources; tackling transboundary pollution, health and the associated challenge of migration and so on – and also a way of securing a longstanding new peace in the region (Browning, 2003). The hope was that cross-border contact would serve to break down enemy images and promote a new shared identity as northern Europeans (Hønneland, 2013).

One of these more pragmatically driven cooperative efforts provides a vivid illustration of the teachers/students hierarchy I am seeking to highlight here. Western actors had watched with concern as communicable diseases, such as tuberculosis and HIV/AIDS, rose dramatically in Eastern Europe and the former Soviet Union. In 2001–2004, the CBSS sought to address this problem through an international task force on health. In coping with the challenge of rising numbers of tuberculosis cases, one of the project's key aspirations was to implement the World Health Organization's (WHO) standardised approach to treatment directly observed treatment, short-course (DOTS). As its name suggests, this was a short-course, directly observed process of tuberculosis treatment that stood in contrast to the practices and medications used under the Soviet Union's extensive tuberculosis-control programmes. Key differences were mass screening of the population, hospitalisation and individually tested cures (the Soviet system) as opposed to the short-term, outpatient and standardised protocol of medicine utilised in DOTS (Hønneland and Rowe, 2004: 50–51).

On the whole, many project participants were satisfied and accepted the WHO's approach (and the hefty Nordic funding associated with it), while others continued to voice vociferous rejection of being put back into a student role with the needed approaches coming from abroad. Many respondents reacted to the presentation of DOTS as a 'magic formula'. Some reported that the project was rooted in a 'degrading attitude' to Russians, and that there must be a hidden agenda for this increased interest (Hønneland and Rowe, 2004: 57). Another high-level Russian official reported consternation at seeing the Nordic countries divide the regions amongst themselves for interventions – 'it is, after all, our country!' ('eto zhe nasha strana!') (Hønneland and Rowe, 2004: 57).

A more circumpolar project between the late 1990s and early 2000s is also indicative of a hierarchical approach to the Russian Arctic, with Russia posited as the target learner of western lessons. Funded by Canada, the project sought to bring together northern indigenous leaders and key civil servants to exchange ideas. Although the notion of exchange was important to how the project was structured, it was Canadian experiences in the Arctic – specifically relating to economic development and co-management – that contained the lessons to be transferred (Wilson Rowe, 2007a).

The project, which operated in Russia in two phases for eight years, involved Canadian and Russian governmental and indigenous representatives participating in a variety of cross-cultural exchanges (travels to northern Canada and northern Russia), targeted training sessions and cross-cultural seminars. The specific ethnographic moment examined here – which I participated in as a Ph.D. student engaged in fieldwork – is a seminar that took place in an oil-rich Siberian district. The aims had been to communicate about key experiences in managing the relationships among oil and gas companies, indigenous peoples, and regional government in resource-rich Arctic areas. Canadian indigenous and non-indigenous members of the delegation gave a variety of lectures, followed by question-and-answer sessions; and Russian bureaucrats, indigenous leaders and oil company representatives from the region described their own activities. The goal of the seminar was to explain and promote the Canadian practice of co-management (multi-stakeholder management) of natural resources.

Canadian development workers involved in the co-management seminar often conceptualised differences they encountered while travelling and working in Russia through temporal or evolutionary analogies. Several Canadian delegates, in casual conversations and interviews, characterised the key difficulty in communicating co-management principles to a Russian audience in this way: it was simply too 'early for the messages of co-management and economic development', as the Russian State and society were at a different point in 'evolution' than the Canadian State. For example, one consultant stated that 'what's going on here is like Canada twenty years ago or even in the 1960s' (Wilson, 2007b: 324). Operating under the assumption that Russia is Canada 'in the past', some in the Canadian delegation made statements along the lines that the Russian system 'could change faster because there are role models, like Canada' (324). Another consultant, while briefing two Canadian indigenous representatives over dinner, asserted that the Canadian indigenous experience was particularly valuable to the indigenous peoples in Russia because

> 'not only do these people not have your level of experience, they also don't have the history of the experience that you draw upon, meaning the history of indigenous political movements in Canada. No discussion followed about what kind of 'history of experience' Russian indigenous peoples might have.
>
> In displacing the Russian/Soviet past and the circumstances of the Russian present, Canadians could imagine that political relationships, such as the relationship between government, oil companies and indigenous peoples that co-management is meant to shape, were undecided or in transition. In reality, such relationships have long been settled,

and the local participants underlined this strongly when asked outside the seminar setting and away from the Canadian guests whom they had appreciated (Wilson, 2007b: 324–325). In the region where the seminar took place, to take one example, there were over forty legislative acts dealing with indigenous peoples, their culture and land, and subsistence issues in relationship to oil and gas extraction (which had begun in that region in the late 1960s). Such a focus on indigenous peoples is not a new phenomenon. The Russian tsarist empire, the Soviet Union and the present Russian State all developed policies and legal acts directed towards indigenous peoples (Blakkisrud and Øverland, 2006; Krupnik, 1993; Slezkine, 1994).

Conceptualising the differences between Canada and Russia as based in time rather than in different political and historical realities allowed them to forgo questioning the extent to which Canadian Arctic knowledge actually was applicable to or realisable in Russia's Arctic. It also allowed them to think about the Canadian position as one of a teacher or role model – not out of intrinsic superiority (which would probably have been seen by all involved as an unpleasant and problematic assumption), but from an advanced position of experience. Imagining that Russia would inevitably become more like Canada through a process of political evolution, these teachers from a rhetorical 'Arctic future' could envision their task as simply speeding up this process of political 'evolution' by delivering information. Unsurprisingly, when I travelled back to the region to conduct follow-up interviews, many of the participants noted that, while they had appreciated the intention of the effort, the lack of interest in and consideration of existing local experience, regional and national legislation, and the specific petroleum history of the region had surprised them (Wilson Rowe, 2007b).

President Putin gave his famous Munich speech in 2007, in which he challenged western hegemony in the world order and also gave a clear message that Russia was 'back' and no longer taking instruction (Tsygankov, 2016). This message was given at a time of sky-high oil prices, a resurgent Russian patriotism and a growing disenchantment with western states, which were framed as having sought to profit – in one way or another – from the post-Soviet power vacuum (Neumann, 2017).

This assertion that Russia would no longer be taking lessons (if it ever did) also gained expression in Arctic cooperative forums. Cooperative initiatives that faced difficulties tended to be those that were premised on the notion of Russia as a developing country that needed to be 'helped' with its northern challenges. For example, AMEC, which had granted unprecedented access for western countries to the military-related challenge of nuclear waste on the Kola Peninsula, was spectacularly suspended, with Norway's representative expelled for spying.

The one enduring way in which Russia has been willing to remain a 'client' of Arctic cross-border politics is in the clean-up of Soviet-era contamination under ACAP (see Chapter 4 for a detailed discussion). Here, however, to be willing to sit in the 'student's chair' Russian policy actors engage in their own kind of temporal distancing. As Khrushcheva and Poberezhskaya (2016) have found, the pollution is seen as a 'Soviet

Union' problem, in which any actor can be involved in amelioration, without threatening Russia's Arctic power status today.

Hierarchy and change

This chapter has shown some of the different ways that hierarchy structures relationships of power in Arctic governance. A hierarchical approach, in my opinion, is useful for Arctic governance. Identifying hierarchy is not about 'testing' whether Arctic politics looks most like different ideal-type conceptualisations (realist, liberal, interdependent) of international relations. Rather, it is a sensitising concept of an enduring structural feature that marks many, if not all, social relations. Hierarchy is also a useful analytic lens, in that it stays open to all kinds of actors and forms of power. In other words, it explores how structured positions figure in power relations, without specifying what performances or resources constitute power in that hierarchical setting.

We have seen how two kinds of club status seem to matter in Arctic international relations as constituted among states – namely the 'Arctic 5' coastal states, and Arctic states in general versus the rest of the globe (the non-Arctic states). Furthermore, we have seen how internationally significant 'great powers', such as the USA and Russia, are best understood as 'resting powers' in an Arctic context. In the quotidian flow of Arctic diplomacy, they act very much like other Arctic coastal states in their preferences and contributions. However, at critical, agenda-setting junctures, their participation is seen by other states as essential and, indeed, the course-setting gestures of the regional great powers have had longlasting significance in the development of Arctic multilateralism.

However, as the case of Norway illustrates, there are other status positions within a hierarchy that can be sought. The country has shown significant creativity around status-seeking in positioning itself as a 'knowledge power' at the leading edge of Arctic politics. One key source of its status was its knowledge of how to cooperate bilaterally with Russia. This gave status vis-à-vis other Arctic states, some of which struggled to maintain effective bilateral relations even in the more positive political climate of the early 2000s. However, as the post-2014 years have shown, this source of status was no longer an available option when the political backdrop changed dramatically and positive East–West relations were not feasible in light of Norway's centrally important alliances to Europe and the United States. An important takeaway about hierarchies illustrated by this case is that, while hierarchies are enduring and durable, they are not impervious to change.

We see also in cross-border people-to-people relations that hierarchies can be contested and also evoke deeply embedded ideas about identity (of self and other). In both Nordic-run projects and one run by Canada in the early 2000s, we see the ways in which an assumption is made by western actors about the fundamental identity of the Russian Arctic. It is 'of the past', and the people there must then, logically, be eager to learn the lessons of teachers from the various European and North American Arctic 'futures'. We see, however, that while this hierarchy could be assumed by one part (the 'teachers') it could be contested or rejected by the counterpart (the putative 'students').

However, the broad lines of the spatialising identity assumed in the hierarchy still colour how other actors think of and approach Russia today, although to a significantly lesser degree than in the heady days of the immediate post-Soviet collapse. How this relationship of teacher and student has played out in another setting – the Arctic Council – is a question that the upcoming chapter explores in detail. And with this we move from the power of position to the subtle workings of norms and diplomatic discipline.

4

Establishing and navigating the rules of the road in Arctic diplomacy

During its 2003–2005 chairmanship of the Arctic Council, Russia – the 'largest' Arctic state – suggested that Arctic cooperation should focus more on the city level. The idea never really garnered any support. This is understandable, on the one hand, in that the idea suited poorly the 'many Arctics' represented by the other countries, most of which include settlements and towns, but very few cities compared to the relatively urbanised Russian Arctic (Orttung, 2017). The urban Arctic also corresponded poorly with dominant framings of the Arctic as a wild and sparsely populated landscape (see Chapter 2).

On the other hand, it is a bit surprising, in that Russia is decidedly the largest Arctic state and the country's involvement was seen as essential to securing effective circumpolar cooperation, as we have seen in Chapter 3. There are few other examples of proposed project ideas in the Arctic Council falling between the cracks publicly as this did. However, if we fast-forward to 2017, Russia has since successfully co-chaired the three binding agreements negotiated formally outside the Arctic Council, but in close conversation and celebration with the forum.

So, why did some of the earlier suggestions and interests of the 'largest' Arctic state fail to carry more weight in this Arctic diplomatic setting? This chapter suggests that such failed or drifting ideas give us a good indication of the impact of norms – shared understandings of appropriate and inappropriate interventions and behaviour – in shaping what is accepted as a legitimate statement or policy option in the Arctic Council. Understanding the ways in which norms exert influence over behaviour in cross-border relations requires reconceptualising the space of global governance as more than a dynamic, inclusive, vast network of governance. Rather, we need to consider how delimited and 'local' the meeting places of cross-border politics – what we can term global governance policy fields – frequently become.

This chapter examines Russia's engagement in the Arctic Council over time to see how its preferences are met (or not), and discusses what this can tell us about the rules of the road in cross-border Arctic diplomacy. Acknowledging that performances of power – including developing and enforcing norms – have an inherently 'local' aspect is important to grounding broad statements about power in global governance. The proposition about power relations here is that Arctic cross-border cooperation *plays out in an environment that has social constraints and norms. These constraints allow for the performance of Arctic diplomacy to a more, or less, successful degree, and shape behaviour, even of the 'great powers', in the region.*

In the first section, we revisit the notion of policy fields to conceptualise how the sporadic meeting places of global governance can indeed become imbued with a site-specific social thickness that matters for shaping behaviour. We then turn to the long lines of Russia's approach to the Arctic, as context for the interventions of Russia's policymakers and diplomatic representatives in Arctic cross-border relations. Some of Russia's key interventions in the politics of the Arctic Council in two separate periods, 1997–2007 and 2007/08–2017, are analysed, based on interviews and Arctic Council archives. This periodisation is chosen as two equally long periods of time – a decade of Arctic diplomacy each. The two periods are also punctuated by key political events in Arctic politics (the Ilullissat Declaration of 2008) and Russian foreign policy (Putin's speech in Munich asserting Russia's return to global power politics). The chapter concludes with a discussion of what Russia's successful and failed interventions tell us about the evolving norms of Arctic cross-border governance – and how Russia has played a role in developing them.

Norms of belonging, speaking and acting

The architecture of acceptable and unacceptable State action in the Arctic is secured in hard and soft laws, such as the UN Convention on the Law of the Sea, and also global conventions on other issues relating to biodiversity, trade, the Polar Code of the International Maritime Organization and so on. Compliance with these rules is often optional and sometimes binding, but, in any case, the content of the rules tends to be developed through formal political processes of negotiation (at the international level). These rules also tend to be anchored to varying degrees at the domestic level, such as through ratification processes for hard law or through involvement of domestic stakeholders in formulating a country's negotiating position for a soft-law process.

However, a good deal of Arctic politics – and governance-development takes place outside such formal strictures – and informal diplomacy is often highly important in bringing a policy problem to the formal nego-tiating table. For example, at the Arctic Council, there are indeed formal procedures for submitting an issue as an agenda item, but if and how proposed issues survive and thrive has much to do with the proposer's position and standing, skills of persuasion and identification of mutual interest, and calling in favours. Overt demonstrations of dominance, as discussed in the preceding chapter, are rare. Rather, the Arctic, and also broader global governance forums in which the Arctic's govern-ance actors are enmeshed, are criss-crossed by norms. These norms may have been promoted by the powerful and adopted by the weak, or generated cooperatively and gradually as certain modes of behaviour are recognised by multiple players in politics as a good match for the social structure of a given field (Bernstein, 2001). In this perspective, norms are best understood as empirical outcomes of many interactions – rather than exhortations or obvious rules (Bernstein, 2001: 467; Finnemore and Sikkink, 1998)

So, how do we get at the practices, norms and relations of power that shape the rules of the road in Arctic cross-border politics in less obvious ways? As discussed in preceding chapters, I suggest that we get important analytical purchase from scholarly work in IR on the idea of policy 'fields'. The notion of a policy 'field' draws upon Bourdieu's work, which defines a field as delineating a realm of interaction with internal rules about appropriate behaviour. Applying this concept from sociology to IR helps us envision the space of global politics as delimited and productive of political culture – shared expectations, shared norms of behaviour and shared framings of/discourses around policy objects.

Sending (2015) argues that fields in global politics should be under-stood as organised around different objects of governance about which actors can hold differing conceptions. What unites them is a 'thin' interest in what is at stake and (more or less) agreed-upon ways of approaching the problem. This is to say that experts may not share the same 'identity' or 'discourse', but rather come together over a shared interest in addressing old or new policy problems. However, over time, policy field participants can establish (or borrow from related fields) a variety of social rules beyond the basic agreement to meet around a par-ticular policy object. They will, therefore, be able to identify, and may react to others' departures from, these well-worn pathways of political participation. To take an example from global climate negotiations, we see that negotiators sent to represent their Government's opinion are also expected to contribute more generally to moving discussions for-ward in their specific areas of expertise (for example, land use or carbon accounting), regardless of whether this is of direct importance to their country's specified national interests (Wilson Rowe, 2013d).

Of course, as discussed in Chapter 3, not all actors (professional networks, interest-based organisations, state representatives, business representatives) involved in global governance will be equally well positioned to 'play the game'. Agents in a field occupy unequal positions, and control over relevant economic, social and symbolic resources is usually unevenly distributed, causing various 'player[s] to play the game more or less successfully' (Pouliot, 2010: 34). We will return to this discussion of the informal norms and uneven terrain of Arctic governance in the final section. First, we consider the kinds of resources, policy traditions and political concerns Russia has brought to the cross-border governance table from its own domestic Arctic.

A large part of many different 'Norths': the Russian Arctic

A key emphasis that is now regularly reiterated by Arctic states is that the Arctic is actually 'many Arctics'. Canadian representatives at conferences in the European Arctic frequently emphasise the remoteness and sparse population of the Canadian Arctic, as a contrast to the relatively highly populated and interconnected reaches of the Nordic Arctic. Russia too has long sought to gain purchase in multilateral settings for its own Arctic specificities – a unique combination of resource-rich, sparsely populated and comparatively highly urbanised (Josephson, 2014; Krivorotov, 2015; Sergunin and Konyshev, 2015). In this section, we take a cue from the actual field participants who point to these many Arctics and first dedicate attention to understanding the long lines of Russia's engagement with its own Arctic, before turning to how the country has intervened in multilateral circumpolar diplomacy.

In today's Russian Arctic, I would argue that there are four main tensions or balancing acts that characterise Russian policymaking around development questions (for an extended discussion, see Wilson Rowe, 2017a). First, there is a tension between traditions of, and continued need for, large State subsidies of Arctic infrastructure and social services, and the desire to have the Arctic primarily as a source of profit for the entire country. Russia inherited from the Soviet Union a North ill-suited to the demands and logic of the market economy. Russian northern policy during the transitional 1990s could be described as haphazard, and focused primarily on emergency measures to alleviate acute fuel and supply shortages, attempting to respond to economic and social crisis in the region. Some areas (Chukotka, for example) experienced conditions of humanitarian crisis, necessitating the involvement of organisations such as the Red Cross (Thompson, 2009). As Helge Blakkisrud (2006) argues in his comprehensive study of Russia's northern policy through the first Putin term, a key aspiration of Arctic policy was to draw a distinction between the 'profitable North' and the 'unprofitable North'. The 'profitable North' – the areas rich in oil and gas and minerals – was to be further developed. The 'unprofitable' North – areas dependent on federal support and without prospects for viable economic activity – was slated to be scaled down, and the non-indigenous population encouraged to resettle. As Lagutina (2013) notes, however, the debate long continued as to how to strike the right balance between State-led, subsidised development and a market-principles-only approach to regional development.

The region's natural resource wealth made the aim of income generation a realisable pursuit – to some extent. The Arctic produces about one-tenth of the world's crude oil and a quarter of its gas. Of this output, 80 per cent of the oil and 99 per cent of the gas come from Russia (AMAP, 2007). However, there are limits to a market-driven development of the North that continuously raise the issue of subsidies versus market mechanisms and private investment. This tension is one that some of the strategy documents presented below address directly and is particularly prominent in large infrastructure projects, such as the rejuvenation of ports along the Northern Sea Route or renewal of the icebreaking fleet (Moe, 2014). The emphasis on shift work (fly-in/fly-out labour) for new sources of natural resource wealth is an indication of this balancing act – pursuing regional profit without committing to the development of social infrastructure (Laruelle, 2013; Saxinger, Nuykina and Ofner, 2017).

A second issue is the locus of decision-making power. Putin's recentralisation of power from the regions to the federal level contrasted sharply with the widespread decentralisation of the 1990s. Moscow, rather than Magadan or Murmansk, now governs this vast territory. At the same time, the cooperation of regional governors is essential for implementing federal policies in far-flung regions of Russia; they are often called upon to front Arctic efforts publicly and, thereby, are likely to exert some behind-the-scenes influence (Sergunin and Konyshev, 2015: 59–78). It is also important to note that centralisation can be understood too as a consolidation of power into the halls of government – and away from civil society. This has consequences, for example, in the Russian indigenous peoples' association RAIPON's participation in Arctic cross-border governance (see Chapter 4).

A third balancing act – between an 'open' and 'closed' Arctic – also characterises the region. Specifically, Russia's evolving relationship to its North entails a tension between the securitisation of northern space and the nationalisation of northern resources working against more international and market-driven orientations (Wilson Rowe, 2009; Baev, 2013). For example, Soviet Arctic industrial cities – in particular those associated with the military complex – were among the more closed places in the Soviet space, requiring special and closely controlled registration permits even for Soviet citizens. At the same time, the natural resources around which many of these cities were built were subject to global affairs and commodity markets, leaving them vulnerable to the vagaries of international politics and price swings.

Marlene Laruelle, in her comprehensive book on the Russian North, describes a similar tension, coining it as one between a 'security first' and a 'cooperation/economics first' reading of the region (Laruelle, 2013: 7). She argues that the Federal Security Service, the military-industrial complex and President Putin prioritise security, since they see the Arctic as a platform from which Russia can assert its 'great power' status. The 'cooperation first' approach draws inspiration from an emphasis on economic opportunities and the necessity of garnering investment and gaining access to foreign expertise. Proponents of this approach include the Ministry of Natural Resources, the Ministry of Regional Development and Prime Minister Medvedev (Laruelle, 2013: 7).

One vivid example of this 'closing' of the Russian North comes from the AMEC, established by the military authorities of Norway, Russia and the USA in 1996. It focuses on spent nuclear fuel containment and remediation of radioactive pollution in the North, with particular attention to the Northern Fleet in northwest Russia and enhancing Russian capacities for handling radioactive waste. In February 2007, a key Norwegian representative within the AMEC project was denied entry to Russia on a routine work visit. The Russian MFA later stated that this representative had been engaged in illegal information gathering, even though all AMEC work had been carried out either on request or agreement from the Russian Northern Fleet and other relevant authorities (Bellona, 2007). This rejection of the AMEC representative sends a signal of changing attitudes in Russian political and security circles towards both being a recipient of 'aid' via capacity-building and the extent to which the Russian North (the military North in particular) is to be open to other actors and multilateral activities. It marks the end of the era of the more open 1990s, which should probably be understood as the exception rather than the norm (Rowe, 2015). Interestingly, however, as we shall see below, Russia continues to accept assistance relating to its environmental pollution problems. This perhaps relates to Khruscheva and Poberezhskaya's finding (2016) that environmental pollution is seen as a legacy of the Soviet Union and that therefore, I would suggest, receiving such assistance does not impinge on Russia's current self-image of a self-sufficient 'great power' state.

Finally, a fourth balancing act is between commercial and environmental concerns. The demise of the Soviet Union in 1991 left Russia with serious environmental issues, as the Soviet regime had largely failed to protect the environment from the negative consequences of industrial development (Rowe, 2013; Oldfield, 2005; Ostergren and Jacques, 2002). As historian Lars Rowe points out in his study of the Soviet nickel industry, environmental protection and coping with pollution were left to the same ministries that were responsible for promoting industrial development, and a deeply utilitarian view of nature prevailed (Rowe, 2013: 11–17).

This is not to say that Soviet society was devoid of concern for nature. Despite being primarily subservient to industrial concerns, the Soviet regime developed environment-monitoring infrastructure, and environmental expertise and practices (Oldfield, 2005; Bruno, 2016). The most influential and noticeable outlet for Soviet environmental interest was a movement that argued for protecting significant tracts of land from industrial development in the first place—the *zapovednik* system. Such a focus on 'pristine' nature was more acceptable to the Soviet leadership, in part because it upheld a division between industrialised areas and wilderness areas (Weiner, 1999).

Today, while the Russian public is concerned with environmental quality and is less willing to 'pay the costs of pollution' (Whitefield, 2003: 102; Crotty and Hall, 2012), these concerns have not been linked to significant action, and environmentalists have been relatively weak political actors throughout the post-Soviet period (Henry, 2010: 764; Yablokov, 2010). At the same time, concern for the environment is not absent and there is a growing correspondence between global and Russian approaches to discussing environmental problems. For example, President Putin's visits to high Arctic islands have often had two components. One is to visit and praise newly modernised infrastructure and feats of military derring-do (Sergunin and Konyshev, 2015), but the other is to call for the 'general clean-up' of old garbage and pollution left from the Soviet period (in Staalesen, 2016). Russian companies are also increasingly aware of their environmental obligations as part of their broader social responsibility, although issues remain on how environmental policy is implemented in practice in areas marked by ageing industrial infrastructure and weak regulatory capacity (Kelman *et al.*, 2016).

Large state, quiet voice in Arctic politics: 1997–2007

So, how did Russia bring its post-Soviet Arctic to the Arctic Council in its first decade of existence? This section examines first Russia's participation in the Arctic Council more generally, then turns to the proposals the country made itself, and finally examines Russia's broader engagement in the areas of cooperation pushed forward by others.

Participation – small but growing

Except for some interventions from RAIPON (which received financial support from the Canadian Government in the early days of the organisation), Russia is almost entirely absent from the official record of the Arctic Council's first three years of operation (1996–1999). The earliest recorded interventions at the Council by Russian representatives suggest a struggle to provide enough relevant actors for the various WGs and other meetings. Russian representatives repeatedly requested a greater streamlining of Arctic Council activities and meetings, and clarification of WG mandates to avoid overlap and ensure effectiveness (Arctic Council, 1999).

Russia began engaging more actively at all levels of the Arctic Council in 1999, but its representatives rarely proposed or, by extension, funded, new projects. This assertion about 1999 as a turning point is based upon a statement by an American representative during the US chairmanship, expressing 'appreciation for the expanded, vigorous Russian participation in the work of the Council' (Arctic Council, 1999). During this period, however, Russia's financial contribution remained largely in the realm of in-kind contributions of administrative and expert services.

A broad range of Russian institutions – both governmental bodies and academic institutes – were involved in the Arctic Council during its first ten years. The Ministry of Natural Resources, Roshydromet (Federal Service for Hydrometeorology and Environmental Monitoring), the Regional Development Ministry, the Ministry of Emergency Situations and the Ministry of Economic Development and Trade all sent representatives to one or more of the six WGs of the Arctic Council. The MFA supplied both the ministerial representative and the Russian SAO. In 2004, a new SAO, Vitaly Churkin, represented Russia during its 2004–2006 chairmanship period. The involvement of this experienced diplomat, who later became Russia's UN envoy, perhaps indicated that greater importance was being attached to the Council's activities, at least during the Russian chairmanship (Churkin was consistently succeeded by Ambassador-level representatives). The Russian Academy of Sciences, the Institute for Arctic and Antarctic Research, and other regional institutes participated at the WG level as well.

Quiet, different proposals

The first proposal that seems to have been actively championed by the Russian side was the *National Plan of Action for the Protection of the Marine Environment from Anthropogenic Pollution in the Arctic Region of the Russian Federation* (NPA-Arctic), which had actually been submitted and funded by the Global Environmental Fund. This proposal, concentrating on the elimination of land-based sources of marine pollution, was included in the sphere of the PAME WG and officially welcomed by the Arctic Council in the Inari Declaration (Stokke *et al.*, 2007: 98). However, although the Russian Arctic Council representatives promoted the project extensively at Council meetings, the NPA-Arctic was never accepted as an official Arctic Council project, because of its exclusive focus on the Russian North.

In 2001, Russia began making its first proposals outside the NPA-Arctic, although very few of them came to fruition as projects. These years also saw some off-beat or perhaps ahead-of-their-time suggestions – such as Russia's proposing that the Arctic Council be promoted via a regular magazine comparable to the US *National Geographic* (Arctic Council, 2000). Likewise, in 2007, Russia presented on satellite cooperation as part of project development taking place under the Russian Federal space programme for 2006–2015. However, it seems the ground was not well prepared for such an idea. Initially, the Russian delegation had sought to bring this up in the relevant SDWG, but had missed the deadline and then sought to bring it up in plenum at an SAOs' meeting shortly thereafter. The proposed project would pinpoint the basic technical parameters for a satellite system for the Arctic region and assist across a broad range of issues including aviation, meteorological monitoring, and radio and TV broadcasting. Presenting the proposal in plenum was done with the aim of generating co-finance of the system building by 'interested Arctic states' (Arctic Council, 2007c).

Russia was 'thanked' for its work on the topic, but the chair noted that the proposal was presented for information only and that a formal proposal would need to be given to the SDWG within the appropriate deadline for proper preliminary handling (Arctic Council, 2007b). The idea was not brought up again at later meetings, although all the Arctic coastal states share communication and 'domain awareness' technology challenges in the High Arctic. Perhaps this was cutting it too close to the business or military interests that had initially been defined as outside the Arctic Council remit.

The most enduring feature of Russia's proposals for the Arctic Council in the 1997–2007 time period, however, is that they were aligned more closely to the sustainable development pillar over the conservation pillar at the heart of the forum (and a key framing of Arctic cross-border governance more generally; see Chapter 2). In describing the accomplishments of the Russian chairmanship, Minister of Foreign Affairs Sergey Lavrov exemplified this emphasis on people and economic development: 'While actively promoting the traditional priority environmental programs, we have sought to build up efforts in the social and economic fields. The aim was to see to it that the people in the North lived comfortably, in a clean natural environment and had a full-fledged access to education, social services and medical assistance' (MFA, Russia, 2006). This focus on 'people' of the North certainly relates to the fact that Russian has the most populous North, and represented a contrast to the Council's established focus on environmental problems. This differing emphasis had been a consistent feature of Russian interventions since 1999. At a November 1999 SAO meeting in Washington, DC, the then chairman of Goskomsever (the State Committee on the North), Vladimir Goman, stated that he 'would like to see projects expanded to focus on people of the North, including indigenous' (Arctic Council, 1999). At the June 2001 meeting, this focus on people was reiterated, as Russia mentioned the sustainability of life of the indigenous peoples as important, and emphasised health and housing issues. At later meetings, the focus on livelihoods (especially reindeer herding) and anything involving the 'human aspect' was stressed (SAO, 2002). This was reiterated at the close of the Russian chairmanship, with the Russian-authored October 2006 SAO report summarising that a major focus of the Russian chairmanship had been to establish a 'more balanced approach to sustainable development in the Arctic', particularly through greater focus on the Arctic peoples and the challenges facing them (SAO, 2006).

On the one hand, Russia's focus on urban people and on the specificities of the country's own northern problems resulted in project proposals that were not always embraced by the other participants in the Arctic Council. The Russian chairmanship was keen to have the Arctic Council link up with the UN urban housing programme, which focused on industrial housing and needier countries, and was, consequently, not relevant to the other less urbanised Arctic states. Although the Russian chair brought it up repeatedly, according to non-Russian interviewees, the issue was eventually dropped because of the other states' lack of interest. On the other hand, Russia's emphasis on people was substantively realised in a project on indigenous peoples and contaminants, involving the Ministry of Health, Roshydromet, the Ministry of Natural Resources and some regional governments. This project, the Persistent Toxic Substances Project, was carried out under AMAP auspices and investigated the significance of aquatic food chains as pathways of pollution exposure for indigenous peoples. Russia, via its Ministry of Health, produced new funding for the effort (SAO, 2006).

Willing partner in low-political cooperation

Participating within the norms of cross-border governance entails, for states and other actors, making not only their own proposals, but also responding to and supporting appropriately initiatives moved forward by others. In understanding Russia's first decade of multilateral engagement, it is useful to consider a classic division used to understand different kinds of issue areas in international governance. On the one hand, it is said that you have 'low-political' dealing with varying ebb and flow of cross-border relations. On the other hand, you have 'high-political' issues that touch on fundamental matters of peace, security and conflict for a given state. Of course, issues can change from high-political to low-political and vice versa – but the division remains usefully descriptive as long as the interest assessed is placed in its historical and broader contexts.

One example of the often rather successful 'low-politics' cooperation that was achieved under the Russian chairmanship on non-strategic issues is that of access to the Russian Arctic under the auspices of the IPY. At an October 2005 SAO meeting, Sweden expressed concern over the high tariffs charged by Russia for icebreaker services in the Northern Sea Route, even for endeavours involving scientific research for the IPY (Arctic Council, 2005). By the closing ministerial meeting in October 2006, Russian explorer Artur Chilingarov could report in his statement that icebreaker fees would be reduced by 50 per cent for IPY research activities (Chilingarov, 2006).

As cooperation moved from these coordination-style issues and into sectors of politics considered more strategic, difficulty increased. The 2007 Oil and Gas Assessment (OGA), which surveyed existing and best practices for High Arctic petroleum extraction and initially enjoyed Russian political support, exemplified how data and coordination were a struggle, for several possible reasons. Russian inability to deliver promised data for this assessment delayed the project by a year (its release had been scheduled for October 2006). While a Russian interviewee described the delay as caused by the difficulty of obtaining information from the private sector (oil and gas companies), other interviewees suggested that this information was considered secret, in that it related to the economy.

One US WG interviewee reflecting on this time period noted that, although Russia consistently sent a scientific expert as a representative, the expert seemed to struggle to pass relevant information up to the *political* level where permission could be gained for particular activities. For example, Russia's slow delivery of data for the PAME Arctic Marine Shipping Assessment delayed release of this assessment, although the data was ultimately provided via Finnish involvement and financing. Except for third-party financing, however, slow data collection was an issue for several countries. An interviewee commented that many countries (including the USA) had difficulties bringing the needed data for an innovative, cross-cutting marine study from multiple sources.

That Russian representatives struggled to traverse the political terrain between low- and high-political issues perhaps relates to the country's longstanding desire to engage in more formal negotiations and treaty-making in the Arctic, as opposed to the more diffuse fields of soft law and best practices. The Arctic Council minutes report several instances where Russian actors pointed to a need to fill 'legislative gaps and problems' at both the international and national level to underpin the various initiatives being undertaken in the Arctic region (e.g. Arctic Council, 1999). This tendency to introduce new concepts and seek internationally binding agreement is evident in two examples from the Arctic Council minutes. An ongoing interest of Russian representatives had been building international cooperation in the field of prevention and elimination of emergency situations in the Arctic. The proposal entailed establishing a network of international base points through an agreement amongst Arctic states (Arctic Council, 2004). In the end, however, participants came to the conclusion that existing treaties and conventions already provide an adequate frame for the work of the EPPR WG and that, instead, the partners should continue to develop cooperation and exchange of experience in relationship to emergency response in the Arctic (SAO, 2006). A US interviewee stated that what Russia had been proposing would entail a treaty process through which other countries were reluctant to go at that period in time. As we will see, the Russian diplomatic interest in new binding agreements absolutely characterised the Arctic Council's second decade and much of Russian leadership in Arctic cross-border governance and cooperation.

In sum, Russia's early engagement in the Arctic Council was marked by capacity issues, a preference for primarily low-political issues/coordination, an unquenched thirst for landing Arctic governance in documents and in international agreements (at a time when most states were satisfied with ongoing discussion and harmonisation of views), and a number of suggestions that did not seem to garner support because they were too closely rooted in specifically Russian Arctic issues and interests to be of interest to other countries. It may be surprising for readers of today to realise that Russia's every word was not heeded or at least carefully considered in an Arctic context. Russia in the 1990s and 2000s was widely perceived by its neighbours and the western world at large as a weakened country in 'transition' – with the ultimate end of that transition expected to be a large democratic state that looked like western states. As historian Lars Rowe suggests, western actors misread the 1990s as a new status for Russia, when the period should rather have been considered a 'state of emergency' for the Russian State, from which its leadership would seek to exit as soon as possible (Rowe, 2015). As we will see now, the second decade of the Arctic Council saw a different kind of fit between Russia's wishes and diplomatic outcomes.

High-level negotiator still receiving 'aid': 2007–2017

In the second decade of its Arctic Council diplomacy, Russia took steps to profile itself as an Arctic leader and worked in tandem with other countries in underlining the governed, peaceful nature of the Arctic. Secondly, as is outlined below, Russia's preference for formal agreement in cross-border Arctic governance grew into a settled aspect of Arctic politics. The country often takes a leadership role in bringing these agreements to fruition. Finally, we will explore how engagement with and external financing of the amelioration of Soviet pollution sites (and more contemporary pollution issues) remained a stable feature of circumpolar cooperation across two decades of post-Cold War Arctic cooperative governance.

Invigorated participation and some key differences

Russia was supportive of and promoted the 2008 Ilullissat Declaration on the peaceful nature of the Arctic and, subsequently, the primacy and sufficiency of the coastal states in stewardship and development of the region. Russia's first Arctic policy document also came out in 2008. This short document spelt out the country's position on the Arctic as a region of peace and cooperation, while at the same time underlining the importance of Russia's pursuing its national interests, broadly defined. More specifically, this includes the centrality of Arctic extractive resources for Russia's economic future.

The pursuit of a 'positive image' in the region was specifically mentioned in the short, 2008 Arctic strategy document (Security Council, 2008). In a set of interviews carried out amongst Arctic diplomats at that time, it seemed clear that an emphasis on positive profiling – and attendant diplomatic and political follow-through – was paying dividends amongst diplomats on the 'receiving' side in the Arctic Council. A North American diplomat formulated it this way in 2012:

> Since 2009, Russia has been at great pains to present that it is back as an Arctic player and has shown more Arctic leadership ... Other countries respond positively because this engagement is occurring through existing, expected vehicles like hosting conferences for discussion of issues or co-chairing initiatives, not through fighters and submarines.
>
> (Wilson Rowe and Blakkisrud, 2014: 79)

A Norwegian diplomat made a similar observation: 'Russia is well served by international law ... Russia has geographical advantages that put it in a beneficial relationship to law of the sea and it was also historically and contemporarily involved in the development of this framework. Russia wants to be seen as modern and at the forefront of international law, taking the lead where they can' (Wilson Rowe and Blakkisrud, 2014: 79).

Russia's annexation of Crimea in the spring of 2014 triggered a low point in Russian–European/North American relations, and a sanctions regime against the country, including measures targeted to hinder development of Russia's Arctic energy sector (Conley and Rohloff, 2015: 2). International military and security-related cooperation was immediately frozen in the region, although low-level safety/security relations continued: for example, coast guard cooperation (Østhagen and Gastaldo, 2015). However, on the level of diplomacy and cross-border relations on non-security issues, Russia continued to engage as before, demonstrating that the region is seen as one where Russian interests are well served by continued cooperation. Russia seemingly sought to minimise spill-over effects from conflict elsewhere (see Chapter 2; and Conley and Rohloff, 2015). On a similar note, Russia's updated submission of its extended continental-shelf claim under UNCLOS in 2016 was accompanied by specific agreements concluded with both Denmark and Canada, indicating these countries' commitment to working cooperatively to settle any disputes (Government of Russia, 2015).

In other words, Russia has continued to signal a commitment to Arctic peace and demonstrate its commitment to international law in the Arctic. However, its statements have been more difficult for other Arctic states – and the broader global community – to take at face value, in light of the country's actions in Ukraine. Furthermore, Russia is still engaged in a decade-long modernisation effort in relation to its ageing Arctic military infrastructure. The resources and attention devoted to this modernisation, some of which could be used to pursue solely national interest and some of which is necessary to support a more open, more cooperative Arctic (e.g. search and rescue capacity), have also become subject to competing representations within other Arctic countries (for example, debating whether Russia's actions represent Arctic militarisation or capacity building, not unlike other countries' efforts, in preparation for a more open Arctic) (Conley and Rohloff, 2015; Pezard et al., 2017).

It is also important to note that Russia's increased engagement in Arctic issues and desire to be seen as a 'play by the rules' Arctic player was nonetheless seen to be selective, not comprehensive, even before the challenging political environment post-2014. Problems relating to openness were also reported by Canadian and Danish interviewees who noted that they had engaged in a successful exchange of information about their respective continental-shelf claims, but that it had proved difficult to establish similar interaction with Russia ('Russians will not share any information or data without agreement from the top'). A US civil servant also noted that the Russian north was more closed to foreign researchers than any other part of the Arctic:

> Russians are not so open to scientific research permits in the Arctic as we would like. The US has never denied a permit for Arctic research, including permits to Russian researchers. I understand how this can be challenging as I also come from a large country with a large bureaucracy and interagency cooperation can be difficult, but it is a bigger problem in Russia, although there has been some improvement of late.
>
> (Wilson Rowe and Blakkisrud, 2014: 81)

Russia's chairmanship of the work on scientific cooperation in the Arctic Council (discussed below) indicated, however, a commitment to ameliorating these problems of interagency communication. This can be seen as an attempted shift towards the 'open' end of the spectrum in Russia's ongoing balancing act between the open and closed nature of Arctic space, even at (or perhaps because of?) heightened tensions with the West on other fronts.

It is also important to note that Russia's engagement with the Council on a general level was still strongly aligned to the sustainable-development side of activities, and perhaps less so on the conservation side. Russia placed more emphasis on the economic opportunities of the Arctic region than the other ministers do, with the possible exception of Norway as illustrated in Chapter 2. To take one example from Minister of Environment Donskoy's intervention at the conclusion of the Canadian chairmanship in 2015:

> Russia is open to collaboration and joint implementation of large-scale projects in the Arctic, particularly in the Arctic region of the Russian Federation.
>
> This entails not just extraction of natural resources, or energy, but also use of the Northern Sea Route as the shortest route for transportation of goods between Europe and Asia ... Climate change and technological breakthroughs make the Arctic, its wealth and resources, accessible for commercial development ... this should happen only in accordance with the highest environmental requirements and with due respect to the people living in the region and their traditional ways of life ... the cost of a failure in the fragile and unique Arctic environment is too high.
>
> (Ministry of Environment, Russian Federation, 2015)

Both conservation and development emphases are there, but economic development occupies the driver's seat in terms of ordering and rhetorical space.

A new era of high-level negotiations

An important feature of public diplomacy and the growing ambitions of the second decade of the Arctic Council's existence was the addition of three binding agreements on Arctic Ocean governance to the suite of best practices and soft law that work in the Council and other Arctic forums had previously generated (for more on these agreements, see Beyers, 2014; and on the most recent agreement on scientific cooperation see Hoel, 2017).

As discussed above, Russia evidenced in its first decade of post-Cold War cooperative governance a strong preference for binding agreements and legislation, and, thus, it is unsurprising that the agreements were welcomed by Russia. Russian representatives have, furthermore, played key roles in chairing all three treaty negotiation processes (co-chairing with the United States and Norway). That the agreements should be binding was not necessarily the intention at the outset as Arctic Council participants began to consider the policy problems. For example, it was initially not seen as necessary that search and rescue coordination – a US proposal that enjoyed fairly immediate support (Arctic Council, 2008: 6) – be supported by formal negotiations or a binding agreement (US Delegation of the Arctic Council, 2008). On a similar note, Russia is seen to have been instrumental in promoting the pursuit of a formal agreement on the topic of marine oil preparedness and response (Rottem, 2013; Arctic Council, 2011a: 8). Russia has been highly involved in the follow-up process (oil-spill pollution prevention framework), even submitting draft framework text early in the process (Arctic Council Task Force on Arctic Marine Oil Pollution Prevention, 2014a).

Likewise, an American interviewee explained in summer 2017 that neither had there been a concrete intention that the science cooperation agreement would need to be a formal treaty. The aim of the Task Force on Scientific Cooperation was to ease the movement of people and equipment and reduce barriers to accessing research areas that are of importance and interest. The co-chair from Russia recommended that the work be extended into the US chairmanship for completion (Arctic Council, 2015a: 10). Both Russia and the US had been heavily involved, with Norway doing key work penning the draft, presenting a draft text that incorporated input from Russia, US and other delegations. At the midpoint of the Canadian chairmanship, one country pushed for a legally binding document, arguing that it would help with the movement of people and equipment across areas which 'may require significant involvement from a wide range of government agencies and stakeholders that do not have science mandates.' This country was heard and the parties pursued a legally binding agreement (Arctic Council Task Force on Scientific Cooperation in the Arctic, 2015).

Dealing with historical trash

An interesting thread that runs throughout this second decade of the Arctic Council is that Russia continued to seek to address the contamination legacy of the Soviet Union, many times as nearly a recipient of 'development aid'. This 'client' state in transition is something that Russia decidedly shrugged off in its bilateral relations to the countries of the Nordic Arctic (Rowe, 2015). It is therefore interesting how durable this cooperation around Arctic contaminants has remained, despite Russia's reassertion of its great power and independent status, and also in light of worsened East–West relations after 2014. Even after Russia's annexation of Crimea and the sanctions regime, US–Russian cooperation under ACAP continued unabated, with the US Environmental Protection Agency even starting a new four-step project to reduce black carbon emissions in the Russian Arctic (ACAP, 2014: 4).

The ACAP WG is an extension of the work started under the AEPS. It also aims to engage in concrete amelioration of contaminated sites, as well as in legislative and regulatory changes to support this work and prevent further pollution. Importantly, AEPS was a product of the times– the 'transitional' 1990s – in which western actors, in cooperation with many Russians themselves, saw post-Soviet Russia as ripe for reshaping into a more western mould (Rowe, 2015; Wilson, 2007b). The ACAP WG is unusual, in that its activities are focused on the Russian Arctic itself, even while being supported by a broader coalition of states. In 2007, all ACAP projects were taking place in Russia, with other countries chairing or leading efforts for work there (ACAP, 2007). Early in the 2007–2017 period, SAO meetings still remained opportunities for 'donor states' to throw their weight around. For example, at an SAO meeting in Svolvær, Norway, a Norwegian delegate highlighted that a project the country contributed to on the packaging of obsolete pesticides in the Komi Republic had recently had an issue with the pesticides being disposed of inappropriately. The ACAP chair responded that it had discussed the issue with the relevant authorities and received 'assurance that it will not reoccur' (Arctic Council, 2008: 2–3).

The work in ACAP has been marked by struggle, with Russian chairs of ACAP being particularly frustrated by and pessimistic about the small amount of progress. For example, the lack of progress on a number of projects resulted in a long report from Andrey Peshkov at the first SAO meeting of the Swedish chairmanship in Luleå (ACAP, 2011). He expressed 'frustration' with the WG and wanted to be told procedures for discontinuing some projects, including one on brominated flame retardants. He noted that there were more of these hazardous materials than ever in Russia, but that there were simply not enough resources to address the problem (Arctic Council, 2011a; ACAP, 2011). He noted that 'to eliminate [brominated flame retardants] in the Arctic would require comprehensive legislative frameworks and additional support from both PSI [Project Support Instrument] and governments' (Arctic Council, 2011a: 6). It also became clear that there had been no actual progress on implementing the carefully developed integrated hazardous waste management strategy (NEFCO, 2009; ACAP, 2013b), but not because the policy problem had disappeared. Reports from ACAP underlined that Russia is storing one of the 'largest stockpiles of obsolete pesticides, which in 2001 was estimated to be more than 21,000 tonnes', because the country has no option for pesticide destruction (ACAP, 2013a).

Despite a high degree of openness about the lack of forward movement and a variety of hindrances, ACAP's work precipitated the first actual funding mechanism under the auspices of the Arctic Council. While, normally, activities are funded on a programme-by-programme basis (as well as some block funding by some countries of WG secretariats and the Arctic Council secretariat), activities under ACAP have their own PSI. This funding mechanism, proposed and managed by NEFCO, had a long development period, with Arctic states initially waiting for Russia to make the first deposit (NEFCO, 2009). In 2011, pledges from other countries had been made to the PSI, and NEFCO was waiting for an agreement to be finalised with Russia on how the fund would operate at its national interface (NEFCO, 2011). By the start of the Canadian chairmanship in 2013, the pledges were in, including matching funds from Russia, but the PSI had yet to fund a project (NEFCO, 2013).

Arctic governance – a social space, a malleable space

Russia today – despite political tensions following the country's annexation of Crimea and violent interventions in Ukraine – has become a steadily more consistent and visible Arctic player in circumpolar diplomacy, fairly aligned with the regional policies and interests of the other states. However, at the beginning of the circumpolar cooperation, Russia regularly made suggestions that fell somewhat outside the remit of the Council. Has Russian diplomacy changed – or have its Arctic counterparts themselves (or their perceptions and understandings of Russia) and the Arctic Council been transformed? What does Russia's engagement in the Arctic Council tell us about the broader rules of the road in Arctic governance?

The first decade of Russia's participation in the Arctic Council was marked by three key features. First, we see issues of low capacity and also the financial constraints of Russia's first post-Soviet decade. Russian participation in WGs and Arctic Council meetings was often sponsored by other states, and these representatives were not always strongly anchored in the rapidly changing governance structures of Moscow. On a related note, and secondly, we also see an emphasis on low-political cooperation: for example, the coordination around reducing icebreaker fees for passage via the Northern Sea Route under activities relating to the IPY. When these lower-stakes cross-border efforts drifted closer to key strategic sectors of the economy, for example in gathering data for the Arctic Council OGA, cooperation became more complicated. Thirdly, Russia's participation increases and intensifies after the first few years of the Arctic Council. However, the activities proposed were often too closely linked to the specificities of the Russian North (urbanised, problems of industrial pollution) to appeal to a broader circumpolar audience. Another challenge was that Russia sought agreements and treaties on paper as a way of anchoring the cooperation, while most states were satisfied with a less labour-intensive and more informal discussion of best practices and harmonisation of views on policy problems.

These Russian experiences point to some of the earlier *norms around procedure* within the forum. These include that projects are expected to have a broader appeal than just one country's North; there is an expectation that low-political (i.e. icebreaker fees) but also more strategic-related cooperation (i.e. sharing data around oil and gas) should be feasible; and there is also an expectation that the entire range of cooperation should be able to take place without additional layers of legal agreement or 'paperwork'.

It is important to note that Russia during this period rarely succeeded in pushing through an unpopular suggestion. This perhaps points to a *taken-for-granted norm of participation* – the expectation that all Arctic countries will participate in circumpolar governance (for whatever reason – interests, moral or ideological commitment). In other words, there may be a shared understanding that real 'exit' is simply not a rational/feasible option from the Arctic multilateral club. Perhaps the club nature – that if one country were to exit all other comparable countries would remain – serves to limit this option. It also points us in the direction of understanding that, of course, the norms of Arctic governance dovetail with broader norms of diplomacy and international relations. There are few countries that elect to recuse themselves from multilateral formats, even if they do not adhere to or support all of the hard- or soft-law obligations produced by that forum.

In the second decade of the Arctic Council, Russia actively profiled itself as an Arctic leader, even in the difficult cooperation atmosphere following Russia's 2014 annexation of Crimea and the western sanctions regime that came about in response. Being a legally minded, play-by-the-rules Arctic actor that fulfils a leadership role was a main aim for Russia. Both western and Russian interviewees at the time noted that Russia had taken a noticeably more positive direction in its role in the Arctic. This also suggests that a *cooperative, coalition-building approach to leadership is seen as the regionally appropriate way for expressing leadership.*

The second decade of the Arctic Council differs from the first primarily in new efforts directed towards *creating binding agreements.* This is an important development to a procedural norm from the first decade: that of minimising formality and instead working towards soft-law and best-practice outcomes only. A number of factors could have contributed to bringing this about: for example, growing awareness of the governance challenge to be addressed in light of a rapidly warming Arctic 'icescape', as well as countering concerns, coming especially from the European Parliament, about the idea of the Arctic as an ungoverned space (Wegge, 2012). I would hazard, however, that Russian interest in such agreements may have also been an important motivating factor. As mentioned above, having legally binding agreements was a diplomatic preference for the actors representing Russia in circumpolar relations, but other countries had been sceptical (perhaps about the existence of a real governance gap or about the resources required to create such agreements). It is important to recall that the USA had originally proposed a non-binding memorandum of understanding on search and rescue, and the same non-binding format was initially considered for an agreement facilitating scientific cooperation. However, both of these areas of policy concern resulted in binding agreement. Here is an area where Russia has perhaps been a norm entrepreneur, turning the Arctic Council into a location where binding, treaty-based agreements can also be proposed and discussed (even if their formal conclusion takes place outside the Arctic Council itself). There may have been other motivating factors and driving forces, but we can at least note with more certainty that the Council's activities have changed in a preferred direction for Russia.

This relates to a second norm, which may be even more pronounced now in the Arctic Council's second decade than its first: that *when the great powers awake and speak, the Council listens.* It could be Russia's growing resurgence on the international stage in this time period that also shaped the country's position on the Arctic Council. As covered above, many of Russia's earlier suggestions (urban housing issues, cooperation on satellites) were seen as off-beat and deflected. Yet, just a few years later, an idea to do an archival memory project based in Russia received support. The project aimed at accumulating information and knowledge available in libraries, archives, museums and specialised collections on the circumpolar world: its history and development, its present and prospective development. When the idea was first presented the following discussion ensued:

> The Chair thanked Russia and encouraged all delegations to contact their appropriate institutions to see if there is an interest in

participating and to contact Russia for more information. Several participants applauded Russia's proposal which in the spirit of IPY would continue the sharing of information with the rest of the world. It was noted that Russia comprises the largest Arctic territory and has the largest Arctic population. There was general interest in working with Russia to develop the proposal further and to determine how best to involve the SDWG and the Arctic Council

(SDWG, 2011: 7, 8).

Interestingly, the project was a departure from previous projects (the Arctic Council does little work on cultural issues like this) and neither was it in keeping with Arctic Council procedures, in that the project focused only on Russia, despite circumpolar ambitions (SDWG, 2011).

The participants specifically referred to Russia's status as the largest geographical Arctic state and also recalled that the Russian Foreign Minister, Sergey Lavrov, had first proposed it on a visit to Tromsø (SDWG, 2009: 7). This may signal an increasing awareness of Russia's status on the global stage and certainly indicates that issues championed at a high-political level by Russian authorities will receive follow-up. It suggests that a norm may be emerging around an especially privileged position for 'major' Arctic countries, perhaps delimiting the room for small states to engage in the policy entrepreneurship that was so important in bringing the AEPS and Arctic Council into existence. It also suggests that any idea that garners high-level engagement from an Arctic country, be it Russia's archival memory project or Canada's desire to focus on economic issues (see Chapter 2), will receive some follow-up.

This demonstrates gradual change in norms. Russia's Arctic has always been vast – and yet Russia's voice mattered more in the latter decade than the former. This probably has to do with the growing assertiveness of Russia on the Arctic stage with Putin's second presidential period (from 2004), but also with the more committed, experienced diplomatic effort that Russia has brought to bear on the Council. As the discussion in SDAP about the archival memory project illustrates, geographical size helps – but only when a country has done the work to make it matter and where the 'rules of the road' indicate that acknowledgement of 'Arctic' power significance is possible or needed. In other words, Russia's engagements – failed and successful – with the Arctic Council do indeed illustrate that Arctic governance takes place in a highly socialised environment layered with field-specific norms.

5

Non-state actors and the quest for authority in Arctic governance

The modern state, as discussed in Chapter 1, can be considered a relative newcomer to the cross-border politics of the Arctic region. However, states have featured prominently in the preceding two chapters. We have come to see how advantageous positions earned by/granted to states vis-à-vis other states matter for shaping the rules of the road in Arctic cooperative governance – and ultimately shape outcomes. In this chapter, I seek to broaden the net to explore the positions of key non-state actors involved in Arctic governance, namely indigenous peoples' organisations and science actors.

I do so, however, with two important caveats derived from developments in IR literature. First, I do not consider power in global governance to be a zero-sum game. This would envision power as a capacity or a quantity, rather than a performance facilitated by relations of dominance and deference. In other words, the power exercised by non-state actors does not come necessarily at the expense of the State and does not result in the 'retreat of the State'. In fact, the influence of non-state actors may be highly symbiotic with or reliant upon relations to states (Neumann and Sending, 2010). One way of getting at these inter-active relations is to consider the question of authority. Authority can be broadly construed as the capacity to secure deference from others in a given setting by wielding successfully whichever forms of capital are highly prized in that particular policy field. Put another way, all actors involved in a policy field are engaged in negotiation over what counts as authority in the first place and, by extension, who is recognised as performing diplomacy authoritatively.

A second caveat relates directly to this idea of authority. Earlier research in global governance tended to posit that different 'kinds' of actors possessed different forms of authority. For example, NGOs or indigenous peoples' organisations would exercise 'moral authority' based on their status as representing affected parties and the original peoples of the Arctic, whereas scientists would exercise 'expert authority', and international organisations a 'delegated authority' derived from their membership (Barnett and Duvall, 2004). Instead, we will look at debates over authority more generally to explore the range of performances that can shape outcomes – without positing at the outset that non-state actors engage in global governance in fundamentally different ways than state actors.

The focus on authority allows us to think about the kinds of resources and performances that shore up power relations in Arctic cross-border governance. We can therefore consider the proposition that *power relations are malleable and constantly enacted, contested and redefined.* Furthermore, authority's common-sense connection to 'knowing what is best' is also helpful in this context. Much of Arctic cooperation has focused around knowledge – be it compilation of knowledge into assessment of the Arctic environment or exchange of policy knowledge across the borders of the North in various people-to-people formats.

The chapter aims to bring contestation over authority into sharp focus by looking at how two non-state actors 'meet the state' directly at high level (SAO, ministerial) within the Arctic Council. We first look at how debates around the 'science–policy interface' manifest themselves more generally. When is discussion of scientific knowledge (or the presence/autonomy of scientists) given weight at the high-political level? Turning to indigenous diplomacy, we analyse and categorise Permanent Participants' diplomatic interventions in the Arctic Council (which is, of course, just one stage upon which the multifaceted politics of indigenous sovereignty is enacted). In the concluding section, I discuss a concept borrowed from science and technology studies that I think serves well to capture the ongoing dynamics around authority in a cross-cutting, regionally based 'umbrella' policy field such as the Arctic. This concept – civic epistemology – is first introduced in the coming section.

Authority in global governance

Rapid globalisation at the end of the Cold War increased and rendered highly visible the multitude of non-state actors and social movements shaping a growing number of transnational policy fields. In coming to grips with this new quantity and visibility, IR scholars working in global governance first operated with implicit (and sometimes explicit) assumptions that the activities of non-state actors in global governance were fundamentally distinct from the functions of states and were perhaps pushing the State out of global governance (see Neumann and Sending, 2010, for a discussion of this notion).

As this scholarship of global politics has developed, there is a growing range of studies that suggest an open approach to the question of authority. This recognises the participation of many actors, but remains agnostic as to the kind of politics that they will be pursuing (e.g. one would not assume that NGOs are engaged in a politics of morality, and experts only in a politics of expertise). Sending suggests that a productive way to approach global governance in a conceptual open way is to envision global politics (and its sub-sets) as an 'ongoing competition for the authority to define what is to be governed, how and why' (2015: 4). Actors are conceived as all engaged in the same quest for authority, even if possessing different interests and more and less advantageous starting points. In other words, rather than assuming that scientists exercise 'expert authority' and indigenous peoples gain from 'moral authority' a different question is needed. Why are some communities of actors perceived of as more credible and relevant in a given policy field than other actors?

Empirically, we see that contestation over knowledge is a key aspect of the contemporary politics of securing authority. In Sending's case, he looks at competing policy communities around population control and peacekeeping (2015). Fourcade (2009) looks at the dominance of economists educated at a small handful of institutions in defining how success in 'development' can be achieved and disseminating this globally through multilateral, national and private institutions. Others have examined how economists and foresters have battled it out in shaping how rainforests will matter for global climate mitigation (Wilson Rowe, 2015) or in defining children's rights (Hakli and Kallio, 2014). All of these studies tend to be fairly tightly focused on one thematic policy field and construct a genealogy of that field as their analytical window on authority. A genealogy is a long-lines tracing back of how different communities of knowledge or networks of actors competed to gain the privileged position of defining what matters in a given global governance field.

A genealogy is a tricky method to apply to contemporary Arctic cross-border governance, although it might be possible if one took a highly specific policy area or actor (e.g. Shadian, 2014, 2017 on the Inuit polity) or worked at a high level of abstraction. In its broadest sense, the regionally defined Arctic policy field is an ecosystem of many intersecting policy fields that overlap with local, national and non-Arctic international policy fields (see Introduction for a discussion of this). In other words, if we are considering the Arctic Council to be a policy field (rather than focusing on its institutional aspects), we have to think about how to capture the authority dynamics brought by many different actors with their own histories of political development to a large suite of policy issues, which have their own local, regional and often global genealogies as well.

Therefore, this chapter explores a systematising 'snapshot' approach, borrowed from science and technology studies, that may be fruitful in bringing problems of Arctic authority to light. In her cross-country comparison of political debates around biotechnology in Germany, the United States and the United Kingdom, Sheila Jasanoff notes persistent differences in national ways of meeting some common questions posed by biotechnology debates, even in relatively similar western states. She asserts that norms of debate, modes of trust, and the roles of and expectations about experts and expertise continue to vary across national borders – and describes this set of attitudes and practices as a 'civic epistemology' (Jasanoff, 2005). These civic epistemology indicators can provide a systematic snapshot view of settled/forgotten, ongoing and upcoming contestations over whose knowledge matters and how it should be presented, thereby providing a good window onto the politics of authority.

Putting debates over the relevance/appropriateness/credibility of knowledge in decision-making settings makes sense in trying to understand authority in an Arctic context, as knowledge has been part of the 'high politics' of the Arctic for centuries. The intertwining of knowledge and science with the pursuit of sovereignty and regional influence has a long history in the Arctic. From the scientific pursuits of early Arctic explorers through to the national emphases on Arctic science in the twentieth century, Arctic state-building has been reliant upon claiming to know the Arctic physical environment via science and through maintaining a physical presence via both military installations and science infrastructure (Bravo and Sörlin, 2002; Bravo, 2005; Shadian, 2009). As one Russian diplomat put it in an interview with the author in October 2011, 'no one knows the Arctic and its challenges like the Arctic states themselves – no one can govern the Arctic better than we can'. And as discussed in Chapter 3, Norway's claim to status in regional hierarchy has been tightly tied to the idea of being at the forefront of knowledge about the High North and the Arctic (MFA, Norway, 2011). Likewise, indigenous peoples' organisations seeking to decolonise relations of power have worked to make space in local, national and international planning and management for the observational and experiential knowledge gathered from close interaction with Arctic ecosystems (traditional knowledge/traditional ecological knowledge) (Huntington, 2000).

As we shall see below, questions of knowledge (whose should count, and who should be heard and how) are, unsurprisingly, actively and explicitly debated at the political level in the Arctic Council, both in terms of science/knowledge actors meeting the State and indigenous sovereignties meeting the State. What do these contours of debate tell us about broader tussles over the effective performance of authority?

Authority at the science–policy interface

This section conveniently refers to these 'what to do politically about the science' interactions in the Arctic Council as being a 'science–policy interface'. However, this handy term has several general shortcomings that the reader should keep in mind before we proceed with the Arctic case.

For one, this tidy division builds on a notion of how roles are played that is often challenged in scholarly writings but is widespread in popular perception: that scientists play a political role (when they choose to) by always 'speaking truth to power', and their 'statements' either being picked up (or ignored) by strategically selective politicians (Lidskog and Sundqvist, 2015). In this perspective, experts involved in international activity are meant to constitute a unified 'epistemic community' and act as agents of knowledge diffusion or informational entrepreneurs, pro-actively disseminating internationally produced information (such as climate assessments) (Adler, 2005; Haas 1992, 2015; Cross, 2013). By contrast, Bernstein's (2001: 487) observation that scientific knowledge may be necessary, requested and supplied in processes 'shaped by politics rather than by science' probably gives more analytical purchase in most science–policy interactions.

Secondly, the idea of a science–policy interface also draws the line between science and politics much more distinctly than the division as it exists in practice, as many studies in the history and sociology of science have shown (see, for example, Barnes *et al.*, 1996; Demeritt, 2001; Collins and Pinch, 1998; Latour, 1987; Shapin and Schaffer, 1985). This scholarship does not say that scientific findings are political or biased, but rather seeks to draw attention to how politics and knowledge production are in constant interplay. For example, the questions of deciding what disciplines or forms of enquiries get funded and to what degree is often subject to political interventions and debates. And there is no purely 'politics only' form of politics, either. Policy debates are often a complex mix of statements and arguments about what we know (science, facts) and what we should value (Dessler and Parson, 2010). This mix of statements is not an accident. Politicians and policy actors prefer to have science on their side, as a way of giving their arguments the added ballast of impartiality (Dessler and Parson, 2010: 56).

The closer one gets to decision-making levels the more extensively reworked and oriented towards policy does the 'science' side of the science–policy interface become. Most of the science presented for consideration in cross-border governance has been vetted or selected before-hand. Higher-level diplomats and politicians do not face piles of unfiltered research or the most recent academic journal articles (nor the academics that produced them). Rather, compilations of research presented with carefully articulated degrees of certainty about change expected and measures that could work are presented. The policy implications of Arctic Council scientific assessment work in the Arctic are often first cleared politically with WG Heads of Delegation (HoDs) to the various Arctic Council WGs interfacing first with their national SAO (see Spence, 2016, for a description of this activity within the AMAP WG). Additionally, we also see commissioned work from independent consultants that includes both the knowledge baseline and policy recommendations, primarily in issue areas closer to technical/governance issues rather than natural processes or environmental change. Examples include reports from the international engineering and management consultancy Det Norske Veritas (DNV) on heavy fuels (DNV, 2011) and specially designated sea areas (DNV, 2013).

This chapter focuses on the 'downstream' where expert knowledge meets political consideration at the international level of Arctic governance. One may expect to find considerably different dynamics within the 'upstream' of the WGs – and also variation across them. For example, one could anticipate that indigenous peoples' organisations are likely to be a strong voice within the Sustainable Development WG, with its emphasis on the 'people politics' of the Arctic Council. The dynamics in the Barents cooperation and certainly at various local and national levels surely possess their own 'local' character. And certainly, the dynamics of the national downstream science–policy interface are even more variable (see Wilson Rowe, 2013c for an example of the reception of Arctic climate science in Russia).

To get at some of the dynamics of authority at the science–policy interface downstream (when knowledge is deployed for policy consideration), I have gathered moments of active discussion/contestation of the function and place of science in the Arctic Council. Arctic Council minutes from the last ten years were analysed for active moments when the position and relevance of science work were debated at high-political meetings. Key themes coming from this analysis centre around the following questions. Who speaks for the Council? When does science become policy – and where do the policy conclusions get vetted? When is there enough science – or even too much – for political action?

Who speaks for the Council?

One window for understanding the science–policy interface at the Arctic Council is to follow discussions over who is meant to speak on behalf of the Council – or represent an Arctic environmental problem – on the global stage. These debates also tie into the broader question of the relationship between the frequently semi-autonomous WGs (with long

institutional memory on Arctic issues) and the regularly shifting diplomatic and political representatives of states.

During the 2015–2017 US chairmanship period, the question of
the Arctic Council's component parts' external relations to other governance bodies was raised in several guises. On one general discussion
of communications and 'who speaks for the AC [Arctic Council]', the
minutes from one SAO meeting indicate that there was 'no agreement':

> Most delegates expressed the view that Working Group Chairs and
> Heads of Delegations are the primary spokespersons for Working
> Group activities and may speak on factual/technical matters relating
> to the work of the Arctic Council, but that they should not speak
> publicly on policy matters on behalf of the Arctic Council writ large.
> Some delegates prefered [sic] that Working Group Chairs, rather than
> secretariats, speak publicly'.
>
> (Arctic Council Secretariat, 2015c: 6)

This last point is interesting, in that WG chairs go through periodic
national-level selection processes in which political voices can be heard,
whereas the secretariats operate at a more arm's-length distance from
political selection processes and often have longer-term employees.

In a more specific context, this issue of representation and voice was
revisited in connection to global climate politics. In the final report of
an SAO meeting held in Anchorage in 2015 (Arctic Council Secretariat,
2015c), the visibility of the Arctic Council at the landmark UNFCCC
Conference of Parties (COP) 21 was discussed. The discussion was triggered
by a WG (AMAP) stating that they wished to participate in a public event
at COP21 organised by the Nordic Council of Ministers. However, 'several delegates thought it would not be appropriate to have a single Arctic
Council working group participate in an event of this kind' organised by an
outside international organisation (Arctic Council Secretariat, 2015c: 5).
The solution landed upon, after some discussion, was that AMAP would
not participate publicly at COP21, but that Iceland would use some of its
own booth space to display Arctic Council publications in Paris.

Similar issues had also been brought up during the 2009–2011 Danish
chairmanship and, once again, in connection to an AMAP effort. It had
made some films that powerfully communicated the environmental
challenges covered in a recent environmental assessment. Concern was
expressed by some SAOs about AMAP having made the films, and there
was a discussion regarding the need for 'more transparency if such films
were to be produced in the future and also as to the geographical areas/
regions shown in the films: films should represent all Artic states and the
full spectrum of affected Arctic ecosystems and priority should be given
to all indigenous peoples, not just one or two'. Interestingly, however,
the indigenous representatives pushed back, arguing that 'they believed

the film on the human dimension captured the conditions of indigenous people very well and expressed its concerns as to the issue of how to adapt to climate change' (Arctic Council, 2011a: 4).

As will be discussed below, speaking/objecting on behalf of indigenous residents of the Arctic can lend a certain moral weight to the argument. In this case, however, an important feature of claiming authority in the Arctic Council made itself plain – indigenous peoples were there to speak on their own behalf, thereby removing the exclusive privilege of state representatives to speak on behalf of the 'people' within their borders.

When does science become policy?

Working groups lay out their plans for assessment and other scientific work, often early in a chairmanship period, for approval and comment. State representatives' commentary on the science tends to be focused on avoiding overlap (trying to get WGs to coordinate more), avoiding duplication and committing resources and data. It is important to keep in mind that states can also withhold resources on topics that they object to for any reason, although this occurs rarely. One example was that the USA was not positively disposed towards a proposed study comparing marine management practices in the Arctic. The reason was perceived duplication of other efforts, and the US representative consequently declared that it would not appoint a chapter author, but would instead submit an existing paper on the topic to the work (PAME, 2007: 4). On the whole, there is often little political-level comment on the planning stages of the WGs' plans or on the specific scientific findings and judgements – at least not reflected in the formal minutes (for a discussion of limitations involved in this source of data, see Introduction).

This dynamic, however, may be different depending on the topic of the assessment, and as the assessment concludes and efforts to formulate policy recommendations are made. The question of how and in what ways Arctic Council-based assessment knowledge was to be vetted at the national level became, for example, an acute issue for the 2007 OGA. Oil and gas production is, of course, a highly technical and economically strategic issue area around which to attempt an international cooperative assessment. The OGA was first presented in a finalised form to the SAOs in 2007 in northern Norway, and the SAO congratulated the authors and also noted that the report was still confidential at that stage.

When the AMAP chair announced plans to release the report at the Arctic Frontiers conference in Tromsø, and then at two regional conferences in Russia and Alaska, a discussion ensued about the difference between the scientific findings and the recommendations in the 'overview report' compiled for policy and public circulation. More specifically, 'clarity was sought as to whether the recommendations in the Overview Report are intended to be scientific or policy recommendations. If the latter, further clarity was sought on Arctic Council process to deal with policy recommendations from/approved within a Working Group and what the SAOs [*sic*] role to respond to the WG recommendations should be' (Arctic Council, 2007b: 9–10). In this field of high socio-economic relevance, it seems that some SAOs felt that the policy recommendations made by the WG were too prescriptive, or had somehow overstepped the mandate of normal procedure and division of labour between expert and political actors in the Arctic Council.

This observation sparked a discussion of how and when the political levels should intervene in shaping the recommendations or dissemination of WG outputs. Then AMAP sought to clarify its

> understanding that the scientists prepare the scientific assessment and write the scientific conclusions and recommendations. The key findings and policy recommendations in the Overview Report were based on the science recommendations in the scientific assessment and negotiated among the AMAP working group heads of delegation with extensive national review.

The minutes further note that a participant argued that 'It has not been the policy for SAOs to alter Working Group reports. The precedent is for the SAOs to receive the work of the working group and recommend elements to bring forward in the SAOs report' (Arctic Council, 2007b: 9–10)

This standing procedure to which the unknown speaker had referred received support from 'most SAOs', and the chair further reiterated that the SAOs' role was to receive the recommendations. Other SAOs felt that the OGA contained statements that 'if intended as policy recommendations, [suggested that] the national review had been insufficient ... that a process for approval of the policy portion of the Assessment within governments was needed' (Artic Council, 2007b: 10). The SAOs agreed to finish their review of the policy portion by mid-January and that the policy recommendations and executive summary could only be released if comments from governments were addressed prior to the planned launch at the Arctic Frontiers conference (Arctic Council, 2007b: 11). At a later meeting, however, the official launch of the OGA was designated as a task of the SAOs (Arctic Council, 2007a).

In releasing the Snow, Water, Ice and Permafrost in the Arctic (SWIPA) assessment in 2010, and perhaps based on the troublesome experience of bringing the OGA to completion, AMAP raised the topic again of how policy recommendations should be developed. The following procedure was established:

AMAP confirmed that AMAP HoDs would develop policy recommendations based on the science report and that these would be included in the summary report ... SAOs stressed that, with respect to the policy recommendations, it is the responsibility of AMAP HoDs to interact closely with their SAOs so that they are more comfortable with the report and its recommendations when it is delivered to SAOs.

Interestingly, however, SAOs sought to bring the natural-science-based SWIPA assessment into close conversation with the Arctic Council, asking for it to be seen as an Arctic Council report. It was noted by AMAP that it does not normally place an Arctic Council logo on science-based reports, but it requested SAO guidance on the topic. The SAOs nonetheless encouraged AMAP to finish the report early enough to allow for 'national consultations' before the next meeting (Arctic Council, 2010a: 6).

Likewise, at different political moments and perhaps involving different diplomats, state representatives have sought to blur the distinction between science and policy – or to be able at least to celebrate scientific cooperation as a political success as well. At an SAO meeting held in Whitehorse in 2015, at a low point in Russia's relations with the West (see Chapter 2 for a discussion of post-2014 Arctic diplomacy) and in response to the presentation of the Arctic Guide on Oil Spill Response in Ice and Snow from EPPR, Russia noted as a positive that the report is both 'technical and political' (Arctic Council Secretariat, 2015a: 18). At this pre-ministerial SAO meeting in Whitehorse, Russia also paid extra attention to AMAP's work and opened a discussion about how AMAP results could be made more accessible to the broader public and politicians (Arctic Council Secretariat, 2015a: 13). The point here is that changing political landscapes more broadly – as well as the regularly shifting diplomats sent by states – probably contribute to the ongoing dynamism of the science–policy interface of the Arctic Council, even twenty years in.

Furthermore, it is important to reiterate that the science–policy interface at the Arctic Council does not seem to be about political actors seeking to control the scientific findings or assessment conclusions themselves. Undergirding this observation is a discussion about two scientific articles produced under ACAP – in which SAOs make it clear they have no intention of seeking to review or judge the validity of scientific findings. ACAP WG raised the question of publications for peer-reviewed journals that had come of the work included in the ACAP working plan, but that did not have or require ACAP or Arctic Council logos or branding. Delegates are reported to have:

agreed that scientific or technical reports that do not contain policy recommendations and that are complete and ready to be released in peer-reviewed journals (or otherwise) could be released when they are

ready. WGs should not feel compelled to delay publication in order to
wait for a Ministerial meeting. Scientific/technical publications that do
not contain policy recommendations do not require SAO approval ...
However, if a product responds directly to a directive from Ministerial
Declaration or contains policy recommendations, it should be saved
for release at the next appropriate Ministerial meeting ... In addition, WG chairs are required to bring any product containing policy
recommendations before SAOs for review.

(Arctic Council Secretariat, 2015c: 9)

Political concern tends, instead, to be much more closely tied to how
results are communicated (by whom and when and after what kind of
process) and, especially, to how policy recommendations are formulated
and communicated (and by whom).

When do you know enough?

It is also important to keep in mind that science or expertise is probably
not always considered useful by policy field participants in global governance – or not beyond a certain point. For example, in international
negotiations around climate change mitigation, diplomats reported
frustration and irritation over negotiation participants who become
too hung up on certain technical nuances when the political drift of the
negotiations had clearly moved forward regardless (Wilson Rowe, 2015;
see Seabrooke and Henriksen, 2017, for a broader discussion).

The Arctic Council archival documents only give us one example of this
kind of limit-drawing about a sufficient evidence basis – at least until political actions start to be taken to 'catch up'. The point was made by the US
chairmanship team at an early SAO meeting during American leadership.
A paper introduced by the chairmanship made the following point about
the sheer number of regulatory and knowledge-based recommendations
that have been made: 'there have been – by one account – some *238
recommendations* made by the Arctic Council on oil and gas activities'
(US Chairmanship of the Arctic Council, 2016a: 2–3 (emphasis in original)). This was celebrated in the report as an indication that the Council
had effectively evolved to 'address real world changes in the realm of oil
and gas. However, the current assemblage of working groups, task forces,
expert groups and bodies outside the Council (e.g., [The Arctic Offshore
Regulators Forum]) that all have involvement in oil and gas issues presents a
coordination challenge to the Council' (3). In other words, the Council had
produced a multitude of well-founded, well-researched recommendations
on oil and gas, but the sheer number of recommendations and actors
involved in producing them limited their practical usage in national-level
politics, where decisions about oil and gas are made.

This brings us back to the point we discussed above about the science policy interface – science may be called upon but be neither decisive nor sufficient as a basis for policymaking in some processes. Before discussing what these various moments of debate over the science–policy interface tell us about the civic epistemology of the Arctic Council, we turn first to a fundamentally important set of governance actors in the Arctic with a substantive claim to authority in the Arctic context – the Permanent Participants representing the indigenous peoples of the region. We then combine these two interfaces to think systematically through what they in combination can tell us about authority in Arctic governance.

Authority at the Peoples–State interface

Several of the organisations taking part as Permanent Participants at the Arctic Council grew out of the social movements around indigenous peoples and their land that emerged in the 1960s and 1970s. Major new economic opportunities bringing further incursions into indigenous lands, such as Alaska's oil wealth and the building of the Trans-Alaska Pipeline System, or seeking to harness the hydroelectric potential of James Bay in northern Quebec, catalysed these movements and had triggered formal negotiation processes between indigenous peoples and the State, such as the Alaska Native Claims Settlement Agreement of 1971 or the James Bay and Northern Quebec Agreement of 1975.

However contested or incomplete these agreements were seen to be at the time, or have come to be seen since, the process of negotiating them forged experienced, powerful, indigenous collective and individual voices calling for justice and equality (Abele and Rodon, 2009). The ICC was pushed forward by a complex set of North American domestic and international factors, and quickly became an important actor within a burgeoning indigenous internationalism taking place in international organisations, such as the United Nations (Smith and Wilson, 2009; Shadian, 2014, 2017). Within the Nordic Arctic, the Saami had for decades become increasingly organised because of internal push factors and also international processes, such as the negotiation of the International Labour Organization's resolution on indigenous peoples (Kuokkanen, 2009).

The genesis of Russian Arctic indigenous peoples' political mobilisation was somewhat different. In the Soviet Arctic, the indigenous peoples of the North, formerly known as *inorodtsy* (aliens) under the tsarist empire, were renamed the 'small-numbered peoples of the North'. Although these peoples were not considered nations, the small-numbered peoples of the Russian North also underwent the Soviet efforts to recruit minority ethnicity/indigenous intelligentsia from the 1930s and onwards (Krupnik, 1993; Slezkine, 1994; Vakhtin, 1994).

This intelligentsia was meant to bridge the gap between indigenous and Soviet cultures (Haruchi, 2002: 86). Simultaneously, there were focused and often brutal efforts to resettle nomadic indigenous groups, primarily reindeer-herding peoples, into villages and to transform nomadism as a way of life into nomadism as a form of Sovietised collective production (Pika, 1999; Vitebsky, 2005).

The end of the Soviet Union witnessed the increased political activity of this indigenous political elite (Haruchi, 2002). With the introduction of perestroika and an accompanying reduction in censorship, the issues facing indigenous Arctic Soviet peoples came to be discussed publicly (Slezkine, 1994). In 1989, a three-day congress of 250 indigenous representatives met to debate and to select representatives for an All-Union Congress of Native Peoples of the North. This was a product of Gorbachev's perestroika and also a response to increasing international pressure (Kaplin, 2002; Murashko, 2002). This congress gradually evolved into RAIPON, in part thanks to practical and financial support from Canadian actors (Wilson, 2007a).

So, how were these organisations representing indigenous peoples of the Arctic to participate in the rapidly expanding cross-border politics of the post-Cold War Arctic? Initially, it was proposed that perhaps the indigenous peoples' organisations should enjoy the same privileges awarded to states. This was seen by many state representatives as a challenging proposition. The USA, for example, partially resisted establishing the Arctic Council, as it raised too pointedly the issue of how indigenous peoples would participate in the proposed new format. There was limited specific concern for the Arctic context, but a broader question of how the inclusion of indigenous peoples as equals could bring a new set of challenges to Alaskan politics and set a diplomatic precedent challenging State authority and existing practices for other international fora. Neither had Norway or Denmark been immediately enthusiastic (English, 2013: 188, 186).

An experienced diplomat and civil servant long engaged with northern questions, Walter Slipchenko, proposed as early as 1992 that indigenous peoples would need to be represented as something more than 'observers' alongside other NGOs, and introduced the category of 'Permanent Participant' for Arctic cross-border settings, which would grant access and participation at all levels of discussion (English, 2013: 167, 181; Shadian, 2014). The United States in turn insisted that the number of Permanent Participants be expanded from the original three (Saami Council, RAIPON, ICC) to also include three new organisations founded to participate in the Arctic Council – the Arctic Athabaskan Council (USA/Canada), the Gwich'in Council International (USA/Canada), and the Aleut International Association (USA/Russia).

Below, I explore three key themes that can be pulled out from the interventions made by these long established and more newly minted

Permanent Participants in high-level Arctic Council meetings in the past ten years, as reflected in minutes and reports. Key topics include the importance of (and challenges to) Permanent Participant participation in the increasing scope of Arctic Council activities, speaking for the peopled Arctic and calling states to account.

Strong political representation in diplomacy, challenged in agenda-setting in the upstream

Within the Arctic Council indigenous participation varies, and this variable participation is frequently linked to problems of capacity. The Indigenous Peoples' Secretariat was established to support the participation of Permanent Participants in Arctic Council work, and how this secretariat is funded and functions has been a frequent focal point for capacity questions. For example, during the Norwegian chairmanship, the Permanent Participants submitted a document clarifying and reminding states about Permanent Participants' role in the leadership of the Indigenous Peoples Secretariat, while underlining that the indigenous leadership role does not dilute the responsibility of the states to continue funding the secretariat (Arctic Council/Indigenous Peoples Secretariat, 2008). In a broader sense, Jim Gamble, Executive Director of the Aleut International Association, notes that every Ministerial Declaration since Ottawa has mentioned the importance of states supporting Permanent Participant capacity. He argues that this testifies to the broadly recognised value that the Permanent Participants bring to the work of the Council and to the unresolved problem of how best to support these small organisations faced with an ever-expanding portfolio of Arctic governance issues (Gamble, 2016).

Across the board, however, Permanent Participant representatives already do participate more consistently than observer states in the various facets of the Arctic Council's work (Knecht, 2017: 9), although at levels less than those of state representatives. Permanent Participants are nearly always present at ministerial meetings and SAO meetings, but with decreased participation in WG meetings (41 per cent average participation) and task force meetings (34.5 per cent) (Knecht, 2017: 8). Coote notes that indigenous peoples' organisations also participate in the upstream of Arctic Council work that takes place in the WGs, although may struggle to set the agenda there because of capacity limitations (2016).

On a related note, it is therefore unsurprising that one topic of debate that sparked 'intensive discussion' was the role of Permanent Participants in conceiving projects. Permanent Participants argued that greater transparency was needed as to whether the indigenous peoples' representatives had been consulted, and whether the inclusion of traditional knowledge had been considered, in early phases of project development. This included making a checklist point on indigenous participation a require-ment for early phases of Arctic Council projects and having this consid-eration (or lack thereof) made visible in the newly established project overview database (the Amarok project tracking document) (Arctic Council, 2015c: 8). Seeking to enshrine consideration of indigenous knowledge, perspectives and participation in the project-planning pro-cess was one way of ensuring that these issues were considered, even if the Permanent Participants themselves could not be at each meeting to place them on the agenda.

Speaking for the living Arctic

There are two main areas of emphasis that we can extract from the formal diplomatic statements and recorded interventions of the Permanent Participants at the Arctic Council. First, as we saw in Chapter 2, indi-genous representatives weighed in heavily on the question of the extent to which Russia's problems with other Arctic countries after 2014 should interfere with or overshadow progress in Arctic cooperation. Permanent Participants' interventions stated that the cooperative cross-border nature of the Arctic region must be preserved, even considering conflict between Arctic countries outside the region.

Another important discursive intervention is insistence on political attention to the 'people' politics that can be addressed at the inter-state level, including questions of economic development. A sampling of statements made by indigenous representatives at the 2011 Nuuk min-isterial meeting serves to illustrate this point. As we saw in Chapter 2, the Greenlandic statement argued for the importance of both pursuing economic opportunities and protecting the environment: 'the Arctic is not just about polar bears and ice. What is often missing from the dis-cussion is the human aspect of the Arctic and the conditions in which we live' (author's translation from Danish, Kleist, 2011: 3). Sergey Kharuchi's statement for RAIPON also highlights the living, human aspect of the Arctic (RAIPON, 2011). A statement from the Saami Council at the same ministerial session raises a key socio-political question of inter-national relevance, given how many of the extractive industries operate in more than one country, calling for the importance of benefit-sharing in extractive industries (Saami Council, 2011).

Calling states to account

Indigenous peoples' organisations also use the Arctic Council setting to hold state representatives to account in facilitating the basis of their participation. This includes attention to the Arctic Council's efficiency and concern over duplicative structures. For example, the Arctic Athabaskan Council pushed hard in 2007 for the WG structure to be revisited and streamlined, calling for the Norwegian chairmanship to devote some serious attention to the question of efficiency (Arctic Athabaskan Council, 2007). For organisations with small staffs, ensuring that the main action starts and finishes in the SAO and ministerial meetings has been important.

Permanent Participants also play a role in on-the-record naming and shaming, something we do not see state representatives doing. Given that public calling-out is unusual in this context, it becomes a powerful way of calling to account. At the Kiruna ministerial meeting, Chief Michael Stickman, once again, as at the Nuuk ministerial session (Arctic Athabaskan Council, 2011), criticises the lack of immediate action on black carbon and the continuous establishment of task forces, rather than a concrete action plan. He specifically asks Prime Minister Lavrov, with the 'greatest respect', to explain why this is the case, as it is Russia who has opposed action on black carbon (Arctic Athabaskan Council, 2013). There are few other settings in the world where a native chief can call the Minister of Foreign Affairs to account.

Likewise, the Swedish Saami representative used the home-turf ministerial meeting to present a negative picture of indigenous rights in Sweden:

> here in the Giron area, industrial development – in particular mining – poses a tremendous challenge to the local Saami reindeer herding people. In our delegation, we have local reindeer herders with us that can witness to the fact that corporate responsibility can be a two-edged sword. The Swedish government says that we expect the mining industry to behave responsibly when operating in the Saami areas. But at the same time, the mining company says we have to follow Swedish law. Here in the Giron area, corporate responsibility equals no responsibility.
>
> (Saami Council, 2013)

RAIPON seems to use sessions of the Arctic Council to make points that many other indigenous organisations would probably have taken care of domestically. For example, in Copenhagen at the 2009 SAO meeting under the Norwegian chairmanship, RAIPON noted that Russia had yet to contribute any data to the flagship ministerial deliverable, the Arctic Marine Shipping Assessment (Arctic Council, 2009a: 2). At a 2010 SAO meeting in Tórshavn, RAIPON took the opportunity to request that they be more involved in Russian governmental work on Arctic issues, for example in ACAP (Arctic Council, 2010b: 11). The centralisation of authority from the regions to Moscow and from multiple branches of government and civil society into the executive in Russia, discussed in the previous chapter, may make the Arctic Council one of the more important meeting spaces for a Russian organisation to meet Russian authorities.

To take an Arctic example of a statement made to a broad audience, including the Arctic Council member states, 'A circumpolar Inuit declaration on sovereignty in the Arctic' made assertions about the peoplehood of the circumpolar Inuit, to mitigate the sovereign claims of states (see Beyers, 2014 for an extended discussion):

> The conduct of international relations in the Arctic and the resolution of international disputes in the Arctic are not the sole preserve of Arctic states or other states; they are also within the purview of the Arctic's indigenous peoples. The development of international institutions in the Arctic, such as multi-level governance systems and indigenous peoples' organizations, must transcend Arctic states' agendas on sovereignty and sovereign rights and the traditional monopoly claimed by states in the area of foreign affairs. Issues of sovereignty and sovereign rights in the Arctic have become inextricably linked to issues of self-determination in the Arctic. Inuit and Arctic states must, therefore, work together closely and constructively to chart the future of the Arctic.
>
> (ICC, 2015a)

Here, we see an interesting feature of the 'civic epistemology' of the Arctic, to which we now turn. In the Arctic Council, states cannot derive authority by speaking on behalf of the populations of their state. Rather they have to interface with and cooperate (or fail to do so at their own expense) with representatives of a 'third space diplomacy' (Beier, 2009) – the Permanent Participants' organisations who are both inside multiple states and outside them at the same time.

A civic epistemology of Arctic governance?

In this concluding section of the chapter, we return to the 'civic epistemology' rubric developed by Jasanoff to point to what may be some enduring features of how authority is negotiated and shaped in Arctic governance. My aim in utilising the civic-epistemology framework is not to deliver the final word on authority in Arctic governance, but rather to bring the observations about the performance and contestation of Arctic power relations by non-state actors into systematic and comparative focus.

Utilising a more dynamic, present-oriented framework is also meant to deliver a supplement to 'field-genealogy'-driven forms of analysis as a historical unpacking of governance fields. A historical approach, while bringing to light important origins of why certain actors, framings or resources brought to a policy field matter more for shaping outcomes, may also reify contestation over authority as a one-time (if uphill) battle and fail to notice that authority remains constantly contested and renegotiated. As we saw above, natural-science and scientific actors have long been enshrined as central actors in Arctic governance, yet when and how they are meant to intercede/interface with the political and diplomatic levels of the Arctic Council remained a debated topic, even twenty years in. Furthermore, given the complexity and interconnectedness of the overlapping policy fields that make up Arctic cross-border governance (and the multitude of actors with their own histories of political development actively shaping these fields), an empirically rigorous genealogy that takes all of this overlap and complexity into account may be challenging to carry out.

In her civic-epistemology framework, Jasanoff compared attitudes and political processes around biotechnology in three countries that one would not necessarily expect to have radically different approaches to questions of what counts for authority. Jasanoff (2005) employed six indicators to unpack expectations about the use of expert knowledge at the national level in the UK, the USA and Germany. The findings of this chapter about tussles around authority science–policy and people–state interfaces at the high-level political meetings of the Arctic Council speak to four of the indicators identified by Jasanoff (slightly adapted for use here):

(1) Trust. How do we discern credibility of statements?
(2) Visibility of expert bodies. Behind the scenes? At the forefront of public debates?
(3) Objectivity. What is the balance between scientifically valid, numerical inputs and other inputs such as social and political concerns in the outcome? How are outcomes negotiated?
(4) Recognition/success. What makes a participant able to secure deference for or support of their claim?

In terms of *trust*, the debates around science-based interventions and Permanent Participant interventions seem to suggest little attention devoted to issues of trust in efforts to gain authority. There are no accusations of 'bad science' or work poorly carried out, or suggestions that Permanent Participants or others are failing to represent their own stated interests or constituencies. The SAOs did indeed take the WGs to task several times, especially AMAP, for what they considered to be a potential overstep of procedures, such as having science findings that seemed to them too much like policy findings, and seeking to take a public stage too frequently or with innovative forms of communication, such as film.

In terms of Permanent Participants' relationship to the states, we see that states are not automatically trusted to do what they have promised or to do what is best for the Arctic based on the science gathered and used as a basis for policymaking. There is never a reason given, however, for why states would not do this, and it is a likely assumption to make that it has more to do with the broad political and economic costs of action for states in, say, climate mitigation, than with a distrust towards the actual representatives of these states. Rather, this ties into a universal issue of politics on long-term environmental problems that outstrip election cycles. Perhaps because the Permanent Participants' diplomatic stakes are more squarely centred on the Arctic, they are more able and willing to challenge states directly on key issues, as in the case of Chief Stickman's comments to Russia on their perceived foot-dragging with regard to black carbon.

The contentious issues relate, rather, to the *visibility of expert bodies* outside the Arctic Council in other global fora. Experts and WG representatives are highly visible at the meetings and associated events of the Arctic Council itself. The tricky question is about their global intersection with other international organisations and professional networks. Monitoring existent and curtailing further expansion in the independent diplomatic networks of the WGs was a pursuit encouraged by both SAOs and Permanent Participants during the American chairmanship. In other words, while science inputs are essential for governing the Arctic, the political representatives operate with a strong sense that scientists should not speak *for* the Arctic, particularly in connection to global audiences.

Ensuring that the wide network of experts surrounding the Arctic Council is first streamlined through the political level may be a particularly important issue for the Permanent Participants in seeking to exercise their special position as the original peoples of the Arctic. Because of their capacity challenges in participating in agenda-setting work within the Arctic Council's WGs, Permanent Participant representation in WGs is nearly half their level of participation in the higher-level political meetings. It thus becomes especially important that the main action, core messages and course-setting decisions are made in those meeting settings. All this ties in well with the characterisation of experts as being appreciated, and 'on tap' but not 'on top' in the driving forward of policymaking or identification of policy consequences (Barnes *et al.*, 1996). In sum, when speaking on behalf of the region to other political settings, Permanent Participants and states seem to be in agreement about retaining that global public voice for themselves.

When it comes to *objectivity*, at the high-level political meetings analysed here, objectivity was less of a concern. Because of the seemingly high levels of trust in the quality of the outputs of WG activity, participants at the meetings were not engaging extensively in issues relating to the balance between natural science and socio-political knowledge, or relating to the balance between quantitative or qualitative inputs. This may be because the mandate at these meetings is to agree on what can be said politically about the evidence basis, rather than to redo the assessment work of the various expert groupings that produced the report. Furthermore, the inclusion of traditional ecological knowledge/traditional knowledge in some of the Arctic Council's work, however incompletely or sporadically, probably introduces a grain of humility about different forms of knowledge and ways of knowing, thus limiting the utility of attempting to raise one form of one source of knowledge high above another. It seems that it is clear to the participants that what is at stake at the higher-level Arctic Council gatherings is not the empirical/scientific basis or validity of the problems presented, but rather what to do about them and how to frame them for broader global and national 'home' audiences.

In sum, *what makes an authority*? Progress in the Arctic Council is highly reliant on agenda-setting and evidence-gathering done by the WGs, and their contributions are trusted and actively used by other policy field participants. However, state representatives and the Permanent Participants all actively engage in efforts to secure their own authoritative positions, particularly vis-à-vis the semi-independent WGs with longstanding secretariats and staff, and markedly less so vis-à-vis one another as explicitly political actors. This occurs primarily along the dimension of who speaks on behalf of the Arctic Council, and is evident especially in contestation over who will address non-Arctic settings and who will be able to draft and disseminate to a global audience evidence-based policy conclusions. Both states and Permanent Participants claim an (overlapping) authority rooted in geography, statehood and peoplehood to speak on behalf of the Arctic and its peoples, extending beyond an expertise-based performance of authority that science actors may bring. In other words, while the Arctic policy field requires scientific input, the policy field has developed in such a way that the most successful performance of authority remains explicitly political, rooted in the logics of sovereignty and statehood.

Conclusion

In October 2016, a US Arctic governmental advisor suggested – at one of the Arctic region's conferences for academics, policymakers and business – that we need to 'shine a light' on the success of Arctic cooperation as an example of peaceful cooperation in a complicated world. Likewise, a high-level representative from Alaska underlined the pressing importance of continued cooperation with Russia, noting that the two countries at their outermost points are only 2.5 miles (3.8 km) apart. To me in the conference audience, this was a striking juxtaposition to the same day's international news. Headlines were of angry chaos in the UN Security Council over Syria and the Obama Administration's decision formally to accuse the Russian Government of stealing and disclosing emails from the Democratic National Committee in an attempt to influence the 2016 presidential elections.

That the Arctic Council has been largely buffered from an all-time post-Cold War low point in Russian–American relations is indeed a remarkable and important achievement. That it has been possible to keep, by and large, broader conflicts out of the Arctic Council can be explained in many ways. The national interests of all Arctic states are reasonably well served by existing political arrangements and the international law provisions of UNCLOS, and few Arctic actors would stand to benefit from bringing external strife to such a stable situation. Both Russia and the USA are large states with traditions of running complex foreign policies that allow for separation of issues and problems, and internal contradictions. The indigenous polities that transect the national borders of the North advocate for (and attest to) the transnational nature of many Arctic concerns, which outstrip the ability of any one geographically bounded country to address alone. However, we have long needed better accounts of the actual diplomatic work – the performances and practices of geopower – that have mattered for maintaining and continuously redefining Arctic cross-border governance in accordance with these broader interests. Hopefully, this book has made a contribution to this knowledge gap.

Power in Arctic cross-border cooperation

This book has sought to show how Arctic cross-border cooperation is marked by power relations – and related norms, representations and hierarchies – that are under constant re-enactment and renegotiation. As discussed in the introductory chapter, the Arctic is often envisioned as on the precipice of conflict. This may be because many governance participants – and especially those outside it – have difficulty buying the notion that a region so valuable and important for many reasons, including those security-related and economy-related, can remain a low-tension one. States' coordinated chorus on the peaceful nature of the region can quickly sound too good to be true. However, if we reveal and understand better the efforts and alliances and inequalities and contestations that shore up this state of cross-border cooperation, the Arctic 'peace' becomes a more recognisable – and possibly more replicable – dynamic.

A focus on power is timely. The Arctic lies in an uncertain zone of the changing post-Cold War global geopolitical imagination. While fostering narratives of circumpolar conflict (and actual conflict in other parts of the world), this untidy geopolitical backdrop of the post-Cold War years has been largely productive in the Arctic. New initiatives, such as the circumpolar Arctic Council, the CBSS and formalised structures for cross-border contact in the Barents region of the Nordic Arctic (discussed in detail in Chapter 1), have been created. Against this dizzyingly positive backdrop of growing cooperation and despite the many important contributions to scholarship from Arctic scholars, power relations as manifested in cross-border cooperative practice have yet to be rigorously analysed using the wide toolkit of concepts developed through studies of global politics elsewhere in the world, as I argued in the introduction.

The growing scholarly interest in bringing to light the performance of power within the liberal institutional order and unmarked by military or open conflict is an analytical cue from the literature that this book has applied to the cooperative politics of the Arctic. Rather than trying to theorise what power *is* in today's global political landscape (or who *has* power), we have utilised perspectives from IR and geography that direct us to understand the performance of power in practice. This entails understanding power as produced through marshalling necessary resources to undergird a performance of dominance (or deference) – and pulling off the performance in such a way that the audience recognises the performance as one of a competent actor. Repeated efforts at this kind of performance – or a very successful one – heighten the ability of actors to shape outcomes after their preferences (including furnishing a policy site with strongly anchored representations, hierarchies, diplomatic norms and scripts of authority, as we saw in Chapters 2, 3, 4 and 5 respectively). Performances of deploying detailed knowledge of or representations about the Arctic landscape and region can be further understood as manifestations of 'geopower', drawing strength from privileged relationships to and representations of the Arctic environment itself.

The book has also conceptualised the location of the enquiry to be an interlinked ecosystem of overlapping fields centred around the Arctic that extends to different levels of governance (global, local, national) to differing degrees. Global policy fields can be understood as delimited spheres of social action, and marked by unequally distributed resources among players within this social field. This kind of open definition suits an enquiry into Arctic cross-border governance well, as the definition of an 'Arctic issue' (and where the Arctic is – and where an issue should be resolved) is often an output of power relations and contestation. Furthermore, the notion of policy field participant remains open to the broad range of Arctic actors engaged in cross-border cooperative work, from people-to-people exchanges, through business associations, to top-level meetings of foreign ministers. The notion of overlapping or nested Arctic policy fields serves to delimit the scope of study in this book, while keeping the sense that these cross-border policy fields are intimately connected to both local and national settings and other global governance issues.

The attention to unequally distributed resources within a policy field, discussed in detail in the Introduction and Chapter 4, also serves to capture the disciplining effects of discourse and norms, while leaving space for the improvisational and instrumental ways in which policy field actors navigate and improvise against a policy field's limitations (or the limitations of their own assumed role and position). This is a different sort of conceptualisation of what is tying actors together than the important scholarship conducted on identity-building taking place alongside region-building in the Arctic during the 1990s. Here, cooperation was often seen as highly structured by mutually constitutive discourses and group- and individual-level Arctic identities. The idea of fields also draws attention to how the field participants are operating in a terrain that does not cater to all participants and all kinds of interventions equally well, making it easier to understand why an actor in the field may seek to innovate (and possibly equipping us better to understand how change happens).

Revisiting the book's four propositions on power

The case-study chapters explored *four propositions* distilled from cues from the broader literature on power relations in global governance from IR, political geography, and science and technology studies. These propositions were designed to shed light on the extent to which and how Arctic cross-border cooperation has been marked by power relations.

In Chapter 2, the proposition that *power relations are manifested in and shaped by the definitions and representations of Arctic policy objects and the region more broadly* was explored. While previous research has identified well the key 'framings' of Arctic space (specific narratives and visual vocabularies), this chapter illustrated how these regional frames are actually actively contested and enthusiastically marshalled by actors seeking to promote a particular perspective on the region in the everyday diplomacy of the region. Reasserting the peaceful Arctic frame in Iqaluit in 2015 was an important message about the commitment of the Arctic states to governing the region peacefully – and primarily amongst themselves.

Furthermore, understanding when broader power relations, as manifested in regional framings, are at stake renders more understandable moments that otherwise seem to be 'policy storms in a teacup', when the importance of immediate interests or magnitude of possible conflicts of interest simply do not match the intensity of the debate. The drawn-out consideration of a new batch of observer applications over two chairmanship periods, and the late-night, last minute discussions of those applications on the eve of the 2013 ministerial meeting are difficult to understand without taking into account how a broader tension between framing the Arctic as global and framing the Arctic as regional was at stake. Likewise, the contention around the development of the AEC can be understood in a similar way. Commercial actors are one of the target audiences of many of the Arctic Council's policy efforts from conservation to economic development, and not newcomers to Arctic affairs, as discussed in Chapter 1. Yet the development of the AEC in its various early iterations attracted high-level debate from a number of key Arctic actors. Chapter 2 illustrated how the AEC was tapping into and activated a longstanding tug-of-war or balancing act between the two pillars of the Arctic Council (and broader associated framings of Arctic space) – conservation/environment and sustainable development. From the cases selected and empirical insights generated, we can see that experienced players in Arctic governance seem highly aware of the importance of 'geopower' – anchoring their preferences in richly weighted narratives about space – to realise preferred power relations and political outcomes. Contestation and debate arise when these narratives are placed under pressure by changing circumstances or new considerations.

The proposition explored in Chapter 3 was that *as policy fields come together and endure, some actors will find themselves in occupation of a more advantageous position for securing desired outcomes – as a result of prior effort and success in defining what matters in the policy field.* Identifying such forms of hierarchy does not necessarily tell us about how this became the case, but rather sensitises us to the extent to which participants in a given policy field find themselves, in rather enduring ways, positioned uniquely. The chapter showed how two kinds of club status seem to matter in Arctic international relations as constituted among states – namely the 'Arctic 5' coastal states and Arctic states in general versus the rest of the globe (the non-Arctic states).

Furthermore, we have seen how internationally significant 'great powers', such as the USA and Russia, are best understood as 'resting powers' in an Arctic context. In the regular flow of Arctic diplomacy, they act very much like other Arctic coastal states in their preferences and contributions. However, at critical, agenda-setting junctures, their participation is seen by other states as essential and, indeed, the course-setting gestures of the regional great powers have had longlasting significance for the development of Arctic multilateralism.

At the same time, there are a number of useful functions and advantageous positions that can be taken below the level of great power. Norway has styled itself as a 'knowledge power' in Arctic politics – and as a bridge to Russia. However, as the post-2014 years have shown, this particular source of status as 'bridge to Russia' was no longer an available option when the political backdrop changed dramatically. This is an important illustration of how politics external to a more delimited policy field may affect the resources available and significant within that narrow policy field, resulting in change.

The chapter also explored how 'deep' hierarchies have long been enacted – and contested – in the people-to-people politics of the region as well. Such 'deep' hierarchies involve identifying peoples or parts of the world as superior and inferior, such as 'developed' and 'developing' world. I have argued that many of the circumpolar development efforts of the 1990s were rooted in such deep hierarchy, envisioning Russia as in transition and the West as having the relevant lessons to bring. We also saw how these spatial framings of teachers and students in an Arctic context were contested at the time, and, even more soundly, as Russia resumed a place on the global stage in the 2000s, as was explored in Chapter 4.

Chapter 4 looked at the informal workings of power by examining what is accepted as a legitimate statement, policy concern or actor in the Arctic Council. The proposition about power explored in this chapter was that Arctic cross-border cooperation *plays out in a social space marked by informal norms. These constraints allow for the performance of Arctic diplomacy to more and less successful degrees and shape behaviour, even of the 'great powers', in the region.* The chapter sought to illustrate some of these key social constraints by examining Russia's role on the Arctic Council, arguing that the country has been disciplined by policy field norm constraints and also sought to transform them. The review of Russia's first decade of participation in the Arctic Council showed low levels of participation, albeit some successful cooperation on 'low-political' cooperation. Russia's own proposals frequently missed the mark, as they were out of step with the emerging norms and procedures of the Council (e.g. focused only on Russia as opposed to multilateral). It is important to note that Russia during this period rarely succeeded in pushing through an unpopular suggestion. This perhaps points to a taken-for-granted norm of participation – the expectation that all Arctic countries will participate in circumpolar governance.

In the second decade of the Arctic Council, Russia actively profiled itself as an Arctic leader. Being a legally minded, play-by-the-rules Arctic actor that fulfils a leadership role was a main pursuit for Russia's Arctic policy actors between 2008 and 2010, and these efforts were warmly received by counterparts in other Arctic states. This also suggests that a cooperative, coalition-building approach to leadership is seen as the regionally appropriate way for expressing leadership. Furthermore, the second decade of the Arctic Council differs from the first primarily in new efforts directed towards creating binding agreements. This is an important development to a procedural norm from the first decade – that of minimising formality and instead working towards soft-law and best-practice outcomes only. This change towards formal agreement is perhaps an area where Russia has been a norm entrepreneur, turning the Arctic Council into a location where also binding, treaty-based agreements can be prepared and concluded. This relates to one further norm, which was decidedly more pronounced in the Arctic Council's second decade than its first: when the great powers speak, the Council listens. How this norm and its enactment will continue to develop is an important avenue for further research.

In Chapter 5, we explored how *power relations are malleable and constantly refined/redefined, especially between different 'kinds' of actors*. To get at a sense of the kind of authority that indigenous organisations and expert actors have achieved in Arctic governance, the chapter examined negotiations across the 'science–policy' and 'peoples–states' interfaces at high-level Arctic Council meetings. These findings of how the lines of responsibility were drawn between different kinds of actors were then systematised using a 'civic epistemology' framework of indicators that helps us think comprehensively about different ways in which authority can be articulated or challenged.

Utilising a more dynamic, present-oriented framework is also meant to deliver a supplement to 'field-genealogy'-driven forms of analysis as a historical unpacking of governance fields. A historical approach lends itself well to understanding how actors have gained certain positions within a policy field. However, carrying out such a genealogy normally involves zooming in on one key actor (see, for example, Shadian, 2014, on the emergence of an Inuit polity) or one particular global policy field (such as Sending, 2015, on population politics). This can be challenging to do given the multitude of actors and issues that are interlinked in 'umbrella policy fields' such as the Arctic Council. Furthermore, tracing the long historical lines can sometimes reify contestation over authority as a one-time (if uphill) battle and make us fail to notice that authority remains constantly contested and renegotiated. As we saw in Chapter 5, expert bodies have long been enshrined as central actors in Arctic governance, yet when and how they are meant to intercede/interface with the political and diplomatic levels of the Arctic Council remained a debated topic, even twenty years in. On the other hand, of course, not all is open to reinterpretation: it is indeed difficult to imagine replacing natural scientists with social scientists, or indigenous peoples' organisations with local government representatives. In any case, the civic epistemology framework gives us a useful tool for understanding contestation over authority, even if it does not tell us the full story of why some actors are more easily heard than others.

Perhaps the most contentious issue identified in Chapter 5 regarding authority relates to the visibility of expert bodies outside the Arctic Council in global fora, part of a broader question of who speaks for the Arctic Council (or the Arctic more generally). The chapter finds that, while science inputs are essential for governing the Arctic, political representatives (of indigenous peoples and of states) operate with a strong sense that scientists should not speak *for* the Arctic, particularly in connection with non-regional or global audiences. Progress in the Arctic Council is highly reliant on agenda-setting and evidence-gathering done by the WGs, and their contributions are trusted by other policy field participants. However, the political level and the Permanent Participants all actively engage in efforts to secure their own authoritative positions as the final stop for Arctic policymaking and, especially, global representation of Arctic issues.

Further research

In the preceding chapters, the emphasis has been on the border-crossing activities of Arctic actors. In many ways, the national and local politics and communities (and professional milieus) that have 'produced' the actors and their dispositions and interests have faded to the background in the effort to bring the social space of Arctic policy fields into clear relief. However, one can hope that Mary Helms' observation on border-crossing holds true: 'emphasis on boundaries ... rather than on the zones themselves, may present sharper symbolic contrasts ... boundaries can make the edge as important as the center' (1988: 28). Hopefully, the research conducted here also provides some useful input to scholars working to understand the national and local dynamics of Arctic politics as well.

Furthermore, the boundaries we have focused on have primarily been political boundaries, conceived of and realised in the landscape through the workings of state power over centuries. With the focus on these constructed boundaries (and the crossing of them), the material landscape of the Arctic (both its expanses and its depths: see Steinberg and Peters, 2015, for a discussion) can easily fade from analytical view. However, the Arctic physical environment is far from a blank canvas against which the powerful can paint any scene. An additional avenue for research would be connecting a study like this book with the agency of the full range of mobilising practices of geopower (from cartography to representation) and the physical materialities of the Arctic itself.

Additionally, some of the concepts used here have only been applied to one actor group or issue area, as this book has sought to go in depth into cases that promised to tell us a bit more about regional policy fields (which comes at the expense of being comprehensive and covering all possible instances that may illustrate similar phenomena). To take one example, Chapter 3, on regional hierarchies, focuses on states as an empirical delimitation. However, research on global politics elsewhere in the world shows that there is indeed also hierarchy amongst civil society actors (NGOs, science organisations, business) that affects their capacity to shape outcomes. Furthermore, such a study of hierarchy as manifested amongst the indigenous polities of the Arctic would be an important contribution both to Arctic understanding and to the emerging literature on the 'third space' of indigenous diplomacy. Likewise, the study of diplomatic norms focused on the interventions of Russia to tell us more about the broader normative landscape of Arctic policy fields. I would anticipate that a similar study of, for example, US interventions may reveal similar, if not identical, findings about these broader inter-subjective norms in Arctic cross-border governance, but the work of checking this assumption remains to be done.

The chapters, taken together, do provide a glimpse into the constant work of maintaining cooperation. They show us how peaceful cooperation is indeed marked by the ongoing conversion of relevant resources into relations of dominance and deference and, ultimately, preferred outcomes. Understanding better how the region 'works' cooperatively, rather than just asserting that it is largely cooperative, has policy implications both for securing progress in Arctic governance and for seeking to see what lessons can be derived for global politics more generally.

Chapter 2 opened with Saami poet Nils-Aslak Valkeapää's envisioning of the Arctic as a highway of movement and conversation, with its treeless expanses providing the opportunity to roam and the long polar nights providing opportunity to talk and listen. This image reminds us of an additional factor that explains this Arctic peace: the socio-political fabric of Arctic cross-border governance is thick, varied and under constant rework. This book has shown that a lot of what happens in Arctic governance requires the efforts and power performances of a wide range of actors. New areas of cooperation are driven forward by broader policy networks, often involving top-level civil servants who have also dedicated their entire professional careers to understanding and achieving progress on a few key areas.

These quiet workings of network politics are important, but probably not enough on their own to manage the magnitude of Arctic change under way. To take one key, region-wide example, the recently released National Oceanic and Atmospheric Association 'report card' on the Arctic once again attempts to draw our attention to a persistently warming Arctic. Average surface air temperature for 2016 was by far the highest since 1900. The sea ice extent at the end of summer 2016 is the second lowest since satellite monitoring of sea ice extent began in 1979, tied with the shock year of 2007.

As we have seen, high-level political interventions have absolutely mattered for big Arctic challenges at many junctures: resolving deadlock on global climate-change negotiations between Copenhagen in 2009 and Paris in 2015; creating global action on transboundary pollutants; and opening up new areas for cooperation, such as the recent Central Arctic Ocean fisheries treaty. The continued engagement of the United States and Russia in regional politics as both active and 'resting' great powers is, in other words, essential for maintaining and expanding cooperation.

Global politics today is marked by enduring, seemingly unresolvable strife and suffering in regional wars and proxy wars; a growing preoccupation with putting domestic politics 'first'; and a populist backlash against expert knowledge, including against the scientific consensus on climate change. Thus, the big risk for Arctic regional politics is not circumpolar military conflict (as one of the oft-repeated Arctic dichotomies suggests), but rather the failure to prioritise and expand the purview of Arctic cooperation in order to generate solutions scaled to the problems at hand.

References

Aalto, P. and I. Jaakkola (2015). 'Arctic energy policy: Global, international, transnational and regional levels', in L. C. Jensen and G. Hønneland (eds.), *Handbook of the Politics of the Arctic*. Cheltenham: Edward Elgar, pp. 128–144.

Aalto, P., S. Dalby and V. Harle (2003). 'The critical geopolitics of northern Europe: Identity politics unlimited', *Geopolitics* 8:1, 7–13.

Abele, F. and T. Rodon (2009). 'Coming in from the cold: Inuit diplomacy and global citizenship', in M. Beier (ed.), *Indigenous Diplomacies*. Basingstoke: Palgrave, pp. 115–132.

ACAP (2007). ACAP progress report to SAOs, Tromsø, Norway, 12–13 April. Arctic Council Archive. http://hdl.handle.net/11374/682 (accessed 29 April 2017).

(2011). Summary of progress report of the ACAP Working Group. Arctic Council Archive. http://hdl.handle.net/11374/1100 (accessed 29 April 2017).

(2013a). 'Environmentally sound management of obsolete pesticides in the Russian Federation. Final report for phases I and II: Inventory and safe storage activities, 2001–2012'. Arctic Council Archive. http://hdl.handle.net/11374/1239 (accessed 29 April 2017).

(2013b). All presentations from the Arctic Council's SAOs' meeting in Whitehorse, Canada, 22–23 October. Arctic Council Archive. https://oaarchive. arctic-council.org/bitstream/handle/11374/1547/6–2_ACAP_WG.pdf? sequence=1&isAllowed=y (accessed 29 April 2017).

(2014). ACAP progress report to SAOs. Arctic Council Archive. http://hdl.handle. net/11374/1293 (accessed 29 April 2017).

Adler, E. (2005). *Communitarian International Relations: The Epistemic Foundations of International Relations*. London and New York: Routledge.

Adler, E. and V. Pouliot (2011). 'International practices', *International Theory* 3:1, 1–36.

Adler-Nissen, R. and V. Pouliot (2014). 'Power in practice: Negotiating the international intervention in Libya', *European Journal of International Relations* 20:4, 889–911.

AEC (2017). Main website. www.arcticeconomiccouncil.com (accessed 29 April 2017).

Airoldi, A. (2014). *The European Union and the Arctic: Developments and Perspectives 2010–2014*. Copenhagen: Norden/Nordic Council of Ministers.

Alaskaweb (2015). 'Diomede'. www.alaskaweb.org/cmtys/diomede.html (accessed 11 February 2017).

Aleut International Association (2013). Statement of Aleut International Association in Kiruna. Arctic Council Archive. https://oaarchive.arctic-council.org/bit-stream/handle/11374/1569/ACMM08_Kiruna_2013_Statement_AIA_Arlene_Gundersen.pdf?sequence=6&isAllowed=y (accessed 29 April 2017).

(2015). Statement of Aleut International Association, Iqaluit, 24 April. Arctic Council Archive. https://oaarchive.arctic-council.org/bitstream/handle/11374/901/ACMMCA09_Iqaluit_2015_AIA_Statement.pdf? sequence=1&isAllowed=y (accessed 29 April 2017).

Alfred, G. (1995). *Heeding the Voices of Our Ancestors: Kahnawake Mohawk Politics and the Rise of Native Nationalism.* Oxford: Oxford University Press.

Alter, K. J. and S. Meunier (2009). 'The politics of international regime complexity', *Perspectives on Politics* 7:1, 13–20.

Althingi (2011). 'A parliamentary resolution on Iceland's Arctic strategy'. http://library. arcticportal.org/1861/ (accessed 14 December 2017).

AMAP (2007). 'Oil and gas assessment 2007'. www.amap.no/oga (accessed 30 April 2012).

Aporta, C., M. Bravo and F. Taylor (2014). *Pan Inuit Trails Atlas.* http://paninuittrails. org (accessed 14 December 2017).

Archer, C. (1988). 'General features of political development and possibilities for cooperation in the Arctic', *Current Research on Peace and Violence* 11:4, 137–145.

Arctic Athabaskan Council (2007). 'Improving the efficiency and effectiveness of the Arctic Council: A discussion paper'. Arctic Council Archive. http://hdl.handle. net/11374/694 (accessed 29 April 2017).

(2011). Statement in Nuuk, Greenland. Arctic Council Archive. https://oaarchive. arctic-council.org/bitstream/handle/11374/1567/ACMM07_Nuuk_2011_AAC. pdf?sequence=1&isAllowed=y (accessed 29 April 2017).

(2013). Ministerial comments, Kiruna. Arctic Council Archive. https://oaarchive. arctic-council.org/handle/11374/1569 (accessed 29 April 2017).

(2015). Remarks by Michael Stickman at the Arctic Council ministerial meeting, Iqaluit, 2015. Arctic Council Archive. http://hdl.handle.net/11374/900 (accessed 29 April 2017).

Arctic Council (1999). Minutes of SAOs' meeting, Washington, DC, 18–19 November. Arctic Council Archive. https://oaarchive.arctic-council.org/bit-stream/handle/11374/273/ACSAO-US02_Minutes_Washington_Nov_1999. pdf?sequence=1&isAllowed=y (accessed 29 April 2017).

(2000). Revised minutes of SAOs' meeting, Fairbanks, Alaska, 27–28 April. Arctic Council Archive. http://hdl.handle.net/11374/280 (accessed 29 April 2017).

(2001). Minutes of SAOs' meeting, Rovaniemi, Finland, 12–13 June. Arctic Council Archive. http://hdl.handle.net/11374/285 (accessed 29 April 2017).

(2004). Draft minutes of SAOs' meeting, Reykjavik, Iceland, 22–23 November. Arctic Council Archive. http://hdl.handle.net/11374/348 (accessed 29 April 2017).

(2005). Minutes of SAOs' meeting, Khanty-Mansiysk, Russia, 12–14 October. Arctic Council Archive. http://hdl.handle.net/11374/361 (accessed 29 April 2017).

(2007a). Draft minutes of SAOs' meeting, Tromsø, Norway, 12–13 April. Arctic Council Archive. http://hdl.handle.net/11374/371 (accessed 29 April 2017).

(2007b). Final report of SAOs' meeting, Narvik, Norway, 28–29 November. https:// oaarchive.arctic-council.org/bitstream/handle/11374/380/ACSAO-NO02_ Narvik_FINAL_Report.pdf?sequence=1&isAllowed=y (accessed 10 January 2018).

(2007c). 'Russian Proposal: "Satellite system development for the Arctic Region"', SAOs' meeting, Narvik, Norway, 28–29 November. Arctic Council Archive. http://hdl.handle.net/11374/812 (accessed 29 April 2017).

(2008). Final report of SAOs' meeting, Kautokeino, Norway, 19–20 November. Arctic Council Archive. http://hdl.handle.net/11374/862 (accessed 29 April 2017).

(2009a). Final report of SAOs' meeting, Copenhagen, Denmark, 10 February. Arctic Council Archive. http://hdl.handle.net/11374/898 (accessed 29 April 2017).

(2009b). Final report of SAOs' meeting, Copenhagen, Denmark, 12–13 April. Arctic Council Archive. https://oaarchive.arctic-council.org/bitstream/handle/11374/960/SAO_report_copehnagen_Nov_2009.pdf?sequence=1&isAllowed=y (accessed 29 April 2017).

(2010a). Final report of SAOs' meeting, Illullissat, Greenland, 28–29 April. Arctic Council Archive. https://oaarchive.arctic-council.org/bitstream/handle/11374/979/SAO_report_illulissat_Apr_2010.pdf?sequence=1&isAllowed=y (accessed 29 April 2017).

(2010b). Final report of SAOs' meeting, Tórshavn, Faroe Islands, 19–20 October. Arctic Council Archive. http://hdl.handle.net/11374/1016 (accessed 29 April 2017).

(2011a). Final report of SAOs' meeting, Copenhagen, Denmark, 16–17 March. Arctic Council Archive. http://hdl.handle.net/11374/1052 (accessed 29 April 2017).

(2011b). Final report of SAOs' meeting, Luleå, Sweden, 8–9 November. Arctic Council Archive. http://hdl.handle.net/11374/1083 (accessed 29 April 2017).

(2015a). Faroe Islands statement of Arctic Council ministerial meeting, Iqaluit, Canada, 24 April. http://hdl.handle.net/11374/903 (accessed 29 April 2017).

(2015b). Greenland statement of Arctic Council ministerial meeting, Iqaluit, Canada, 24 April. Arctic Council Archive. http://hdl.handle.net/11374/905 (accessed 29 April 2017).

(2015c). Iceland statement of Arctic Council ministerial meeting, Iqaluit, 24 April. Arctic Council Archive. http://hdl.handle.net/11374/907 (accessed 29 April 2017).

Arctic Council/Indigenous Peoples Secretariat (2008). Draft memorandum of understanding between the Arctic Council Permanent Participants and the Arctic Council member states. https://oaarchive.arctic-council.org/handle/11374/882 (accessed 1 August 2017).

Arctic Council Secretariat (2013). *Arctic Council Observer Manual for Subsidiary Bodies*. Arctic Council Archive. http://hdl.handle.net/11374/939 (accessed 29 April 2017).

(2014). Final draft report of Arctic Council SAO meeting, Yellowknife, Canada, 22–23 October. Arctic Council Archive. http://hdl.handle.net/11374/1363 (accessed 29 April 2017).

(2015a). Plenary report of Arctic Council SAO meeting, Whitehorse, 4–5 March (final version, 22 April). Arctic Council Archive. http://hdl.handle.net/11374/1412 (accessed 29 April 2017).

(2015b). Summary of Working Groups' relationships to external bodies. Arctic Council Archive. https://oaarchive.arctic-council.org/bitstream/handle/11374/1487/EDOCS-2640-v2-ACSAOUS201_Anchorage_2015_3–1–2a_Summary_of_working_group_relations_external_bodies.pdf?sequence=1&isAllowed=y (accessed 29 April 2017).

(2015c). Summary report of Arctic Council SAO plenary meeting, Anchorage, Alaska, 21–22 October. Arctic Council Archive. http://hdl.handle.net/11374/1576 (accessed 29 April 2017).

(2016a). AMAROK tracking tool maxi report. Arctic Council Archive. http://hdl.handle.net/11374/1822 (accessed 29 April 2017).

(2016b). 'Arctic Council funding: An overview'. Arctic Council Archive. http://hdl. handle.net/11374/1721 (accessed 1 August 2017).

(2016c). Summary report of SAO plenary meeting. Fairbanks, Alaska, 16–17 March. Arctic Council Archive. http://hdl.handle.net.11374/1762 (accessed 1 August 2017).

Arctic Council Task Force on Arctic Marine Oil Pollution Prevention (2014a). 'Two-pager' submitted by the co-chairs of first meeting of the Arctic Council Task Force on Oil Pollution Prevention, Oslo, Norway, 16–17 January. Arctic Council Archive. http://hdl.handle.net/11374/1309 (accessed 29 April 2017).

(2014b). 'Summary two-pager' of third meeting of Arctic Council Task Force on Oil Pollution Prevention, Ottawa, Canada, 12–13 June. Arctic Council Archive. http://hdl.handle.net/11374/1396 (accessed 29 April 2017).

(2014c). 'Summary two-pager' of fourth meeting of Arctic Council Task Force on Oil Pollution Prevention, Nuuk, Greenland, 10–11 September. Arctic Council Archive. http://hdl.handle.net/11374/1395 (accessed 29 April 2017).

Arctic Council Task Force on Scientific Cooperation in the Arctic (2015). Task force report to the SAOs. Arctic Council Archive. http://hdl.handle.net/11374/1428 (accessed 29 April 2017).

Åtland, K. (2008). 'Mikhail Gorbachev, the Murmansk initiative, and the desecuritization of interstate relation in the Arctic', *Cooperation and Conflict*, 43:3, 289–311.

(2011). 'Russia's armed forces and the Arctic: All quiet on the Northern Front?', *Contemporary Security Policy* 32:2, 267–285.

Axworthy, L. and M. Simon (2015). 'Is Canada undermining the Arctic Council?', *Globe and Mail*, www.globeandmail.com/opinion/is-canada-undermining-the-arctic-council (accessed 10 February 2017).

Baev, P. (2013). 'Russia's Arctic ambitions and anxieties', *Current History* 112:76, 265–270.

Bailes, A. and L. Heininen (2012). 'Strategy papers on the Arctic or High North: A comparative study and analysis'. Reykjavik: Centre for Small State Studies.

Balzer, M. M. (1999). *The Tenacity of Ethnicity: A Siberian Saga in Global Perspective*. Princeton: Princeton University Press.

Bankes, N. and T. Koivurova (2014). 'Legal systems', in J. Nymand Larsen and G. Fondahl (eds.), *Arctic Human Development Report*. Copenhagen: Nordic Council of Ministers, pp. 221–247.

Barnes, B., D. Bloor and J. Henry (1996). *Scientific Knowledge: A Sociological Analysis*. London: Athlone Press.

Barnett, M. and R. Duvall, eds. (2004). *Power in Global Governance*. Cambridge: Cambridge University Press.

Barnett, M. and M. Finnemore (2005). *Rules for the World: International Organizations in Global Politics*. Ithaca and London: Cornell University Press.

Beier, J. M. (2009). 'Introduction: *Indigenous* diplomacies as indigenous *diplomacies*', in J. M. Beier (ed.), *Indigenous Diplomacies*. Basingstoke: Palgrave, 1–10.

Bekkevold, J. I. and K. Offerdal (2014). 'Norway's High North Policy and new Asian stakeholders', *Strategic Analysis* 38:6, 825–840.

Bellona (2007). 'Norwegian AMEC Co-Chair expelled from Russia'. www.bellona.org/articles/kroken (accessed 29 April 2017).

Bennett, M. (2015). 'How China sees the Arctic: Reading between extraregional and intraregional narratives', *Geopolitics* 20:3, 645–668.

Berbrick, W. (2015). 'Strengthening US Arctic policy through US–Russia maritime cooperation', in L. C. Jensen and G. Hønneland (eds.), *Handbook of the Politics of the Arctic*. Cheltenham: Edward Elgar, pp. 26–50.

Berger, T. R. (1985). *Village Journey: The Report of the Alaska Native Review Commission*. New York: Hill and Wang.

Bernstein, S. (2001). *The Compromise of Liberal Environmentalism*. New York: Columbia University Press.

Bertelsen, R., J. C. Justinussen and C. Smits (2015). 'Energy as a developmental strategy: Creating knowledge-based energy sectors in Iceland, the Faroe Islands and Greenland', in L. C. Jensen and G. Hønneland (eds.), *Handbook of the Politics of the Arctic*. Cheltenham: Edward Elgar, pp. 3–25.

Beyers, M. (2014). *International Law and the Arctic*. Cambridge: Cambridge University Press.

Biermann, F. (2006). 'Whose experts? The role of geographic representation in global environmental assessments', in R. B. Mitchell, W. C. Clark, D. W. Cash and N. M. Dickson (eds.), *Global Environmental Assessments: Information and Influence*. Cambridge, MA: MIT Press, pp. 87–112.

Blakkisrud, H. (2006). 'What's to be done with the North?', in H. Blakkisrud and G. Hønneland (eds.), *Tackling Space: Federal Politics and the Russian North*. Lanham, MD: University Press of America, pp. 25–52.

Blakkisrud, H. and G. Hønneland, eds. (2006). *Tackling Space: Federal Politics and the Russian North*. Lanham, MD: University Press of America.

Blakkisrud, H. and I. Øverland, I. (2006). 'The evolution of federal indigenous policy in the post-Soviet North', in H. Blakkisrud and G. Hønneland (eds.), *Tackling Space: Federal Politics and the Russian North*. Lanham, MD: University Press of America, pp. 175–192.

Blakkisrud, H. and E. Wilson Rowe, eds. (2017). *Russia's Turn to the East*. Palgrave: Basingstoke.

Blunden, M. (2012). 'Geopolitics and the Northern Sea Route', *International Affairs* 88:1, 115–129.

Bodenhorn, B. (1990). 'I'm not the great hunter, my wife is: Inupiat and anthropological models of gender', *Inuit Studies* 14:1/2, 55–74.

Bonhomme, B. (2012). *Russian Exploration, from Siberia to Space: A History*. Jefferson, NC: McFarland.

Bravo, M. (2005). 'Mission gardens: Natural history and global expansion, 1720–1820', in L. L. Schiebinger and C. Swan (eds.), *Colonial Botany*. Philadephia: University of Pennsylvania Press, pp. 49–65.

Bravo, M. and S. Sörlin, eds. (2002). *Narrating the Arctic: A Cultural History of Nordic Scientific Practices*. Canton, MA: Science History Publications.

Brigham, L. (n.d. [2015]). 'IMO Polar Code for ships operating in polar waters'. ACCESS Policy Brief 4. www.access-eu.org/modules/resources/download/access/fichiers_pdf/ACCESS-PolicyBrief4-Final.pdf (accessed 18 December 2017).

Brody, H. (2000). *The Other Side of Eden*. New York: North Point Press.

Brosnan, I. G., T. M. Leschine and E. L. Miles (2011). 'Cooperation or conflict in a changing Arctic?', *Ocean Development and International Law* 42:1/2, 173–210.

Browning, C. S. (2003). 'The region-building approach revisited: The continued othering of Russia in discourses of region-building in the European North', *Geopolitics* 8:1, 45–71.

Bruno, A. (2016). *The Nature of Soviet Power: An Arctic Environmental History.* Cambridge: Cambridge University Press.

Burke, D. (2017). 'Leading by example: Canada and its Arctic stewardship role', *International Journal of Public Policy* 13:1/2, 36–52.

Bush. G. (2009). National security presidential directive and homeland security presidential directive. http://georgewbush-whitehouse.archives.gov/news/releases/2009/01/20090112–3.html (accessed 5 January 2012).

Caron, D. D. (1993). 'Toward an Arctic environmental regime', *Ocean Development and International Law* 24:4, 377–392.

Carothers, T. (2002). 'The end of the transition paradigm', *Journal of Democracy* 13:1, 5–21.

Chater, A. (2017). 'Why 2016's US–Canada joint Arctic statement still matters in the Trump era', *Arctic Now.* www.arcticnow.com/voices/analysis/2017/02/05/why-2016s-us-canada-joint-arctic-statement-still-matters-in-the-trump-era/#_=_ (accessed 10 February 2017).

Chen, G. (2016). 'Asian economic interests in the Arctic: Singapore's perspective', in L. Lunde, L. Y. Jiang and I. Stensdal (eds.), *Asian Countries and the Arctic Future.* New Jersey: World Scientific, pp. 203–216.

Chernenko, E. (2013). 'Rossiya ogranichivaet polyarniy krug'. *Kommersant,* www.kommersant.ru/doc/2187097 (accessed 16 May 2013).

Chilingarov, A. (2006). Concluding statement by Mr Artur N. Chilingarov, Deputy Chairman of the State Duma of the Russian Federation. Arctic Council Archive. https://oaarchive.arctic-council.org/bitstream/handle/11374/1564/ACMM05_Salekhard_2006_Chilingarov_En.pdf?sequence=6&isAllowed=y (accessed 29 April 2017).

Churchill, R. (2015). 'The exploitation and management of marine resources in the Arctic: Law, politics and the environmental challenge', in L. C. Jensen and G. Hønneland (eds.), *Handbook of the Politics of the Arctic.* Cheltenham: Edward Elgar, pp. 147–184.

Collins, H. and T. Pinch (1998). *The Golem: What You Should Know about Science.* Cambridge: Cambridge University Press.

Conley, H. and C. Rohloff (2015). *The New Ice Curtain: Russia's Strategic Reach to the Arctic.* CSIS. www.csis.org/analysis/new-ice-curtain (accessed 7 April 2017).

Cooley, A. (2005). *Logics of Hierarchy: The Organization of Empires, States and Military Occupation.* Ithaca: Cornell University Press.

Cooley, A. and D. Nexon (2013). 'The Empire will compensate you: The structural dynamics of the US overseas basing network', *Perspectives on Politics* 11:4, 1034–1050.

Coote, M. (2016) 'Environmental decision-making in the Arctic Council: What is the role of indigenous peoples?', *Arctic Yearbook.* www.arcticyearbook.com/images/Articles_2016/scholarly-articles/1-AY2016-Coote.pdf (accessed 29 April 2017).

Craciun, A. (2009). 'The scramble for the Arctic', *Inteventions* 11:1, 103–114.

Cross, M. (2013). 'The military dimension of European Security: An epistemic community approach', *Millennium: Journal of International Studies* 42:1, 45–64.

Crotty, J. and S. M. Hall (2012). 'Environmental awareness and sustainable development in the Russian Federation', *Sustainable Development* 22:5, 311–320. http://onlinelibrary.wiley.com/journal/10.1002/%28ISSN%291099–1719/earlyview. DOI: 10.1002/sd.1542 (accessed 1 March 2012).

Damas, D. (2002). *Arctic Migrants/Arctic Villagers: The Transformation of Inuit Settlement in the Central Arctic.* Montreal: McGill-Queen's University Press.

Darst, R. (2001). *Smokestack Diplomacy: Cooperation and Conflict in East–West Environmental Politics.* Cambridge, MA: MIT Press.

Davies, J. and A. Spicer (2015). 'Interrogating networks: Towards agnostic perspective on governance research', *Environment and Planning C: Government and Policy* 33, 223–238.

De Carvalho, B. and Neumann, I., eds. (2015). *Small States and Status-Seeking: Norway's Quest for International Standing.* Basingstoke: Routledge.

De Certau, M. (2011). *The Practice of Everyday Life.* Berkeley, Los Angeles and London: University of California Press.

Demeritt, D. (2001). 'The construction of global warming and the politics of science', *Annals of the Association of American Geographers* 91:2, 307–337.

Depledge, D. and K. Dodds (2017). 'Bazaar governance: Situating the Arctic Circle', in K. Keil and S. Knecht (eds.), *Governing Arctic Change.* Basingstoke: Palgrave, pp. 141–158.

Dessler, A. and E. A. Parson (2010). *The Science and Politics of Global Climate Change: A Guide to the Debate.* Cambridge: Cambridge University Press.

Deudney, D. (2006). *Bounding Power: Republican Security Theory from the Polis to the Global Village.* Princeton: Princeton University Press.

Dittmer, J., S. Moisio, A. Ingram, and K. Dodds (2011). 'Have you heard the one about the disappearing ice? Recasting Arctic geopolitics', *Political Geography* 30:4, 202–214.

DNV (2011). 'Report: Heavy fuel in the Arctic (phase 1)'. Arctic Council Archive. http://hdl.handle.net/11374/1059 (accessed 29 April 2017).

(2013). 'Report: Specially designated marine areas in the Arctic high seas'. Arctic Council Archive. http://hdl.handle.net/11374/1341 (accessed 29 April 2017).

Dodds, K. (2010). 'Flag planting and finger pointing: The law of the sea, the Arctic, and the political geographies of the outer continental shelf', *Political Geography* 29:2, 63–73.

(2013). 'Anticipating the Arctic and the Arctic Council: Pre-emption, precaution and preparedness', *Polar Record* 49:2, 193–203.

Dodds, K. and M. Nuttall (2015). *The Scramble for the Poles: The Geopolitics of the Arctic and the Antarctic.* London: Polity.

Dongmin, J., S. Won-Sang and L. Seokwoo (2017). 'Arctic policy of the Republic of Korea', *Ocean and Coastal Law Journal* 22:1, 85–96.

Ducharme, S. (2017). 'Louis Kamookak: How Inuit knowledge led the way to Franklin's wrecks', *Nunatsiaq Online*, www.nunatsiaqonline.ca/stories/article/65674louis_kamookak_how_inuit_knowledge_led_the_way_to_franklins_wrecks/ (accessed 1 February 2017).

Duyck, S. (2012). Participation of non-state actors in environmental governance. *Nordica Geographical Publications* 40:4, 99–110.

Elliot-Meisel, E. (2009). 'Politics, pride and precedent: The United States and Canada in the Northwest Passage', *Ocean Development and International Law* 40:2, 204–232.

Elzinga, A. (2013). 'The Nordic nations in polar science: Expeditions, international polar years and their geopolitical dimensions', in S. Sörlin (ed.), *Science, Geopolitics and Culture in the Polar Region: Norden beyond Borders.* London and New York: Routledge, pp. 357–391.

English, J. (2013). *Ice and Water: Politics, People and the Arctic Council.* Toronto: Penguin Random House Canada.

Epstein, C. (2008). *The Power of Words in International Relations: Birth of an Anti-Whaling Discourse.* Boston, MA: MIT Press.

Finnemore, M. and K. Sikkink (1998). 'International norm dynamics and political change', *International Organization* 52:4, 887–917.

Fitzhugh, W. and A. Crowell (1988). *Crossroads of Continents: Cultures of Siberia and Alaska*. Washington, DC: Smithsonian Institution Scholarly Press.

Foucault, M. (1980). 'Questions on geography', in M. Foucault, *Power/Knowledge: Selected Interviews and Other Writings*, ed. C. Gordon. New York: Pantheon, pp. 63–77.

Fourcade, M. (2009). *Economists and Societies: Discipline and Profession in the United States, Britain and France, 1890s–1990s*. Princeton: Princeton University Press.

Friedheim, R. (1988). 'The regime of the Arctic: Distributional or integrative bargaining?', *Ocean Development and International Law* 19:6, 493–510.

Gahr Støre, J. (2011a). 'Hva vil vi med Arktis?'. Speech in Stavanger, Norway, 19 October. www.regjeringen.no/nb/dep/ud/aktuelt/taler_artikler/utenriksministeren/2011/arktis_refleks.html?id=661268 (accessed 29 April 2017).

(2011b). 'Norsk nordområdepolitikk'. Speech at Hof Culture and Conference Centre, Akureyri, Iceland. www.regjeringen.no/nb/dep/ud/aktuelt/taler_artikler/utenriksministeren/2011/akureyri_innlegg.html?id=656935 (accessed 5 June 2012).

Gamble, J. (2016). 'Commentary. The Arctic Council permanent participants: A giant step forward in capacity and support'. *Arctic Yearbook*. www.arcticyearbook.com/commentaries-2016/222-the-arctic-council-permanent-participants-a-giant-step-forward-in-capacity-and-support (accessed 29 April 2017).

Gerhardt, H., P. Steinberg, J. Tasch, S. Fabiano and R. Shields (2010). 'Contested sovereignty in a changing Arctic', *Annals of the Association of American Geographers* 100, 992–1002.

Goddard, S. E. and D. H. Nexon (2016). 'The dynamics of global power politics: A framework for analysis', *Global Security Studies* 1:1, 4–18.

Government of Canada (2010). 'Statement on Canada's Arctic foreign policy: Exercising sovereignty and promoting Canada's northern strategy abroad'. www.international.gc.ca/polar-polaire/canada_arctic_foreign_policy-la_politique_etrangere_du_canada_pour_arctique.aspx?lang=eng&view=d (accessed 5 January 2012).

Government of Norway (2017). 'Nordområdestrategi: Mellom geopolitikk og samfunnsutvikling' ['High North strategy: Between geopolitics and societal development']. www.regjeringen.no/no/dokumenter/strategi_nord/id2550081/ (accessed 14 December 2017).

Government of Russia (2015). 'Executive summary: Partial revised submission of the Russian Federation'. www.un.org/depts/los/clcs_new/submissions_files/rus01_rev15/2015_08_03_Exec_Summary_English.pdf (accessed 29 April 2017).

Government Office of Sweden (2011). 'Sweden's strategy for the Arctic region'. www.government.se/contentassets/85de9103bbbe4373b55eddd7f71608da/swedens-strategy-for-the-arctic-region (accessed 15 December 2017).

Graczyk, P. and T. Koivurova (2014). 'A new era in the Arctic Council's external relations? Broader consequences of the Nuuk observer rules of governance', *Polar Record* 50:3, 225–236.

Graczyk, P., M. Śmieszek, T. Koivurova and A. Stępień (2017). 'Preparing for the global rush: The Arctic Council, institutional norms and socialization of observers', in K. Keil and S. Knecht (eds.), *Governing Arctic Change*. Basingstoke: Palgrave, pp. 121–136.

Grant, S. (2002). *Arctic Justice: On Trial for Murder, Pond Inlet, 1923*. Montreal: McGill-Queens University Press.

(2010). *Polar Imperative: A History of Arctic Sovereignty in North America*. Vancouver: D&M.

Greenpeace (2015). 'Looking back: Canada's Arctic Council chairmanship'. *Greenpeace*. www.greenpeace.org/sa/looking-bac-canadas-arctic-council-chairmanship (accessed 20 April 2015).

Griffiths, F., R. Huebert and W. Lackenbauer (2011). *Canada and the Changing Arctic: Sovereignty, Security, and Stewardship*. Ontario: Wilfrid Laurier University Press.

Guzzini, S. (1993). 'Structural power: The limits of neorealist power analysis', *International Organization* 47:3, 443–478.

Haas, P. M. (1992). 'Introduction: Epistemic communities and international policy coordination', *International Organization* 46:1, 1–35.

(2015). *Epistemic Communities, Constructivism and International Environmental Politics*. Abingdon: Routledge.

Hakli J. and K. P. Kallio (2014). 'The global as a field: Children's rights advocacy as transnational practice', *Environment and Planning D: Society and Space* 32:2, 293–309.

Harders, J. E. (1987). 'In quest of an Arctic legal regime: Marine regionalism – a concept of international law evaluated', *Marine Policy* 11:4, 285–298.

Haruchi, G. (2002). 'The indigenous intelligentsia', in T. Kohler and K. Wessendorf (eds.), *Towards a New Millennium: Ten Years of the Indigenous Movement in Russia*. Copenhagen: IWGIA, pp. 86–93.

Heininen, L., ed. (2015). *Future Security of the Global Arctic: State Policy, Economic Security and Climate*. Basingstoke: Palgrave.

Held, D. and A. McGrew (2002). *Governing Globalization: Power, Authority and Global Governance*. Chichester: Wiley.

Helms, M. (1988). *Ulysses' Sail: An Ethnographic Odyssey of Power, Knowledge, and Geographical Distance*. Princeton: Princeton Legacy Library.

Henry, L. A. (2010). 'Between transnationalism and state power: The development of Russia's post-Soviet environmental movement', *Environmental Politics* 19:5, 756–781.

Hobson, J. and J. C. Sharman (2005). 'The enduring place of hierarchy in world politics: Tracing the social logics of hierarchy and political change', *European Journal of International Relations* 11:1, 63–98.

Hoel, A. H. (2015). 'Oceans governance, the Arctic Council and ecosystem-based management', in L. C. Jensen and G. Hønneland (eds.), *Handbook of the Politics of the Arctic*. Cheltenham: Edward Elgar, pp. 265–280.

(2017). 'Op-ed: Strengthened research cooperation in the Arctic Council'. *High North News*. www.highnorthnews.com/op-ed-strengthened-research-cooperation-in-the-arctic-council/ (accessed 18 August 2017).

Holmes, M. (2013). 'The force of face-to-face diplomacy: Mirror neurons and the problem of intentions', *International Organization* 67:4, 829–861.

Holtsmark, S., ed. (2015). *Naboer i frykt og forventning: Norge og Russland 1917–2014 [Neighbours in Fear and Expectation: Norway and Russia 1917–2014]*. Oslo: Pax.

Hønneland, G. (2005). *Barentsbrytninger: Norsk nordområdepolitikk etter den Kalde Krigen [Barents Breaking: Norwegian Foreign Policy in the North after the Cold War]*. Kristiansand: Høyskoleforlaget.

(2013). *Borderland Russians: Identity, Narrative and International Relations*. Basingstoke: Palgrave Macmillan.

(2017). *Arctic Euphoria and International High North Politics*. London: Palgrave.

Hønneland, G. and L. Rowe (2004). *Health as International Politics*. Burlington, VT: Ashgate.

(2010). *Nordområdene – hva nå? [The High North – What Now?]*. Trondheim: Tapir Academic Press.

Hønneland, G. and O. Stokke, eds. (2010). *International Cooperation and Arctic Governance: Regime Effectiveness and Northern Region Building*. London: Routledge.

Hoogensen Gjørv, G., G. D. Bazely, M. Goloviznina and A. Tanentzap, eds. (2013). *Environmental and Human Security in the Arctic*. New York: Routledge.

Huebert, R., H. Exner-Pirot, A. Lajeunesse and J. Gulledge (2012). 'Climate change and international security: The Arctic as a bellwether'. www.c2es.org/publications/climate-change-international-arctic-security (accessed 29 April 2017).

Humrich, C. (2017). 'Coping with institutional challenges for Arctic environmental governance', in K. Keil and S. Knecht (eds.), *Governing Arctic Change*. Basingstoke: Palgrave, pp. 81–95.

Huntington, H. (2000). 'Using traditional ecological knowledge in science: Methods and applications', *Ecological Applications*, 10:5, 1270–1274.

Huskey, L., I. Mäenpää and A. Pelyasov (2014). 'Economic systems', in J. Nymand Larsen and G. Fondahl (eds.), *Arctic Human Development Report*. Copenhagen: Nordic Council of Ministers, pp. 151–180.

ICC (2013). Kiruna statement. Arctic Council Archive. https://oaarchive.arctic-council.org/handle/11374/1569 (accessed 29 April 2017).

(2015a). 'A circumpolar Inuit declaration on sovereignty in the Arctic'. http://www.inuitcircumpolar.com/sovereignty-in-the-arctic.html (accessed 29 April 2017).

(2015b). 'One Arctic: Shared opportunities, challenges and responsibilities'. Statement of Okalik Eegeesiak, Arctic Council ministerial meeting, Iqaluit, Canada, 24 April 2015. Arctic Council Archive. http://hdl.handle.net/11374/906 (accessed 29 April 2017).

Irlbacher-Fox, S. (2009). *Finding Dashaa: Self-Government, Social Suffering and Aboriginal Policy in Canada*. Vancouver: University of British Columbia Press.

Jakobsen, L. (2010). 'China prepares for an ice-free Arctic'. *SIPRI Insights on Peace and Security* 2:1, www.polar-academy.com/Publication/SIPRIInsight1002(2).pdf (accessed 10 February 2017).

Jakobsen, L. and S. Lee (2013). 'The North East Asian states' interests in the Arctic and possible cooperation with the Kingdom of Denmark', *SIPRI*. www.sipri.org/research/security/arctic/arcticpublications/NEAsia-Arctic%20130415%20full.pdf (accessed 2 May 2013).

Jasanoff, S. (2005). *Designs on Nature: Science and Democracy in Europe and the United States*. Princeton: Princeton University Press.

Jasanoff, S. and B. Wynne (1998). 'Science and decisionmaking', in S. Rayner and E. Malone (eds.), *Human Choice and Climate Change*, Vol. I. Columbus, OH: Battelle Press, pp. 1–87.

Jensen, L. C. (2013). 'Seduced and surrounded by security: A post-structuralist take on Norwegian high north securitizing discourses', *Cooperation and Conflict* 48:1, 80–99.

Jensen, L. C. and G. Hønneland (2011). 'Framing the High North: Public discourses in Norway after 2000', *Acta borealia* 28:1, 1–17.

Jensen, L. C. and P. W. Skedsmo (2010). 'Approaching the North: Norwegian and Russian foreign policy discourses on the European Arctic', *Polar Research* 29, 439–450.

Jensen, Ø. (2015). 'The seaward limits of the continental shelf beyond 200 nautical miles in the Arctic Ocean: Legal framework and state practice', in

L. C. Jensen and G. Hønneland (eds.), *Handbook of the Politics of the Arctic*. Cheltenham: Edward Elgar, pp. 227–246.

Joenniemi, P. and A. Sergunin (2015). 'Paradiplomacy as a capacity-building strategy', *Problems of Post-Communism* 61:6, 18–33.

Jones, A. and J. Clark (2015). 'Mundane diplomacies for the practice of European geopolitics', *Geoforum* 62, 1–12.

Josephson, P. (2014). *The Conquest of the Russian Arctic*. Cambridge, MA: Harvard University Press.

Kaplin, N. (2002). 'RAIPON today', in T. Kohler and K. Wessendorf (eds.), *Towards a New Millennium: Ten Years of the Indigenous Movement in Russia*. Copenhagen: IWGIA, pp. 30–34.

Keil, K. and S. Knecht (2017). 'Introduction: The Arctic as a globally embedded space', in K. Keil and S. Knecht (eds.), *Governing Arctic Change*. Basingstoke: Palgrave, pp. 1–15.

Kelman, I., J. Loe, E. Wilson Rowe, E. Wilson, N. Poussenkova, E. Nikitina and D. Fjærtoft (2016). 'Local perceptions of corporate social responsibility for Arctic petroleum in the Barents region', *Arctic Review on Law and Politics* 7:2, 152–178.

Keohane, R. O. and J. S. Nye (1989). *Power and Interdependence*. New York: HarperCollins.

Kerr, J. (2014). 'Greenpeace apology to Inuit for impacts of seal campaign'. *Greenpeace*, www.greenpeace.org/canada/en/blog/Blogentry/greenpeace-to-canadas-aboriginal-peoples-work/blog/53339/ (accessed 1 February 2017).

Keskitalo, C. (2007). 'International region-building: Development of the Arctic as an international region', *Cooperation and Conflict* 42:2, 187–205.

Keskitalo, E. C. H. (2004). *Negotiating the Arctic: The Construction of an International Region*. New York and London: Routledge.

Khrushcheva, O. and M. Poberezhskaya (2016). 'The Arctic in the political discourse of Russian leaders: The national pride and economic ambitions', *East European Politics* 32:4, 547–566.

Kleist, K. (2011). 'Formanden for Naalakkersuisut Kuupik Kleist: På vegne af Danmark, Færøerne og Grønland', seventh ministerial meeting of the Arctic Council, ministerial round table meeting, 12 May. Arctic Council Archive. https://oaarchive.arctic-council.org/bitstream/handle/11374/1567/ACMM07_Nuuk_2011_Address_Kuupik_Kleist_Arctic_Council_DANISH.pdf?sequence=2&isAllowed=y (accessed 29 April 2017).

Knecht, S. (2017). 'The politics of Arctic international cooperation: Introducing a dataset on stakeholder participation in Arctic Council meetings, 1998–2015', *Cooperation and Conflict* 52:2, 202–223. DOI: 10.1177/00108367 16652431.

Koivurova, T. and G. Alfredsson, eds. (2014). *Yearbook of Polar Law*. Leiden: Brill.

Koivurova, T. and E. J. Molenaar (2009). *International Governance and the Regulation of the Marine Arctic*. Oslo: WWF International Arctic Programme.

Kommersant (2013). 'Rossiya priotkryla Arktiku' ['Russia opened up the Arctic']. www.kommersant.ru/doc/2188538 (accessed 29 April 2017).

Kraska, J., ed. (2011). *Arctic Security in an Age of Climate Change*. Cambridge: Cambridge University Press.

Krasner, S. D. (1982). 'Structural causes and regime consequences: Regimes as intervening variables', *International Organization* 36:2, 185–205.

Kristoffersen, B. and O. Langhelle (2017). 'Sustainable development as a global–Arctic matter: Imaginaries and controversies', in K. Keil and S. Knecht (eds.), *Governing Arctic Change*. Basingstoke: Palgrave, pp. 21–38.

Krivorotov, A. (2015). *Politika gosudarstva kak faktor konkurentosposobnosti arkticheskikh regionov [Government policy as a factor for the economic competitivieness of Arctic regions]*. Apatity: Russian Academy of Sciences.

Krupnik, I. (1993). *Arctic Adaptations: Native Whalers and Reindeer Herders of Northern Eurasia*. Hanover: University of New England Press.

Kuokkanen, R. (2009). 'Achievements of indigenous self-determination: The case of Sami parliaments in Finland and Norway', in J. M. Beier (ed.), *Indigenous diplomacies*. Basingstoke: Palgrave, pp. 97–114.

Lagutina, M. (2013). 'Russian Arctic policy in the 21st century: From international to transnational cooperation?', *Global Review*, winter. www.academia.edu/28182112/Lagutina_M._Russian_Arctic_Policy_in_the_21st_Century_From_International_to_Transnational_Cooperation (accessed 1 January 2018).

Lahn, B. (2016). 'Forests through the papermill: Assembling REDD+ through the production of documents'. Master's thesis, University of Oslo. www.duo.uio.no/handle/10852/51274 (accessed 29 April 2017).

Lahn, B. and E. Wilson Rowe (2014). 'How to be a "front-runner": Norway and international climate politics', in B. de Carvalho and I. B. Neumann (eds.), *Small States and Status Seeking: Norway's Quest for International Standing*. Oxford: Routledge, pp. 126–145.

Lahsen, M. (2004). 'Transnational locals: Brazilian experiences of the climate regime', in S. Jasanoff and M. Martell (eds.), *Earthly Politics: Local and Global in Environmental Governance* (Cambridge, MA: MIT Press), pp. 151–172.

Lajus, J. (2013). 'Field stations on the coast of the Arctic Ocean in the European part of Russia from the first to the second IPY', in S. Sörlin (ed.), *Science, Geopolitics and Culture in the Polar Region: Norden beyond Borders*. Basingstoke: Routledge, pp. 111–141.

Lake, D. (2009). *Hierarchy in International Relations*. Ithaca: Cornell University Press.

(2017). 'Laws and norms in the making of international hierarchies', in A. Zarakol (ed.), *Hierarchies in World Politics*. Cambridge: Cambridge University Press, pp. 17–42.

Lanteigne, M. (2014). 'China's emerging Arctic strategies: Economics and institutions'. Reykjavik: Centre for Small State Studies. http://ams.hi.is/wp-content/uploads/2014/11/ChinasEmergingArcticStrategiesPDF_FIX2.pdf (accessed 29 April 2017).

Larson, D. and A. Shevchenko (2010). 'Status seekers: Chinese and Russian responses to US primacy', *International Security* 34:4, 63–95.

Laruelle, M. (2013). *Russia's Arctic Strategies and the Future of the Far North*. Armonk, NY: M. E. Sharpe.

Latour, B. (1987). *Science in Action: How to Follow Scientists and Engineers through Society*. Cambridge, MA: Harvard University Press.

LeFebvre, H. (1991). *The Production of Space*. Malden: Blackwell.

Legvold, R. (2016). *Return to Cold War*. Cambridge: Polity.

Leonard, D. and T. Fenge (2003). *Northern Lights against POPs, Combatting Toxic Threats in the Arctic*. Montreal: McGill-Queen's University Press.

Lidskog, R. and G. Sundqvist (2015). 'When does science matter? International relations meets science and technology studies', *Global Environmental Politics* 15:1, 1–20.

Loukacheva, N. (2015). 'The Arctic Economic Council: The origins', in G. Alfredsson, T. Koivurova and J. Jabour (eds.), *The Yearbook of Polar Law* 7:1, 225–248.

Luard, E. (1976). *Types of International Society*. Ann Arbor: University of Michigan.

Luedtke, B. (2013). 'An ice-free Arctic Ocean: History, science and skepticism', *Polar Record* 51:257, 130–139.

Lunde, L. (2016). 'Nordic perspectives on Asia's Arctic interests', in L. Lunde, L. Y. Jiang and I. Stensdal (eds.), *Asian Countries and the Arctic Future*. New Jersey: World Scientific, pp. 7–12.

MacDonald, P. (2018). 'Embedded authority: A relational network approach to hierarchy in world politics', *Review of International Studies* 44:1, 128–150.

Mamadouh, V. and G. Dijink (2006). 'Geopolitics, international relations and political geography: The politics of geopolitical discourse', *Geopolitics*, 11:3, 349–366.

Manicom, J. and P. W. Lackenbauer (2013). 'East Asian states, the Arctic Council and international relations in the Arctic'. CIGI Policy Brief 26. www.cigionline.org/sites/default/files/no26.pdf (accessed 18 December 2017).

Marcus, A. R. (1995). *Relocating Eden: The Image and Politics of Inuit Exile in the Canadian Arctic*. Hanover: University of Dartmouth Press.

Mattern, J. and A. Zarakol (2016). 'Review essay: Hierarchies in world politics', *International Organization* 70:3, 1–32.

Mauer, R. (2010). 'Soviet ships drive a path through ice'. *Anchorage Daily News*. www.adn.com/projects/article/soviet-ships-drive-path-through-ice/2010/09/25/ (accessed 11 February 2017).

McConnell, F., T. Morea and J. Dittmer (2012). 'Mimicking state diplomacy: The legitimizing strategies of unofficial diplomacies', *Geoforum* 43, 804–814.

McGhee, R. (2006). *The Last Imaginary Place: A Human History of the Arctic World*. Oxford: Oxford University Press.

Medby, I. A. (2014). 'Arctic state, Arctic nation? Arctic national identity among the post-Cold War generation in Norway', *Polar Geography* 37:3, 252–269.

MFA, Canada (2015). Address by Minister Aglukkaq to Arctic Council ministerial meeting on Canada's chairmanship achievements, Iqaluit, Canada, 24 April. Arctic Council Archive. http://hdl.handle.net/11374/896 (accessed 29 April 2017).

MFA, China (2010). 'China's view on Arctic cooperation'. *Ministry of Foreign Affairs of the People's Republic of China*. www.fmprc.gov.cn/eng/wjb/zzjg/tyfls/tfsxw/t812046.htm (accessed 10 May 2013).

MFA, Denmark (2011). 'Kongeriget Danmarks strategi for Arktis 2011–2020'. http://um.dk/da/udenrigspolitik/lande-og-regioner/arktisk-portal/arktisk-strategi (accessed 29 April 2017).

    (2013). Ministerial intervention. Arctic Council Archive. https://oaarchive.arctic-council.org/handle/11374/1569 (accessed 29 April 2017).

    (2015). Ministerial meeting in the Arctic Council: Intervention by the Danish Foreign Minister, Iqaluit, Canada, 24 April. Arctic Council Archive. http://hdl.handle.net/11374/902 (accessed 29 April 2017).

MFA, Finland (2015). Statement by Mr Erkki Tuomioja, Minister for Foreign Affairs, Finland, Iqaluit, Canada, 24 April. Arctic Council Archive. http://hdl.handle.net/11374/904 (accessed 29 April 2017).

MFA, Iceland (2013). Ministerial intervention, Kiruna, Sweden, 15 May. Arctic Council Archive. https://oaarchive.arctic-council.org/handle/11374/1569 (accessed 29 April 2017).

MFA, Japan (2012). Statement at meeting between the Swedish chairmanship of the Arctic Council and observers/ad hoc observers. Ministry of Foreign Affairs of Japan. www.mofa.go.jp/announce/svm/pdfs/statement121108.pdf (accessed 15 April 2013).

MFA, Norway (2006). 'Regjeringens nordområdestrategi' ['The Government's northern strategy']. www.regjeringen.no/upload/kilde/ud/pla/2006/0006/ddd/pdfv/302927-nstrategi06.pdf (accessed 29 April 2017).

(2009). 'Nye byggesteiner i nord'. www.regjeringen.no/no/dokumenter/nordstrategi_trinn2/id548803/ (accessed 29 April 2017).

(2011). 'Nordområdene: Visjon og virkemidler. Melding til Stortinget (No. 7)' ['The high north: Vision and instruments. Paper to Parliament, no. 7']. www.regjeringen.no/nb/dep/ud/dok/regpubl/stmeld/2011–2012/meld-st-7–20112012.html?id=663433 (accessed 29 April 2017).

(2014). 'Nordkloden: Verdiskaping og ressurser. Klimaendringer og kunnskap. Utvikling nord på kloden angår oss alle' ['Northworld: Creating value and resources. Climate change and knowledge. Developments at the north of the globe affect us all']. www.regjeringen.no/no/dokumenter/nordkloden/id2076193/ (accessed 29 April 2017).

(2015). 'Arktisk råds ministermøte, Iqaluit 24 April'. Arctic Council Archive. http://hdl.handle.net/11374/908 (accessed 29 April 2017).

MFA, Russia (2006). Address by Minister of Foreign Affairs of the Russian Federation Sergey Lavrov at the fifth ministerial session of the Arctic Council, Salekhard, Russia, 26 October 2006. Arctic Council Archive. https://oaarchive.arctic-council.org/bitstream/handle/11374/1564/ACMM05_Salekhard_2006_Lavrov_Speech_in_Yamal_ENG.pdf?sequence=12& isAllowed=y (accessed 29 April 2017).

(2013). Speech of the Russian Foreign Minister Sergey Lavrov, eighth ministerial session of the Arctic Council, Kiruna, Sweden, 15 May 2013. Arctic Council Archive. https://oaarchive.arctic-council.org/bitstream/handle/11374/1569/ACMM08_Kiruna_2013_Statement_Russia_Sergey_Lavrov_Russian.pdf?sequence=17&isAllowed=y (accessed 29 April 2017).

MFA, Singapore. (2012). 'Singapore's fulfillment of the "Nuuk Criteria", non-paper'. Unpublished document.

Milner, H. (1991). 'The assumption of anarchy in international relations theory: A critique', *Review of International Studies* 17, 67–85.

Ministry of Environment, Russian Federation (2015). Statement by Minister S. E. Donskoy at the Arctic Council ministerial meeting, Iqaluit, Canada, 24 April. Arctic Council Archive. http://hdl.handle.net/11374/909 (accessed 29 April 2017).

Mitchell, M. (1996). *From Talking Chiefs to a Native Corporate Elite: The Birth of Class and Nationalism among Canadian Inuit*. Montreal: McGill-Queen's University Press.

Moe, A. (2014). 'The Northern Sea Route: Smooth sailing ahead?', *Strategic Analysis* 38:6, 784–802.

Moe, A., D. Fjærtoft and I. Øverland (2011). 'Space and timing: Why was the Barents Sea delimitation dispute resolved in 2010?', *Polar Geography* 34:3, 145–162.

Muller, M. (2012). 'Opening the black box of the organization: Sociomaterial practices of geopolitical ordering', *Political Geography* 31:6, 379–388.

Murashko, O. (2002). 'Introduction', in T. Kohler and K. Wessendorf (eds.), *Towards a New Millennium: Ten Years of the Indigenous Movement in Russia*. Copenhagen: IWGIA, pp. 20–30.

Murphy, A., M. Bassin, D. Newman, P. Reuber and J. Agnew (2004). 'Is there a politics to geopolitics?', *Progress in Human Geography* 28:5, 619–640.

Natural Resources Canada (2017). 'Map of north circumpolar region'. www.nrcan.gc.ca/earth-sciences/geography/atlas-canada/wall-maps/16870 (accessed 29 April 2017).

NEFCO (2009). 'Draft 2009.02.22: Update on PSI – Arctic Council's Project Support Instrument'. Arctic Council Archive. http://hdl.handle.net/11374/933 (accessed 29 April 2017).

—— (2011). 'SAO fall meeting, Luleå, Sweden, 8–9 November: Update on PSI – Arctic Council's Project Support Instrument'. Arctic Council Archive. http://hdl.handle.net/11374/1090 (accessed 29 April 2017).

—— (2013). 'Ag. [7.1]: Update on the Arctic Council Project Support Instrument (PSI) (Presented by NEFCO)'. Arctic Council Archive. http://hdl.handle.net/11374/657 (accessed 29 April 2017).

Neumann, I. (2017). *Russia and the Idea of Europe: A Study in Identity and International Relations*. Abingdon: Routledge.

Neumann, I. and B. de Carvalho (2015). 'Introduction: Small states and status', in B. de Carvalho and I. Neumann (eds.), *Small States and Status-Seeking: Norway's Quest for International Standing*. Basingstoke: Routledge, pp. 1–21.

Neumann, I. B. (1994). 'A region-building approach to northern Europe', *Review of International Studies* 20:1, 53–74.

Neumann, I. B. and O. J. Sending (2010). *Governing the Global Polity*. Ann Arbor: University of Michigan Press.

Nexon, D. and I. B. Neumann (2017). 'Hegemonic-order theory: A field-theoretic account', *European Journal of International Relations*, 1–25. DOI: 10.1177/1354066117716524.

Nexon, D. and T. Wright (2007). 'What's at stake in the American Empire debate', *American Political Science Review* 101:2, 253–271.

Nicol, H. and L. Heininen (2013). 'Human security, the Arctic Council and climate change: Competition or co-existence?', *Polar Record* 50:1, 80–85.

Nilsen, T. (2017). 'Brende: Law of the sea and international law is the "constitution" of the Arctic'. https://thebarentsobserver.com/en/arctic/2017/01/brende-law-sea-and-international-law-constitution-arctic (accessed 7 April 2017).

Nilsson, A. (2009). 'A changing Arctic climate: Science and policy in the Arctic climate impact assessment', in T. Koivurova, E. Keskitalo and N. Bankes (eds.), *Climate Governance in the Arctic*. New York: Springer.

Norsk Telegrambyrå (2017). 'Brende til Arkhangelsk konferanse i mars' ['Foreign Minister Brende to Arkhangelsk Conference in March'], 17 February. www.dn.no/nyheter/2017/02/17/1514/Norge/brende-til-arkhangelsk-konferanse-i-mars (accessed 7 April 2017).

Nuttall, M. (2015). 'Subsurface politics: Greenlandic discourses on extractive industries', in L. C. Jensen and G. Hønneland (eds.), *Handbook of the Politics of the Arctic*. Cheltenham: Edward Elgar.

Nye, J. (2002). *The Paradox of American Power: Why the World's Only Superpower Can't Go It Alone*. Oxford: Oxford University Press.

Nymand Larsen, J. and G. Fondahl, eds. (2015). *Arctic Human Development Report: Regional Processes and Global Linkages*. Copenhagen: Nordic Council of Ministers.

Obama, B. (2013). National strategy for the Arctic region. https://obamawhitehouse.archives.gov/sites/default/files/docs/nat_arctic_strategy.pdf (accessed 29 April 2017).

Ohnishi, F. (2016). 'Japan's Arctic policy development: From engagement to a strategy', in L. Lunde, L. Y. Jiang and I. Stensdal (eds.), *Asian Countries and the Arctic Future*. New Jersey: World Scientific, pp. 171–182.

Oldfield, J. (2005). *Russian Nature: Exploring the Environmental Consequences of Societal Change*. Aldershot: Ashgate.

Olsen, I. H. and J. Shadian (2016). 'Greenland and the Arctic Council: Subnational regions in a time of Arctic Westphalianism'. *Arctic Yearbook* 2016. www.researchgate. net/publication/309764163_Greenland_and_the_Arctic_Council_Subnational_ regions_in_a_time_of_Arctic_Westphalianisation (accessed 19 December 2017).

Orttung, R. W., ed. (2017). *Sustaining Russia's Arctic Cities: Resource Politics, Migration and Climate Change*. New York: Berghahn.

Ostergren, D. and P. Jacques (2002). 'A political economy of Russian nature conservation policy: Why scientists have taken a back seat', *Global Environmental Politics* 2:4, 102–124.

Østhagen, A. (2016). 'High north, low politics: Maritime cooperation with Russia in the Arctic', *Arctic Review on Law and Politics* 7:1, 83–100.

Østhagen, A. and V. Gastaldo (2015). 'Coast guard co-operation in a changing Arctic'. Munk-Gordon Arctic Security Program Report. http://gordonfoundation.ca/ resource/coast-guard-co-operation-in-a-changing-arctic/ (accessed 7 April 2017).

O'Tuathail, G. and S. Dalby, eds. (1998). *Rethinking Geopolitics*. London and New York: Routledge.

Palosaari, T. and N. Tynkkynen (2015). 'Arctic securitization and climate change', in L. Jensen and G. Hønneland (eds.), *Handbook of the Politics of the Arctic*. Edward Elgar, pp. 87–104.

PAME (2007). PAME progress report to SAOs, Narvik, Norway, 28–29 November. Arctic Council Archive. http://hdl.handle.net/11374/793 (accessed 29 April 2017).

(2015a). Arctic Council: Arctic Marine Strategic Plan. Arctic Council Archive. http://hdl.handle.net/11374/413 (accessed 29 April 2017).

(2015b). 'Arctic Council Arctic Marine Strategic Plan 2015–2025: Protecting marine and coastal ecosystems in a changing Arctic'. Arctic Council Archive. http://hdl. handle.net/11374/1467 (accessed 29 April 2017).

Pan Inuit Trails (2017). 'Introduction to Pan Inuit Trails'. www.paninuittrails.org/ index.html?module=module.intro (accessed 29 April 2017).

Pape, R. (2005). 'Soft balancing against the United States', *International Security* 30:1, 7–45.

Paul, T. V. (2005). 'Soft balancing in the age of US primacy', *International Security* 30:1, 46–71.

Pedersen, T. (2006). 'The Svalbard contintental shelf controversy: Legal disputes and political rivalries', *Ocean Development and International Law* 37:3–4, 339–358.

(2012). 'Debates over the role of the Arctic Council', *Ocean Development and International Law* 43:2, 146–156.

Persson, K. (2015). Arctic Council ministerial meeting: Statement by Sweden, Iqaluit, Canada, 24 April. Arctic Council Archive. http://hdl.handle.net/11374/912 (accessed 29 April 2017).

Pezard, S., A. Tingstad, K. Van Abel and S. Stephenson (2017). *Maintaining Arctic Cooperation with Russia: Planning for Regional Change in the Far North*. Santa Monica: RAND Corporation. www.rand.org/pubs/research_reports/RR1731. html (accessed 18 August 2017).

Pika, A. (1999). *Neotraditionalism in the Russian North*. Edmonton and Seattle: Canadian Circumpolar Institute and the University of Washington Press.

Poelzer, G. and G. Wilson (2015). 'Governance in the Arctic: Political systems and geopolitics', in J. Nymand Larsen and G. Fondahl (eds.), *Arctic Human Development Report*. Copenhagen: Nordic Council of Ministers, pp. 183–218.

Pouliot, V. (2010). *International Security in Practice: The Politics of NATO–Russia Diplomacy*. Cambridge: Cambridge University Press.

Powell, R. and K. Dodds, eds. (2014). *Polar Geopolitics: Knowledges, Resources and Legal Regimes*. Cheltenham: Edward Elgar.

Prime Minister's Office, Finland (2013). 'Finland's strategy for the Arctic region 2013: Government resolution on 23 August 2013'. Prime Minister's Office Publications 16. http://vnk.fi/documents/10616/334509/Arktinen+strategia+2013+en.pdf/6b6fb723-40ec-4c17-b286-5b5910fbecf4 (accessed 19 December 2017).

Quinn, E. (2016). 'How will the Arctic Economic Council shape business future of the North?'. *Anchorage Daily News*, www.adn.com/arctic/article/how-will-arctic-economic-council-shape-business-future-of-the-North (accessed 1 August 2017).

RAIPON (2011). Statement at Nuuk ministerial meeting (in Russian). Arctic Council Archive. https://oaarchive.arctic-council.org/bitstream/handle/11374/1567/ACMM07_Nuuk_2011_RAIPON.pdf?sequence=9&isAllowed=y (accessed 29 April 2017).

Roginko, A. Y. and M. J. LaMourie (1992). 'Emerging marine environmental protection strategies for the Arctic', *Marine Policy* 16:4, 259–276.

Rottem, S. V. (2013). 'The Arctic Council and the search and rescue agreement: The case of Norway', *Polar Record* 50:3, 284–292.

Rowe, L. (2013). 'Pechenganikel: Soviet industry, Russian pollution and the outside world'. Doctoral thesis, University of Oslo.

(2015). 'Fra unntakstilstand til en ny normal' ['From state of emergency to new normalcy'], in S. Holtsmark (ed.), *Naboer i frykt og forventning: Norge og Russland 1917–2014 [Neighbors in Fear and Expectation: Norway and Russia 1917–2014]*. Oslo: Pax forlag, pp. 628–632.

Russian Embassy to Norway (2017). Open letter. www.norway.mid.ru/press_17_011.html (accessed 29 April 2017).

Saami Council (2011). 'The changing Arctic: Challenges and opportunities for the Arctic Council', statement by Olav Mattis Eira, President of the Saami Council, seventh ministerial meeting of the Arctic Council, Nuuk, Greenland, 12 May. Arctic Council Archive. https://oaarchive.arctic-council.org/bitstream/handle/11374/1567/ACMM07_Nuuk_2011_SAAMI_Statement.pdf?sequence=10&isAllowed=y (accessed 29 April 2017).

(2013). Statement by Ms Áile Javo, President of the Saami Council, eighth ministerial meeting of the Arctic Council, Giron [Kiruna], Sweden, 15 May. Arctic Council Archive. https://oaarchive.arctic-council.org/bitstream/handle/11374/1569/ACMM08_Kiruna_2013_Statement_Saami_Council_Aile_Javo.pdf?sequence=18&isAllowed=y (accessed 29 April 2017).

(2015). Statement by Ms Áile Javo, President of the Saami Council, ninth ministerial meeting of the Arctic Council, 24 April. Arctic Council Archive. http://hdl.handle.net/11374/911 (accessed 29 April 2017).

SAO (2002). Report of SAOs to Arctic Council ministers, Inari, Finland, 7–8 October. Arctic Council Archive. http://hdl.handle.net/11374/1552 (accessed 29 April 2017).

(2006). Report of SAOs to Arctic Council ministers, Salekhard, Russia, 26 October. Arctic Council Archive. http://hdl.handle.net/11374/1554 (accessed 29 April 2017).

Saxinger, G., E. Nuykina and E. Ofner (2017). 'The Russian north connected: The role of long-distance commute work for regional integration', in R. W. Orttung (ed.), *Sustaining Russia's Arctic Cities: Resource Politics, Migration and Climate Change*. New York: Berghahn, pp. 112–138.

Schia, N. N. (2013). 'Being part of the parade: "Going native" in the United Nations Security Council', *Political and Legal Anthropology Review (PoLAR)* 36:1, 138–156.

Schweitzer, P., P. Sköld and O. Ulturgasheva (2015). 'Cultures and identities', in J. Nymand Larsen and G. Fondahl (eds.), *Arctic Human Development Report*. Copenhagen: Nordic Council of Ministers, pp. 105–145.

Scrivener, D. (1999). 'Arctic environmental cooperation in transition', *Polar Record* 35:1, 51–58.

SDWG (2009). Status report of the SDWG, SAOs' meeting, Copenhagen, Denmark, 12–13 November. https://oaarchive.arctic-council.org/bitstream/handle/11374/969/ACSAO-DK01_9_SDWG_Progress_Report.pdf?sequence=1&isAllowed=y (accessed 16 January 2018).

(2011). 'Doc 5.1d: Electronic memory of the Arctic/SDWG. Request for endorsement of the project by SDWG'. Arctic Council Archive. http://hdl.handle.net/11374/1097 (accessed 29 April 2017).

Seabrooke, L. and L. Henriksen, eds. (2017). *Professional Networks and Transnational Governance*. Cambridge: Cambridge University Press.

Security Council (2008). 'The fundamentals of state policy of the Russian Federation in the Arctic in the period up to 2020 and beyond' ['Osnovy gosudarstvennoi politiki RF v Arktike na period do 2020 i dal'neishuyu perspektivu']. https://rg.ru/2009/03/30/arktika-osnovy-dok.html (accessed 1 April 2017).

Selin, H. (2017). 'Global environmental governance and treaty-making: The Arctic's fragmented voice', in K. Keil and S. Knecht (eds.), *Governing Arctic Change*. Basingstoke: Palgrave, pp. 101–118.

Sending, O. J. (2015). *The Politics of Expertise: Competing for Authority in Global Governance*. Ann Arbor: University of Michigan Press.

Sending, O. J., I. B. Neumann and V. Pouliot, eds. (2015). *Diplomacy: The Making of World Politics*. Cambridge and New York: Cambridge University Press.

Sergunin, A. and V. Konyshev (2015). *Russia in the Arctic: Hard or Soft Power?* Stuttgart: IBIDEM.

Shadian, J. (2009). 'Revisiting politics and science in the poles: IPY and the governance of Science in post-Westphalia', in J. Shadian and M. Tennberg (eds.), *Legacies and Change in Polar Sciences: Historical, Legal and Political Reflections on the International Polar Year*. London and New York: Routledge, 35–61.

(2014). *The Politics of Arctic Sovereignty: Oil, Ice and Inuit Governance*. Abingdon: Routledge.

(2017). 'Navigating political borders old and new: The territoriality of indigenous Inuit governance', *Journal of Borderlands Studies*. http://www.tandfonline.com/doi/full/10.1080/08865655.2017.1300781. DOI: https://doi.org/10.1080/08865655.2017.1300781.

Shapin, S. and S. Schaffer (1985). *Leviathan and the Air-Pump: Hobbes, Boyle and the Experimental Life*. Princeton: Princeton University Press.

Shkilnyk, A. (1985). *A Poison Stronger than Love: The Destruction of an Ojibwa Community*. New Haven: Yale University Press.

Slezkine, Y. (1994). *Arctic Mirrors: Russia and the Small Peoples of the North*. Ithaca and London: Cornell University Press.

Śmieszek, M. (2016). '25 years of the International Arctic Science Committee (IASC)'. *Arctic Yearbook*. www.arcticyearbook.com/briefing-notes2015/ 173–25-years-of-the-international-arctic-science-committee-iasc (accessed 15 February 2017).

Smith, H. and G. Wilson (2009). 'Inuit transnational activism: Cooperation and resistance in the face of global change', in J. M. Beier (ed.), *Indigenous Diplomacies*. Basingstoke: Palgrave, pp. 171–186.

Soja, E. (2003). *Postmodern Geographies: The Reassertion of Space in Critical Social Theory*. London: Verso.

Solli, P. E., E. Wilson Rowe and W. Y. Lindgren (2013). 'Coming into the cold? The Arctic interests of Asian states', *Polar Geography* 36:4, 253–270.

Sörlin, S. (2013). 'Introduction: Polar extensions, Nordic states and their polar strategies', in S. Sörlin (ed.), *Science, Geopolitics and Culture in the Polar Region: Norden beyond Borders*. London: Routledge, pp. 1–19.

Spence, J. (2016). 'Finding a place in the Arctic Council for non-Arctic actors: A social network analysis of the Arctic Monitoring and Assessment Programme'. *Arctic Yearbook*. www.arcticyearbook.com/scholarly-papers-2016/233-finding-a-place-in-the-arctic-council-for-non-arctic-actors-a-social-network-analysis-of-the-arctic-monitoring-and-assessment-programme (accessed 29 April 2017).

Spencer, H. (1988). 'Russia mulls opening Siberian door to Alaska'. *The New York Times*, 1 May, 137.

Staalesen, A. (2016). 'Putin prepares for Arctic visit 8. September'. *Independent Barents Observer*. https://thebarentsobserver.com/en/arctic/2016/09/putin-prepares-arctic-visit (accessed 7 April 2017).

Steinberg, P. and K. Peters (2015). 'Wet ontologies, fluid spaces: Giving depth to volume through oceanic thinking', *Environment and Planning D: Society and Space* 33:2, 247–264.

Steinberg, P., J. Tasch and H. Gerhardt (2015). *Contesting the Arctic: Politics and Imaginaries in the Circumpolar North*. London: I. B. Tauris.

Stokke, O. (1990). 'The northern environment: Is cooperation coming?', *Annals of the American Academy of Political and Social Science* 512, 36–38.

    (2011). 'Environmental security in the Arctic: The case for multi-level governance', *International Journal* 66:4, 835–848.

    (2015). 'Institutional complexity in Arctic governance: Curse or blessing?', in L. C. Jensen and G. Hønneland (eds.), *Handbook of the Politics of the Arctic*. Cheltenham: Edward Elgar, pp. 328–351.

Stokke, O., G. Hønneland and P. Schei (2007). 'Pollution and conservation', in O. Stokke and G. Hønneland (eds.), *International Cooperation and Arctic Governance: Regime Effectiveness and Northern Region Building*. London: Routledge, pp. 78–111.

Strandsbjerg, J. (2012). 'Cartopolitics, geopolitics and boundaries in the Arctic', *Geopolitics* 17:4, 818–842.

Stuhl, A. (2016). *Unfreezing the Arctic: Science, Colonialism, and the Transformation of Inuit Lands*. Chicago: University of Chicago Press.

Swedberg, R. (2014). *The Art of Social Theory*. Princeton: Princeton University Press.

Sweeney, T. and T. Vauraste (2016). 'Arctic Economic Council: Creating parameters for sustainable economic development in the Arctic'. *The Arctic Yearbook*. www.arcticyearbook.com/commentaries-2016/216-arctic-economic-council-creating-parameters-for-sustainable-economic-development-in-the-arctic (accessed 10 February 2017).

Tennberg, M. (2000). *Arctic Environmental Cooperation: A Study in Governmentality*. Burlington: Ashgate.

    ed. (2012). *Politics of Development in the Barents Region*. Rovaniemi: University of Lapland Press.

(2015). 'Arctic change through a political reading', in L. C. Jensen and G. Hønneland (eds.), *Handbook of the Politics of the Arctic*. Cheltenham: Edward Elgar, pp. 408–420.

Thompson, N. (2009*). Settlers on the Edge: Identity and Modernization on Russia's Arctic Frontier.* Vancouver: UBC Press.

Thrift, N. (2000). 'It's the little things', in D. Atkinson and K. Dodds (eds.), *Geopolitical Traditions: A Century of Geopolitical Thought.* London: Routledge, pp. 380–387.

Tonami, A. and S. Watters (2012). 'Japan's Arctic policy: The sum of many parts', in L. Heininen (ed.), *Arctic Yearbook 2012*. Akureyri: Northern Research Forum, pp. 93–103.

(2013). 'Singapore: The Arctic newcomer', *The Circle WWF* 1:1, 13–15. http://awsassets.panda.org/downloads/the_circle_2013_1_web.pdf (accessed 10 May 2013).

Trudeau, J. (2016a). 'United States–Canada joint Arctic leaders' statement'. http://pm.gc.ca/eng/news/2016/12/20/united-states-canada-joint-arctic-leaders-statement (accessed 10 February 2017).

(2016b). 'US–Canada joint statement on climate, energy and Arctic leadership', http://pm.gc.ca/eng/news/2016/03/10/us-canada-joint-statement-climate-energy-and-arctic-leadership (accessed 10 February 2017).

Tsygankov, A. P. (2016). *Russia's Foreign Policy: Change and Continuity in National Identity*. Lanham: Rowman and Littlefield.

Unwin, T. (2000). 'A waste of space: Towards a critique of the social production of space', *Transactions of the Institute of British Geographers* 25:1, 11–29.

US Chairmanship of the Arctic Council (2016a). Discussion Paper on the Arctic Council's work on oil and gas issues. Arctic Council Archive. http://hdl.handle.net/11374/1730 (accessed 29 April 2017).

(2016b). 'Issue paper: Toward clarity and transparency in relationships with other bodies'. https://oaarchive.arctic-council.org/bitstream/handle/11374/1525/EDOCS-2696-v1-ACSAOUS201_Anchorage_2015_3–1–1_Issue_Paper_Relationships_with_Other_Bodies.pdf?sequence=1&isAllowed=y (accessed 6 January 2018).

US Delegation of the Arctic Council (2008). 'Concept for an Arctic search and rescue memorandum of understanding'. http://hdl.handle.net/11374/870 (accessed 29 April 2017).

US Department of State (2013). 'Remarks with Swedish Foreign Minister Carl Bildt and Russian Foreign Minister Sergey Lavrov at the Arctic Council ministerial session'. https://2009-2017.state.gov/secretary/remarks/2013/05/209402.htm (accessed 21 December 2017).

(2015). 'Remarks at the presentation of the US Chairmanship Program at the Arctic Council Ministerial. John Kerry, Secretary of State. Iqaluit, Canada, 24 April'. Arctic Council Archive. http://hdl.handle.net/11374/913 (accessed 29 April 2017).

US Fish and Wildlife Service (2013). 'Birds connect Arctic refuge with the world'. Map. www.fws.gov/refuge/arctic/birdworldmig.html (accessed 29 April 2017).

Vakhtin, N. (1994). 'The native peoples of the Russian far north', in Minority Rights Group (ed.), *Polar Peoples: Self-Determination and Development*. London: Minority Rights Publications, pp. 29–80.

Valkeapää, N. A. (1998). *The Sun, My Father*. Seattle: University of Washington Press.

Vik, H. and A. Semb (2013). 'Who owns the land? Norway, the Sami and the ILO indigenous and tribal peoples convention', *International Journal on Minority and Group Rights* 20:4, 517–550. DOI: 10.1163/15718115–02004002.

Visible Earth Project (NASA) (2017). MISR sights the Bering Strait. https://visibleearth.nasa.gov/view.php?id=1050 (accessed 29 August 2017).

Vitebsky, P. (2005). *Reindeer People: Living with Animals and Spirits in Siberia.* London: HarperCollins.

Vorob'ev, V (2013). 'Zapolyarniy krug interesov' ['A polar circle of interests'], *Rossiskaya gazeta*, 16 May 2013.

Watters, S. and A. Tonami (2012). 'Singapore: An emerging Arctic actor', in L. Heininen (ed.), *Arctic Yearbook 2012.* Akureyri: Northern Research Forum, pp. 105–114.

Wegge, N. (2010). 'The political order in the Arctic: Power structures, regimes, and influence', *Polar Record* 47:241, 165–176.

——— (2012). 'The EU and the Arctic: European foreign policy in the making', *Arctic Review on Law and Politics* 3:1, 6–29.

Wehrmann, D. (2017). 'Non-state actors in Arctic Council governance', in K. Keil and S. Knecht (eds.), *Governing Arctic Change.* London: Palgrave Macmillan, pp. 187–206.

Weiner, D. R. (1999). *A Little Corner of Freedom: Russian Nature Protection from Stalin to Gorbachev.* Berkeley: University of California Press.

Wenzel, G. (1991). *Animal Rights, Human Rights: Ecology, Economy and Ideology in the Canadian Arctic.* Toronto: University of Toronto Press.

Whitefield, S. (2003). 'Russian mass attitudes towards the environment, 1993–2001', *Post-Soviet Affairs* 19:2, 95–113.

Willis, M. and D. Depledge (2015). 'How we learned to stop worrying about China's ambitions: Understanding China's admission to the Arctic Council, 2004–2013', in L. C. Jensen and G. Hønneland (eds.), *Handbook of the Politics of the Arctic.* Cheltenham: Edward Elgar, pp. 388–407.

Wilson, E. (2006). 'Building an Arctic community of knowledge: The promotion and reception of Canadian resource management and economic development models in the Russian North'. Doctoral thesis, University of Cambridge.

Wilson, E. (2007a). 'Indigenousness and the mobility of knowledge: Promoting Canadian governance practices in the Russian North', *Sibirica* 6:2, 26–50.

——— (2007b). 'Time, idealization and international development: Promoting Canadian co-management in Northern Russia', *Area* 39:3, 323–330.

Wilson, E. (2015). *Energy and minerals in Greenland: Governance, corporate responsibility and social resilience.* London: IIED.

Wilson Rowe, E. (2009). 'Russian regional multilateralism: The case of the Arctic Council', in E. Wilson Rowe and S. Torjesen (eds.), *The Multilateral Dimension of Russian Foreign Policy.* London: Routledge, pp. 142–152.

——— (2013a). 'A dangerous space? Unpacking state and media discourses on the Arctic', *Polar Geography* 36:3, 232–244.

——— (2013b). 'Arctic hierarchies? Norway, status and the "High North"', *Polar Record* 1, 72–79.

——— (2013c). *Russian Climate Politics: When Science Meets Policy.* Basingstoke: Palgrave.

——— (2013d). 'A sylvan superpower: Russian forests in international climate negotiations', *Geoforum* 48:1, 216–224.

——— (2015). 'Locating international REDD+ power relations: Debating forests and trees in international climate negotiations', *Geoforum* 66:1, 64–74.

——— (2017a). 'The Arctic in Moscow', in R. W. Orttung (ed.), *Sustaining Russia's Arctic Cities: Resource Politics, Migration and Climate Change.* New York: Berghahn, pp. 25–41.

(2017b). 'Promises, promises: Murmansk and the unbuilt petroleum environment', *Arctic Review on Law and Politics,* 1.

Wilson Rowe, E. and H. Blakkisrud (2014). 'A new kind of Arctic power? Russia's policy discourses and diplomatic practices in the circumpolar North', *Geopolitics* 19:1, 66–85.

Wohlforth, B. and D. Kang (2009). 'Hypotheses on status competition'. American Political Science Association, Toronto meeting paper. http://papers.ssrn.com/sol3/papers.cfm?abstract_id=1450467## (accessed 15 November 2011).

Wolf, R. (2011). 'Respect and disrespect in international politics: The significance of status recognition', *International Theory* 3:1, 105–142.

Wråkberg, U. (2013). 'Science and industry in northern Russia from a Nordic perspective'., in S. Sörlin (ed.), *Science, Geopolitics and Culture in the Polar Region: Norden beyond Borders.* London: Routledge, pp. 195–223.

WWF (2014). 'New Arctic Economic Council could be a missed opportunity', www.panda.org/wwf_news/?218590/aec-missed-opportunity (accessed 1 February 2017).

Yablokov, A. (2010). 'The environment and politics in Russia', *Russian Analytical Digest* 79, 2–4.

Young, O. (1985). 'The age of the Arctic', *Foreign Policy* 61:1, 160–179.

   (1992). *Arctic Politics: Conflict and Cooperation in the Circumpolar North.* Hanover: Dartmouth College Press.

   (1998). *Creating Regimes: Arctic Accords and International Governance.* Cornell: Cornell University Press.

   (2002). 'Can the Arctic Council and the Northern Forum find common ground?'. *Polar Record* 38, 289–296.

   (2005). 'Governing the Arctic: From Cold War theatre to mosaic of cooperation'. *Global Governance: A Review of Multilateralism and International Organizations* 11:1, 9–15.

   (2009). 'Whither the Arctic? Further developments'. *Polar Record* 45, 179–181.

Zarakol, A. (2017). 'Theorising hierarchies: An introduction', in A. Zarakol (ed.), *Hierarchies in World Politics.* Cambridge: Cambridge University Press, pp. 1–14.

Zhang, P. and J. Yang (2016). 'Changes in the Arctic and China's participation in Arctic governance', in L. Lunde, L. Y. Jiang and I. Stensdal (eds.), *Asian Countries and the Arctic Future.* New Jersey: World Scientific, pp. 217–236.

Zhao, J. (2013). Speech by Ambassador Zhao Jun at the Arctic Frontiers Conference, 21 January. http://archive.arcticfrontiers.com/index.php?option=com_docman&task=doc_download&gid=713&Itemid=516 (accessed 1 March 2013).

Zysk, K. (2011). 'Military aspects of Russia's Arctic policy: Hard power and natural resources', in J. Kraska (ed.), *Arctic Security in an Age of Climate Change.* Cambridge: Cambridge University Press, pp. 85–106.

Index

155